DIVORCE GUIDE FOR ONTARIO

DIVORCE GUIDE FOR ONTARIO

Sandra J. Meyrick, LL.B.

Self-Counsel Press
(a division of)
International Self-Counsel Press Ltd.
Canada U.S.A.

Self-Counsel Press acknowledges the financial support of the Government of Canada through the Book Publishing Industry Development Program (BPIDP) for our publishing activities.

Printed in Canada.

First edition: 1973
Tenth edition: 1993
Fifteenth edition: 1998; Reprinted: 1998
Sixteenth edition: 2000

Canadian Cataloguing in Publication Data

Meyrick, Sandra J.
    Divorce guide for Ontario

    (Self-counsel legal series)
    First-2nd eds. by Ronald J. Reid; 3rd-5th eds. by J.D. James; 6th-10th eds.
by Gloria J. Epstein; 1st ed. has title: Ontario divorce guide; 2nd-15th eds. have title:
Divorce guide for Ontario.

    ISBN 1-55180-296-1

    1. Divorce — Law and legislation — Ontario — Popular works. 2. Divorce —
Law and legislation — Ontario — Forms. I. Title. II. Title: Divorce guide for Ontario.
III. Series.
KEO224.Z82E67 2000   346.71301'66   C00-910248-5
KF535.Z9E67 2000

Self-Counsel Press
(a division of)
International Self-Counsel Press Ltd.

1481 Charlotte Road   1704 N. State Street
North Vancouver, BC V7J 1H1   Bellingham, WA 98225
Canada   U.S.A.

CONTENTS

SAMPLES

ACKNOWLEDGMENT

Thanks to Kim, without whom this
edition would have taken much longer.
SCP Editors

NOTICE TO READERS

SERVICES AVAILABLE FROM THE PUBLISHER

To obtain your divorce, you will have to file certain forms with the divorce court. You may type all of these forms yourself, but it is easier and quicker to fill in preprinted forms. The use of preprinted forms is common in the legal profession as it eases the typing load considerably.

Self-Counsel Press stocks two sets of forms suitable for use in most cases: one set if you are filing for divorce as a sole petitioner and one set if you and your spouse are filing as joint petitioners. **Note:** If you and/or your spouse live in one of the areas of Ontario now under the jurisdiction of the *Ontario* Superior Court of Justice, Family Court Branch (see chapter 6 for the list of areas), the forms needed for joint and sole applications are the *same* and copies of those forms are included in *both* the kits.

MAKE SURE YOU HAVE THE CORRECT SET OF FORMS BEFORE OPENING THE KIT. Please read chapters 5 and 6 of this book for further information about which set of forms you need. When you fill out these forms, read them carefully and complete them by following the instructions and samples in this book.

Included in the set of preprinted forms is a 3 ½" disk version of the forms for use on a PC with WordPerfect (6.1 or higher), MS Word (6.0 or higher), or Acrobat pdf.

1. Divorce Forms and Disk for Ontario
   (Sole Petitioner) $26.95

2. Divorce Forms and Disk for Ontario
   (Joint Petitioners) $26.95

To obtain any of these packages of preprinted forms, complete the form on the next page and mail it with your money order or MasterCard or Visa number, or purchase them where you bought this book.

(Prices subject to change without notice.)

✂ . . . .

ORDER FORM

TO: Self-Counsel Press
4 Bram Court
Brampton, ON L6W 3R6

Enclosed is a money order for $ _____ which is payment
in full for:

_____   set(s) of Divorce Forms and Disk for Ontario (Sole Petitioner) at
              $26.95 each   _____

_____   set(s) of Divorce Forms and Disk for Ontario (Joint Petitioners) at
              $26.95 each   _____

              plus $3.00 postage and handling   _____
              Subtotal   _____
              Add 7% GST to subtotal   _____
              Add 8% PST to subtotal   _____
              TOTAL: _____

Name: _____

Address: _____

City: _____

Province: _____ Postal code: _____

Telephone: _____ _____

MasterCard/Visa number: _____

Expiration date: _____ Validation date: _____

Signature: _____

1
CAN I DO MY OWN DIVORCE?

a. DO I NEED A LAWYER?

Although the philosophy of this publication is self-help, there are cases in which you *cannot* handle the divorce yourself and will require professional advice or assistance. Specifically, if your divorce will be contested by your spouse, you should not attempt to handle it without the services of a lawyer. This publication is intended to help you decide whether or not your case is one in which the assistance of a lawyer is necessary and then how to process your divorce effectively.

Even if your divorce is uncontested, there may be procedural complications that will require the services of a lawyer. For example, if you have no idea where your spouse is living, you may have trouble serving the Petition for Divorce on him or her.

There may also be maintenance payments to be negotiated or, perhaps, problems of proof in certain circumstances. If you require special advice, you can retain the services of a lawyer for limited purposes only, while you complete the bulk of the work yourself.

In some cases, no court appearance will be necessary. However, if your case is one in which a court attendance is required, you should consider retaining a lawyer to handle the actual hearing in court. For approximately $600, most divorce lawyers will read your documents, take the case into court, and file the Divorce Judgment (i.e., the judge's order for divorce). You are, of course, entitled to represent yourself in court in any action. The choice is yours.

If, however, you do elect to retain a lawyer to handle your court case, you should do the following:

(a) Be sure to choose a lawyer who carries on a matrimonial practice.

(b) Ask for a quotation beforehand (this applies to any legal service).

(c) Make sure your lawyer agrees to handle only those parts of the procedure with which you are not comfortable.

If you decide to handle your divorce yourself, remember that even with the recent changes to the law and rules, obtaining your own divorce still requires a good measure of intelligence, perseverance, and concentration.

b. THINK BEFORE YOU START

Think twice about everything you are doing. Be fully aware of all the consequences but particularly what the position of you, your spouse, and your children will be as a result of your decision to bring a divorce action. Seek help from a marriage counsellor or other qualified person if you feel there is any chance of reconciliation.

If you are determined to proceed with a divorce, you may wish to pursue mediation. In any event, follow all the suggested procedures very carefully; they are all important. Likewise, all forms must be completed with meticulous attention to detail. If you do sloppy work, you could end up paying a lawyer twice as much to correct your mistakes. Be methodical and well prepared at all times.

Be persistent. Don't be afraid to ask questions about the law, even though there may be people who try to discourage your inquiries. Your sincerity and politeness will encourage the proper responses. Contrary to what you might have heard, the divorce courts are quite efficient. Let's keep them that way by not clogging the process with defective papers and pleadings.

If you must appear in court and you intend to represent yourself, you must be especially well prepared. The judge is not there to block your efforts to obtain a divorce. However, the judge does have a specific job to do and must be satisfied that the requirements of the Divorce Act have been complied with. This book provides an outline of the types of questions that will be asked. However, you should make a point of attending at least one court session of uncontested divorces in order to familiarize yourself with the conduct of a divorce trial.

If you find yourself getting in over your head, you will have to make a decision —

(a) to consult a lawyer, or

(b) to drop the action.

The choice is entirely a personal one but, in any event, don't proceed if you do not have a clear understanding of what you are doing. The consequences of errors can be serious and permanent.

c. HOW CAN THIS BOOK HELP ME?

This book is divided into two basic parts. The first part outlines the existing law concerning a divorce action. It discusses the various grounds on which you may proceed. The second part deals with the step-by-step procedure leading to the securing of the Divorce Judgment.

There are various objective tests to meet before you have the right to a divorce. A copy of the Divorce Act is provided in Appendix 4 for your information. Make sure you understand the grounds under which you are proceeding and that you satisfy the requirements of the particular section you are using. You cannot immediately obtain a divorce just because you and your spouse have agreed to break up.

Marriage breakdown is the sole ground for divorce. There are, however, limitations on the means of proving marriage breakdown. There are three different ways you can declare marriage breakdown: one-year separation, adultery, or cruelty. If you have lived apart for less than one year you must either wait until one year has passed before the divorce can be granted or establish your case based on adultery or cruelty.

You do not have to wait that long if your spouse has left and you wish to collect support, if custody of children must be determined, or if you want an early division of matrimonial property. If you wish, these areas of relief can be pursued separately under the Family Law Act, which is provincial legislation. This book does not cover these remedies, and if you decide that any of these remedies offers the most appropriate form of relief for you, you will have to see a lawyer, legal aid office, or family court official. You might also refer to the Ontario edition of *Marriage, Separation, and Divorce*, another title in the Self-Counsel Series.

It is important to recognize that the problems of proof vary according to the section of the act you use as the basis of your divorce. Obviously, it will be easy for you to start your divorce, all things being equal, under a section that sets out simple and straightforward grounds. But, if you run into any serious difficulties in preparing your Petition, or any serious problems of proof, it will be necessary for you to consult a lawyer to put you back on the proper course.

If you feel that there are two or more sections of the Divorce Act you can use to plead marriage breakdown, you should use them all as your chances of success will increase accordingly.

The second part of the book is where you will find step-by-step procedures. Directions are given for starting your action and all the stages up to the completed divorce. The procedure is similar, but not the same, depending on where you live in Ontario. Chapters 5 and 6 detail the regional differences.

Your divorce will be heard in the region where either you or your spouse is living. The local registrar's office where you begin your action is located in the regional courthouse.

Each step outlined in this book is important, and each one must be completed before you proceed to the next. Failure to do so will only result in a great deal of delay and confusion at a later stage.

Do not allow technical words to confuse you. If you encounter terms or phrases foreign to you, look them up in a legal dictionary, which can be found at any library, or consult another professional source. A glossary of the most common terms is provided at the back of this book for your use. Keep a notebook of such information. It will pay you to research your divorce carefully. Again, it is emphasized that ignorance in the early stages can "snowball" into later difficulties.

This book also shows all the forms you will need and illustrates how they should be completed. These are included as samples only of commonly used sentences and phrases. If your specific situation does not fit these examples, do not copy from the forms, just use them as guides to the general style and form required.

It is not difficult to draft your own clauses. Put a little work into writing properly structured sentences and, generally, if they state the truth, they will be accepted.

While you are following the step-by-step procedure, you will find it necessary to refer constantly to these forms. You may not see the reason for some of them, but they are all necessary for the successful completion of your action.

d. SUMMARY

The following is a list of circumstances that must apply to you if you want to process your own divorce:

(a) You can prove marriage breakdown in a straightforward way (see chapter 2).

(b) You can serve your spouse without undue difficulty (i.e., your spouse lives in Canada and isn't avoiding service of the documents).

(c) There are no contentious issues between you and your spouse in areas such as custody of and access to the children or support for you and/or the children.

(d) You are not advancing a claim to property that is being opposed by your spouse.

2
GROUNDS FOR DIVORCE

Under the Divorce Act, there is only one ground for divorce. The Divorce Act, in subsection 8(1), establishes marriage breakdown as the sole criterion for divorce. However, subsection 8(2) does limit the ways you can prove a marriage breakdown. Marriage breakdown can be established in these cases:

(a) If you and your spouse have lived separately for at least one year before the Divorce Judgment (although you may begin the paperwork any time after your separation begins)

(b) If the spouse against whom a divorce is sought has committed adultery or has treated you with physical or mental cruelty of such a kind as to make it intolerable for the two of you to live together.

a. ONE-YEAR SEPARATION (Section 8(2)(a))

Under section 8(2)(a) of the Divorce Act, the period during which you and your spouse must have been separated to qualify for a divorce is one year, and either you or your spouse may commence proceedings without waiting until that period has expired. All that is necessary is that you and your spouse be separated at the time the proceedings are started. The one-year period of separation will be satisfied provided that 12 months have elapsed before the Divorce Judgment is granted.

It is important to note that the period of separation must be uninterrupted up to the time the Divorce Judgment is granted. However, the Divorce Act does make provisions for efforts to reconcile. You and your spouse may live together after separation without eliminating the accumulation of time toward the one-year period as long as each temporary period or periods of living together do not exceed 90 days in total. When determining whether you and your spouse have been separated for one year, any and all total periods of attempted reconciliation lasting 90 days or less will be included. This is the case even though there may, in addition, have been casual acts of sexual intercourse.

For example, if you and your spouse were living apart for ten months, then resumed cohabitation for more than 90 days, and then separated again, the first ten months could not be used to establish a period of separation. In this case, you would have to begin calculating your period of separation at the start of your second separation.

It does not matter whether the separation has occurred by consent of the spouses or by seemingly totally unjustified "desertion" by one spouse. In the event of a unilateral separation, either spouse or both can commence divorce proceedings.

Often people are confused about what separation means and when it starts. If one spouse leaves the matrimonial home, that is usually a clear sign of the commencement of separation. However, spouses may have been living "separate and apart" and remain in the same dwelling as long as they have been living independent lives.

Finally, it is significant that *both* spouses may apply for divorce when the ground is marriage breakdown based on a one-year separation. You cannot obtain a divorce on the basis of your own adultery (nor can your spouse on the ground of his or her own adultery).

b. ADULTERY (Section 8(2)(b)(i))

Under the Divorce Act, marriage breakdown can also be established if you can prove that your spouse has committed adultery.

You do not have to name the person with whom your spouse has allegedly committed adultery. However, if you decide to name the person as a co-respondent (your spouse would be the other respondent), then you must serve that person with a copy of the Petition. The only case in which it is necessary to name the third party is when you are making a claim against that party.

The situation may arise where you know that your spouse has committed adultery and you want to assert a specific claim against that person but you do not know the name of the other person involved. You can, in these circumstances, simply serve your spouse with the Petition for Divorce and then, when you later find out the name of the person with whom the adultery was committed, amend your Petition and serve the document on the other party to the proceeding.

It is not necessary for you to find your spouse in bed with another person to corroborate your own evidence of your spouse's adultery. You need only establish the probability that such adultery occurred. Circumstantial evidence such as a mutual friend seeing men's and women's clothing in the bedroom closet after you have already separated from your spouse is usually enough to establish adultery.

If your spouse has an illegitimate child, obtain a copy of the birth certificate from the Registrar General, P.O. Box 4600, Thunder Bay, Ontario, P7B 6L8 if the birth was in Ontario, and use the certificate to corroborate your evidence of adultery. Refer to Appendix 2 for a list of Vital Statistics Departments in the various provinces to write to for information.

Send a money order with your request. The amount will vary according to the province. The payee differs by province — for instance, in Ontario the money order should be made payable to the Minister of Finance; in Alberta the payee is the Provincial Treasurer — you might wish to leave the payee space blank.

If your only corroboration is a birth certificate, you may run into difficulties, as a judge may be hesitant to accept the illegitimacy of a child. In this case, I recommend that you do not proceed unless your spouse is prepared to admit the alleged adultery under oath (i.e., orally at trial or in an affidavit or an examination for discovery as will be described later), or there is an independent witness available to testify. A private detective can be hired to obtain the evidence or, if you are short of funds, you can ask a friend. One drawback of using a friend is that he or she may be reluctant to become involved. The best and cheapest witness is one not connected to either party, such as a landlord or a next-door neighbor.

1. By affidavit evidence

The simplest way to obtain a divorce on the grounds of marriage breakdown based on adultery is by the affidavit evidence of your spouse and, preferably, by the person with whom your spouse is alleged to have committed adultery. The affidavit of your spouse should state that he or she understands that there is no obligation to provide the evidence given. Your spouse should also say that he or she has received a copy of the Petition for Divorce and has reviewed the facts alleged with respect to adultery and that these facts are correct. Alternatively, any corrections to those facts should be indicated. Your spouse should also confirm the date you separated and that the adultery has not been condoned. Further, it should be stated that there is no possibility of reconciliation.

If possible, an affidavit from the person with whom your spouse is alleged to have committed adultery should also be filed with the court. The affidavit should state that this person is not obliged to give evidence of adultery, but has reviewed the facts alleged in the Petition with respect to adultery and that the facts are correct or, again, any corrections required should be indicated.

Alternatively, an affidavit can be filed by someone who is in a position to confirm the adultery alleged against your spouse. For example, a friend may be able to provide the evidence proving that your spouse is living common-law.

2. By examination for discovery

Adultery can also be proved to the court by filing a transcript of an examination for discovery. This is the process you would use if you feel that a court appearance will be necessary to settle certain contested matters, but your spouse, although prepared to admit to the allegation of adultery, is unwilling or unable to attend court. In this instance, you may want to hire a lawyer who practises in the city or town where your spouse lives to conduct the examination for discovery. Your spouse, if he or she is co-operative, can call around to find out the fees of lawyers in the area for this service and forward the information to you so that you can hire the lawyer of your choice. Otherwise your nearest large library will have books with lists of names of lawyers who practise in different areas.

The lawyer will make an appointment to meet with a court reporter and your spouse. The court reporter will put your spouse under oath, just as a judge would if your spouse appeared in court. The lawyer will then ask the questions that will show on the transcript of the examination for discovery that your spouse is the proper respondent to the action and that the acts of adultery complained of in the Petition are admitted to. The court reporter will take down all of the questions and answers. In order to have as strong corroborative evidence as possible, a similar examination of the person with whom the adultery is alleged to have been committed is advisable. Arrangements can usually be made to have the two examinations proceed one after the other.

The question and answer period usually takes less than half an hour, even if two people are being examined. In a few weeks, you will receive a copy of the questions and answers. The cost of hiring a lawyer to do this should range from $300 to $500 plus the cost of the court reporter and the transcript of the examination for discovery.

Once you receive the transcript you can make a photocopy for yourself; if a court appearance is still necessary you should take the transcript to court with you and hand the original to the clerk. When the judge requests evidence of the grounds on which the divorce is proceeding, the transcript of the examination for discovery will be marked as an exhibit.

Alternatively, it may appear, after the examination for discovery, that the divorce can proceed without a court appearance. In this instance you can file the transcripts instead of the affidavits.

The judge will read over the transcript either privately or in court to make sure that the proper party was served and that he or she made the admissions under oath. If you are in court, the judge will then proceed with questions on the rest of the Petition. You will be asked few, if any, questions about the grounds for divorce.

3. By court appearance

Finally, adultery can be proved by your appearance and testimony in court, preferably with your spouse who is prepared to corroborate the adultery. If your spouse is unwilling or unable to come to court to corroborate and you do not have transcripts of an examination for discovery, then you may be able to have the adultery corroborated through the testimony of a person with whom adultery is alleged to have been committed or through the testimony of an independent third person. In a court appearance as well, the filing of the birth certificate of a child of your spouse and another person would be helpful.

As you can appreciate, the court must be entirely satisfied that your spouse is being truthful in this type of situation before a divorce will be granted. Your spouse's evidence, whether through an affidavit, examination for discovery, or appearance in court, *must* be voluntary, and there must be no suggestion that you and your spouse have entered into an agreement to fabricate evidence.

Therefore, as a safeguard, it is essential that you do not enter into an agreement with your spouse that he or she will provide evidence in court until after you have commenced divorce proceedings and have had all the necessary documents served. This will indicate that admissions made by your spouse under oath are admissions of fact as set out in your Petition and that there was no fabrication of evidence. (When you allege that "there has been no collusion" in your Petition for Divorce, you are stating that no evidence has been fabricated, nor have you and your spouse joined together to "create" evidence.)

4. Summary

In conclusion, if you intend to obtain your own divorce on the grounds of your spouse's adultery, you must be able to provide independent proof that the adultery you are alleging actually took place. A written letter of confession from your spouse is not sufficient. One of the following types of proof is required.

(a) Where a court appearance is not necessary you may file —

(i) an affidavit sworn by your spouse confirming the particulars of the alleged adultery,

(ii) an affidavit sworn by the person who is alleged to have committed the adultery with your spouse, again confirming the particulars of the adultery,

(iii) transcripts of the examinations for discovery of the spouse and the person with whom the adultery is alleged, or

(iv) an affidavit from a person or persons in a position to confirm the adultery.

(b) Where a court appearance is necessary, you may —

(i) call your spouse as the witness to the adultery complained of if he or she is willing to come to court and admit to the adultery alleged in your Petition,

(ii) call as a witness the person with whom your spouse is alleged to have committed adultery if he or she is willing to come to court and admit to the adultery alleged,

(iii) use transcripts from an examination for discovery,

(iv) call a witness who has seen your spouse living with the other person as husband and wife, or

(v) call a witness who has seen the other person stay overnight on various occasions at your spouse's residence.

It would be inadvisable for you to attempt to obtain your own divorce on the grounds of marriage breakdown based on adultery unless you can provide the court with suitable evidence as outlined above. If none of these procedures is available to you, you must consult a lawyer.

c. CRUELTY (Section 8(2)(b)(ii))

Breakdown of the marriage may be established if your spouse has treated you with physical or mental cruelty of such a kind as to make continued cohabitation intolerable.

It is impossible to describe all types of contact that may constitute cruelty or those falling short of cruelty. The courts have not tried to define cruelty. However, an ordinary understanding may signify the disposition to inflict suffering, to delight in or exhibit indifference to your misery, or to demonstrate hard-heartedness. If, in your marriage relationship, your spouse causes unnecessary pain to your body or emotions, his or her conduct may constitute cruelty that will entitle you to dissolution of a marriage if such actions render your cohabitation intolerable.

If you decide to proceed under this section, you must be able to establish that the cruelty is of grave nature and not merely conduct that can be characterized as incompatibility of personalities. The whole matrimonial relationship must be considered, especially if the cruelty consists of complaints, accusations, or what may be called nagging.

The courts will want to consider what effect the allegedly cruel conduct has had on you. In the final analysis, determination of what constitutes cruelty must depend on the circumstances of each case while considering the personal characteristics of you and your spouse and your attitude toward the marriage relationship.

To demonstrate a marriage breakdown based on cruelty you must, therefore, specify the conduct on the part of your spouse that makes living together intolerable, provide as accurately as possible the times and places of the cruelty, and have a witness who can corroborate the conduct complained of and its effect on you. The evidence of a physician, psychiatrist, or other professional person is invaluable.

In many cases there may be no other person who knows of your spouse's cruelty. You may still proceed with your Petition; however, your evidence must be very strong to obtain a divorce without corroborating evidence. It is very important to give an accurate and detailed account in both your Petition and your evidence of the cruel conduct of your spouse and the effects on you of such conduct.

As with the other manifestations of marriage breakdown, you can proceed either by way of affidavit evidence or by a court appearance. If you use an affidavit, you must file one that indicates the relationship of the person swearing the affidavit to you (e.g., a friend, relative, employer, doctor) and gives details of any acts of cruelty or evidence of cruelty witnessed by the person. Alternatively, a copy of a medical report signed by a medical practitioner licensed to practice in Ontario may be attached as an exhibit to your affidavit.

3
ADDITIONAL MATTERS

a. CUSTODY

Both natural parents of the child have equal rights to custody. This situation remains until a court makes an order to the contrary or until the parents enter into a written agreement giving sole custody, care, and control of the children to either the mother or the father, or agreeing to a joint custody arrangement.

It used to be that in most cases the mother had custody of the children, particularly when they were very young. But times have changed, and in an increasing number of cases, custody is being granted to the father. There are, as well, an increasing number of situations where the parents agree to co-operate in the joint upbringing of their children. In these cases a joint custody arrangement is entered into in which all the major decisions pertaining to the children are shared by the parents even though care and control may predominately be with one parent or split between both parents.

If a custody agreement cannot be reached, the issue must be heard by a judge. In any contested hearing before the court, the judge is concerned with one matter only: the best interests of the children.

If there is any suggestion whatsoever that there is to be a contested custody hearing, you must consult a lawyer. However, it may be that you wish to obtain an uncontested divorce and leave the issue of custody and support to another hearing. In this case, you can proceed and obtain a divorce on your own and then start a corollary relief action for a decision pertaining only to custody and support. If you decide to go this route, it would be wise to consult a lawyer beforehand, as certain of your rights, particularly those of property, may be affected. The division of property is not discussed in detail in this book as it falls under provincial legislation called the Family Law Act, which is not covered here. Also, it is important to retain a lawyer for the corollary relief action as it is complicated and generally requires a court appearance.

Once a court order is made awarding either the husband or the wife custody, the issue is not necessarily final. The spouse who does not have custody or day-to-day care and control of the children can, at a later date, if circumstances have changed considerably, apply to the court to have the issue of custody reviewed. If satisfied that a change in custody would be in the best interests of the child or children, the judge can vary the original custody order whether or not it was obtained on consent.

You should note that the Divorce Act expressly empowers the court to order joint or shared parenting privileges between spouses, although it falls short of endorsing any presumption in favor of joint custody. There are decisions from Ontario courts that support joint custody and others that do not. It is clear that the trend is to support joint custody arrangements, especially where the parents are able to co-operate. In Ontario, some courts have ordered alternating monthly custody arrangements in a joint custody situation notwithstanding that each parent had sought an order for sole custody.

Under the Divorce Act, the court may grant joint custody to the spouse or to one or both of the spouses and any other person such as a close relative. You should keep in mind that orders allowing custody and/or access to third parties will not be made unless that person consents and an opportunity has been given to the court to assess the qualifications of the third party to enjoy custodial or access privileges.

According to the Divorce Act, the courts must apply the principle that a child of the marriage should have as much contact with each parent as is consistent with the best interests of the child. For that purpose the court shall take into consideration the willingness of the person for whom custody is sought to facilitate such contact.

These provisions were intended to encourage maximum access between the child and the non-custodial parent. If one spouse is prepared to facilitate maximum contact between the child and the other spouse, whereas the other spouse is opposed to allowing generous access privileges and both spouses are equally competent parents, then the court should grant sole custody to the spouse who will promote maximum contact provided that this is consistent with the best interests of the child.

The act also gives broad discretion to the court to make custody or access orders for specified periods and subject to other terms or conditions. The court has the express authority to grant a temporary or fixed-term order for custody or access, which may be reviewed at a later date. In other words, in some circumstances, the court could order an independent assessment of the family to try to determine the needs of the child and the ability of the respective parents to fulfill those needs. Alternatively, the court could refer the parties to a mediator who might assist in working out custody and access arrangements.

You should keep in mind that it is rare for the courts to grant custody orders for children over the age of 16 years.

It is most unusual for a spouse not having custody of the children to be deprived of the right to see them. The judge is more likely to consider it in the best interests of the children to have a relationship with both parents. As has been said earlier, if you interfere with your spouse's access to the children, you stand the chance of losing custody as, all else being equal, a court is going to be inclined to award custody to the spouse who will provide the greatest opportunity for access.

The courts also often prefer the parents to work out their own arrangements for access and will grant an order for "reasonable," "liberal," or "generous" access. Such an order provides the flexibility to accommodate the interests of the parents and the children.

If the parents are unable to work out the terms of access themselves, the court will fix appropriate times and places if necessary. The court may also impose additional restrictions such as limiting the custodial parent's right to take the children out of the jurisdiction or directing that access privileges be exercised under the supervision of a third party if the non-custodial parent has abused his or her access privileges.

b. FINANCIAL RELIEF

1. In general

Read the provisions of sections 15 to 19 of the Divorce Act (see Appendix 4). These sections regulate the jurisdiction of the court to order relief in terms of support for you and/or the children, custody, and access.

An original application for temporary or permanent support for you or the child or children of the marriage may be made by either or both spouses or former spouses. Apparently, a joint application is possible. There is no longer a distinction between payments made before divorce and after.

Accordingly, the terms "alimony" and "maintenance" have been replaced by the term "support."

Neither party to a divorce action is automatically entitled to spousal support. The court will look at any fact it feels is relevant to a person's request for support. The court will likely consider the "needs" of the party seeking support and the "means" or ability to pay of the other spouse (the "payor" spouse). Detailed statements of finances and property must be submitted by both spouses to allow a court to determine whether support is appropriate.

A husband may be able to secure support on his own behalf from his wife or, as is more often the case, the wife from the husband. A support order can be for a fixed period of time within which the wife is expected to rehabilitate herself and put herself in a position where she is self-supporting.

The judge will be concerned with factors such as the earnings of both parties, the ability of the spouse seeking support to hold a job or to secure employment, his or her education level, training, health, and other related matters.

The judge can order either the husband or the wife to make monthly payments in an amount specified by the judge and/or a lump sum settlement instead of support payments.

Sometimes, if the petitioner successfully obtains an order for support, the judge will not specify an amount at the time of the hearing, but will refer the matter to a family court judge, or to a family law reference for the determination of the proper sum to be paid. The petitioner must then appear before the court officer who will hear all necessary evidence regarding respective incomes and expenses of the spouses and will then arrive at the amount of support payments to be made. If your spouse is working and living in the province, you should retain the services of a lawyer to conduct the hearing on your behalf. However, if your spouse is not employed or his or her actual whereabouts are not known, you are probably wasting your time and money trying to collect support.

Many people do not realize that they can often use the facilities of family courts in Ontario to obtain an order requiring their spouses to make support payments on their behalf and/or on behalf of the children of the marriage. If you are unsure whether or not you wish to start divorce proceedings, but you do require support, you should contact the family court officials in your district. They will advise you of your rights and will help you exercise those rights as quickly as possible. You do not require a lawyer and should have no difficulty presenting your case.

Your children have a right to support that cannot be bargained away by you or your spouse. This means simply that any agreement made between the spouses for support of the children may be completely disregarded by the court.

This right to support can quite easily be enforced by the family court. All support orders made by the *Ontario* Superior Court of Justice or the *Ontario* Superior Court of Justice Family Court are enforced by automatic payroll deduction through the government payroll office of the Family Support Plan. Certain forms must be filed with your other documents to make sure this is done. Payments usually continue until the children are 18 years of age, become self-supporting, or marry, whichever event occurs first. Children who are not married or self-supporting and who remain in school past the age of 18, up to and including three years of post-secondary school, would also be entitled to support.

You will note from reading section 2, subsection (d) of the Divorce Act, that in divorce proceedings children have a basic right to support up to the age of 16 years.

However, support may continue beyond this age if the children are unable to provide for themselves and are dependent on either the husband or the wife. Obviously, the age to which children remain entitled to support varies from case to case. Generally speaking, a child is not entitled to support beyond the age of 18 years.

An order of support for either you or the children of the marriage can be varied at any time if there has been a material change in circumstances. The onus of proving a material change in circumstances lies on the applicant.

The jurisdiction to hear and determine a variation proceeding rests in the court of a province where either former spouse is ordinarily a resident at the commencement of the variation proceeding or in a court whose jurisdiction is accepted by both spouses. An application to vary or suspend a support order or any term of an order may be brought by either or both former spouses. The Divorce Act gives the courts the power to vary or suspend a spousal or child support order retroactively. This allows a court to eliminate support arrears that may have fallen due.

A support order may be for a fixed term or until the occurrence of a specific event, such as the remarriage of the spouse receiving support. The act imposes strict limitations on the court's ability to make a variation order after the expiration of the fixed term or the occurrence of the stipulated event.

The court must be satisfied that a variation order is necessary to relieve economic hardship arising from a change that is related to the marriage and that the changed circumstances would have resulted in a different order had they occurred at the time the original order was made. Hardship that arises from circumstances unconnected with the marriage, such as the inability to find a job, would not support a variation order. If, for example, after the fixed term you lose your job because of economic conditions, this will not allow you to return to the courts for a variation of a fixed-term support order.

Keep in mind that the courts are reluctant to interfere with the terms of a negotiated settlement. This is particularly true where the settlement is supposed to finally resolve all property and support rights between the parties. A court will intervene, however, where a change of circumstances makes the settlement unjust.

There is no requirement in the act for the court to vary a support order if one of the spouses remarries or begins living with someone. The remarriage or cohabitation of a divorced spouse is a relevant but not a decisive factor on any subsequent application to vary a support order.

It is very important to note that in an application for support, the conduct of the parties is irrelevant. However, the persistent failure of a financially dependent spouse to acquire the skills necessary to achieve economic self-sufficiency may constitute a basis for the variation or suspension of a support order, as one of the objectives of the Divorce Act is to put each party in a position where they are economically self-sufficient.

2. The Family Law Act

If you do not wish to immediately petition for divorce, or if you wish to obtain a division of property, you may decide to commence proceedings under the Family Law Act, which is provincial legislation. This act requires that when support or division of property is involved, the petitioner and the respondent must file a financial information form.

Some people find the relationship between the Family Law Act and the Divorce Act very confusing. Consider, for instance, the situation where you and your spouse separate and you wish to have exclusive possession of the matrimonial home, custody of the children, and support for you and the children. You have not yet made the decision to apply for a divorce. In this instance you should retain the services of a lawyer and he or she will commence an action on your behalf under the Family Law Act for relief such as exclusive possession of the matrimonial home, custody, equalization of net family property, and support for you and the children. It is hoped you will eventually resolve these particular issues by agreement or court order and then, if you so desire, divorce proceedings can be initiated.

In this case, the only issue in the divorce proceedings will be the grounds for the actual divorce; all other matters will have been determined under the Family Law Act. The minutes of settlement, separation agreement, or court order that has disposed of the Family Law Act proceedings will be part of the record before the court in the divorce action, and the final Divorce Judgment will incorporate any appropriate provisions of this agreement.

The Family Law Act also applies to cases where a claim to property is being made. Because the Divorce Act is federal legislation and the federal government has no jurisdiction over property rights, the property claim must be made through provincial legislation or the Family Law Act. The claim, however, must be made in the *Ontario* Superior Court of Justice. If you and your spouse separate and you decide to apply for a divorce immediately, your Petition for Divorce must state that you are also commencing Family Law Act proceedings to claim an equalization of net family property. Again, if you decide to go this route, the services of a lawyer are recommended.

3. Canada Pension Plan benefits

A divorced person may be entitled to share Canada Pension Plan credits with his or her former spouse. A division of pension credits may increase a person's benefit or even create one where none previously existed.

Eligibility for credit splitting depends on the length of your relationship, when it ended, if there was a marriage agreement, and other factors. For more information on CPP credit splitting, contact the Income Security Programs office nearest you.

4. Separation agreements

As many individuals do not want to start divorce proceedings immediately, they often seek advice about being "legally separated." Practically speaking, a husband and wife are legally separated when they are simply living apart.

In a situation where the husband and wife are living apart, they would often be well advised to have a lawyer write what is commonly called a "separation agreement." Such an agreement is simply a contract between a husband and wife determining certain issues such as support, custody of children, and the division of assets. This document sets out the rights and obligations of the parties but does not make the separation any more "legal."

Before such an agreement can be entered into, certain issues have to be settled between the parties. You should consider the following matters:

(a) A clause should be inserted that stipulates that neither party will annoy, molest, or interfere with the other.

(b) If there are children of the marriage, agreement should be reached about custody and access.

(c) The issue of support for the children should be agreed on, including the amount to be paid and the age to which payments will continue. When discussing this matter with your spouse, you should also consider the requirements of the children beyond high school and, in particular, the question of financial assistance to the children should they wish to attend post-secondary institutions. While an agreement covering support payments for the children may have little effect in family court, the matter should nevertheless be discussed by the parties and agreed on if possible.

(d) If there are assets such as cars, investments, and furnishings, an agreement will have to be reached for disposing of them.

(e) If there is a family home, agreement should be reached about whether —

(i) the house will be sold and the proceeds of the sale divided equally between the parties;

(ii) one party will buy out the other; or

(iii) one party will continue to live in the home with the children until the family is grown and self-supporting. If the wife is to have sole custody of the children, it is often agreed that she will continue to live in the family home with them. In this case, definite agreement should be reached about who will pay for the mortgage and for major repairs, such as a new roof or new furnace, which might be required from time to time.

(f) If one spouse is claiming support and the other agrees to pay, then some provision should be included in the agreement on the amount to be paid, the times of payments, and under what circumstances the payments will cease (e.g., remarriage or the supported spouse living with another person).

(g) If there are debts outstanding prior to the separation of the parties, there should be a clause in the agreement stating who is responsible for such debts. Provision should also be made for indemnifying each party against responsibility for debts incurred by the other after the agreement has been signed.

(h) There should be a clause in the agreement determining the effective period of the agreement (e.g., whether it is to be an interim agreement to be terminated on dissolution of the marriage, or whether it is to continue in effect after a divorce judgment has been granted), particularly in regard to property settlement and support for the spouse and children.

The best way to approach the drafting of a separation agreement is for you and your spouse to sit down and discuss the issues mentioned above. There will undoubtedly be other matters to consider, but the issues set out should be your first considerations.

If you can reach agreement on these basic issues, I suggest that you then retain a lawyer to put in writing what you and your spouse have already agreed on. Then your spouse must retain a lawyer for the sole purpose of providing him or her with independent legal advice on how the agreement affects his or her rights.

You must remember, however, that the separation agreement is, in fact, a contract, and it is presumed that the parties know and thoroughly understand what they are entering into. While you and your spouse should talk over the main areas of the proposed agreement beforehand, if support for you and/or your children is involved, you should see a lawyer.

It is essential to keep in mind that a separation agreement may not be enforceable and therefore may not be worth the paper it is printed on if, for example, one party was forced to sign it, if there was incomplete disclosure of assets, if the effect of the agreement is grossly unfair, or if both spouses have not had independent legal advice. The chances of having a worthless separation agreement may be too great for you to take the chance of doing it yourself.

Remember, whatever you are told about your rights, it is up to you to decide whether or not you want to exercise them to their fullest extent.

c. TAX ASPECTS OF SEPARATION AND DIVORCE

1. Support payments

If you are planning to separate or have already done so and support payments are involved for your spouse or your children, you should take time to read this section.

(i) Spousal support

The tax department allows one person to deduct spousal support if the other includes the income for tax purposes in his or her return. You should, however, be aware of the following required formalities (and see section (ii) following).

If you agree to pay monthly support (called "periodic payments") to your spouse, you will be able to deduct those payments when calculating your taxable income if —

(a) the payments are made according to a court order, Divorce Judgment, or a written agreement;

(b) the payments are made by you to your spouse, or in certain circumstances, to a third party (such as a mortgage company) for the benefit of the spouse, on a periodic basis (note that these third-party expenses must be specifically identified in the document creating the obligation to pay);

(c) you are separated from your spouse at the time the first payment is made and remain separated throughout the year; and

(d) you were legally married, or you and your spouse are of opposite sexes and have cohabited continuously in a common-law situation for three years or more, or are cohabiting and have a child. In common-law situations, the payments must be made pursuant to an order of the court.

As has been said, the support payments are deductible only if they are periodic in nature, for example, $500 per month for a spouse during his or her lifetime. A lump sum support payment such as a once and for all payment of $10 000 in lieu of future support claims is not deductible. Neither is it included in the recipient's income for tax purposes.

As you can see, it is important to define in your separation agreement that you will pay a specific amount of support at regular intervals, for example, biweekly or monthly. This will ensure that payments are properly deductible.

Your agreement can be worded in such a way as to allow tax deductions for payments made prior to the date of the agreement. This has certain limitations. Payments made in the year in which the agreement is signed and for the previous 12 months are deductible, but you cannot go back further than that. In other words, if an agreement is signed in May 1997, and specifies that prior payments are deductible, then those prior payments going back only as far as January 1, 1996, can be deducted. When filing your tax returns, always be certain to include a copy of your agreement or court order.

Also, if you are considering reconciling with your spouse, you may lose the deduction for the year unless you remain separated "throughout the remainder of the year." To give a simple illustration, if you and your spouse separated according to a written agreement in February, and the two of you got back together for the month of November in an attempt to reconcile, you would not be able to claim support payments as a deduction because you were not separated "throughout the remainder of the year." A reconciliation attempted in January of the following year would be more beneficial — at least financially.

Remember, if you are able to deduct support payments, your spouse will have to include the same amount in his or her income. In the above example, however, as you were not able to deduct the payments made from February through to November, your spouse would not have to claim them as income.

(ii) Child support

The federal government has passed a series of changes to the tax treatment of child support payments for those whose separation agreement or court order is made after May 1997. Recipients will no longer include such payments in their income; payors will not claim a deduction for the payments. Child support payments will be determined net of tax, in accordance with a schedule of child support guidelines which are shown in Appendix 6.

2. Single parents

Your family situation can have a great impact on the amount of income tax that you have to pay each year. If you are separated or divorced you may have some special tax complications that do not affect the majority of the population, especially if there are children involved. The income tax department's free booklet *Income Tax and the Single Parent* provides useful information for these situations.

The amount of personal exemptions that single parents can claim is a complicated issue, especially in the year that a divorce or separation occurs. Support payments, family allowance payments, claims for child care expenses, and the income tax

aspects of various kinds of property settlements should all be checked carefully.

If you are divorced or separated during the year and both you and your spouse have taxable income to report and children who were dependent on one of you for part of the year and on the other for part of the year, it is possible that a double claim may be made for each child.

3. The child tax benefit

If there are children of your marriage, it is quite likely that you will have already submitted a child tax benefit application to Revenue Canada, and depending upon the joint income of you and your spouse, you may or may not have qualified for this benefit. You must now notify Revenue Canada of the date your marital status changed. The person with whom your child has his or her primary residence, and who is responsible for the care and upbringing of the child, is the person eligible for the child tax benefit. You will need to advise Revenue Canada of the date that the child began residing with you, the date that you entered into a separation agreement, or the date of your divorce.

Although you may not previously have been eligible for this benefit because your joint family income was too high, your change in marital status will have an impact on your financial situation. Once you are legally separated by a separation agreement or divorce, Revenue Canada will calculate the child tax credit solely on the person's income who has custody of the child, or in the case of joint custody, the person with whom the child has his or her primary residence.

To claim this benefit, you must file a personal income tax return each year, whether or not you have any income to report. When claiming the credit for the year in which your marital status changed, you should include the net income of your spouse only up to the day on which the divorce was made final, or date of your separation agreement, whichever occurred first.

For more information, a pamphlet called *Your Child Tax Benefit* can be obtained from Revenue Canada.

4. Child care expenses

If you are a single parent, divorced, or separated, and if you have children to care for, you will probably want to claim child care expenses. Remember, though, that you can make a claim only if you report income from employment, self-employment, adult training allowances, or some form of grant; these expenses must have been incurred and paid in the taxation year in Canada. You do not have to file receipts, but you should keep them in case the tax department wants to see them.

Children for whom you claim must not be over 16 years of age in the taxation year, unless they are infirm, and you may not deduct child care payments to anyone you or your spouse claim as a dependant or to a relative who is under 21. If you are claiming payments being made to a boarding school or camp, the maximum allowance is $30 per week per child.

Only those expenses incurred to allow the parent to work, to take occupational training courses, or to do research work (if grants are received) are claimable. Babysitting expenses incurred for other purposes, such as attending school, usually don't qualify.

The tax department publishes a pamphlet called *Child Care Expenses* which is available free from any district taxation office.

4

PRELIMINARY NOTES ON PROCEDURE

a. GENERAL

All documents submitted to court must be on letter-size paper. It is permissible to use any type of bond paper except the easily erasable type, which is not acceptable at the court office. (Any stationer will help you select the proper type of paper.)

Photocopies are acceptable and you should, wherever possible, type one original only and then photocopy this original to obtain the desired number of copies. If you do not have access to a photocopying machine, carbon copies are, of course, still acceptable. However, even though the documents may be photocopied, you must personally sign all copies. You must not photocopy your signature; it will not be accepted.

Note: Certain types of photocopies are not acceptable to the court. (Xerox and other dry copiers are acceptable.) If you plan to use "wet" photocopies, take a sample copy to your local court or registrar's office and ask if it is acceptable. Only the kind that have passed the 20-year preservation test will be approved by the courts; be certain that the kind you plan to use fits into this category. Most copies now pass the test.

b. TITLE OF PROCEEDING

All legal documents must have a heading known as the "title of proceeding." This allows documents to be properly identified. Specifically, the title of proceeding in a divorce action will contain the following information:

(a) The court registry number, which will be stamped or written on the original and all copies of the Petition when it is filed, and which should be used on all subsequent documents filed in the registrar's office

(b) Name of the court, *Ontario* Superior Court of Justice

(c) Full names of the petitioner and the respondent (or husband and wife if you are joint petitioners)

The title of proceeding should head all of your documents. In many of the examples I refer simply to "title of proceeding." When preparing all your documents, head them with a title of proceeding similar to that shown in Sample #1.

c. BACKING SHEETS
(Document backs)

Every document filed in the registrar's office is required to have a document back, which is an extra page placed behind the last page of your document. It has the title of proceedings, the name of the particular document, and the name, address, and telephone number of the petitioner — or, in the case of a Joint Petition, of the husband and wife — typed on it.

A document back is shown in Sample #2. Note that the title of proceedings is typed across the top of the page, and the title of the document, etc. is typed down the right-hand side.

If you are typing your own documents and document backs, position the information in the same way that is shown in

Sample #2. The backing pages face outward and are attached to the complete document.

All documents submitted to the registrar's office for filing must have backs. The only exception to this rule will be when you file what is called your Record. It is not necessary to include copies of the backs of the documents in the Record.

d. IDENTIFICATION OF JUDGES

This section applies only if a court appearance is necessary. The Ontario Court (General Division) has exclusive jurisdiction to hear divorce cases and the registrar of the court will help you process the paperwork for doing this.

When the matter is being heard before a judge, he or she will be referred to in the Judgment for Divorce as "The Honourable Mr. or Mdm. Justice_____."

e. FORMAT FOR COURT ORDER

In addition to the requirement to use ordinary bond paper (not the easily erasable type) for your orders, it is essential that when you prepare and submit any order for the approval of the court, you leave three to four inches (about seven to ten centimetres) of space at the bottom of the document. This space is required for the stamps and signatures of various officials as well as the judge. There have been occasions where orders submitted by lawyers have been rejected because insufficient space was allowed for the stamps and signatures.

It is also necessary to allow a one-and-a-half- to two-inch margin (four to five centimetres) on the left side of your documents. This is also to allow for any necessary registry stamps and/or notations.

Note: All typewritten documents submitted to the court must be double-spaced.

SAMPLE #1
TITLE OF PROCEEDING

Court file no._____

ONTARIO SUPERIOR COURT OF JUSTICE

BETWEEN:

Joan Public

PETITIONER
(Wife   )

- and -

John Que Public

RESPONDENT
(Husband   )

(Court Seal)

Joan Public
PETITIONER (Wife

and

John Que Public
RESPONDENT (Husband

)

)

Court file no.____

(Short title of proceeding)

ONTARIO **SUPERIOR COURT OF JUSTICE**

Proceeding commenced at

(NAME OF DOCUMENT)

Name, address, and telephone number of petitioner

Joan Public
322 Lakeshore Road
Toronto, Ontario
555-5666

Petitioner appearing in person

5

STEP-BY-STEP PROCEDURE

for *Ontario* **Superior Court of Justice**

Note: Divorce law has recently changed in Ontario with the implementation of the new Family Law Rules. If you and/or your spouse live in a region that is not referred to in Chapter 6, your case will come under the *Ontario* Superior Court of Justice and the Rules of Civil Procedure and this chapter is for you. If you live elsewhere in the province you are in an area where the new Family Law Rules are in effect and you may have to file different forms. (See chapter 6.)

If you have decided that your situation is simple enough for you to do your divorce yourself, and you can foresee no complications with proof, etc., you are now ready to begin the step-by-step procedure. (See Appendix 1 for a detailed checklist of steps.)

Samples of the forms you will have to submit are illustrated in this chapter. If you are confused by any section of a form, seek professional advice. Do not proceed if you are uncertain; the consequences of making an error could be costly.

a. OBTAINING YOUR MARRIAGE REGISTRATION

The Certificate of Marriage given to you at the time of your marriage may not be adequate for proving the marriage in court.

If you were married in Canada or in a country that is a member of the Commonwealth, you should get a copy of the registration of your marriage. If you were married in Ontario, write to the Office of the Registrar General, P.O. Box 4600, Thunder Bay, Ontario, P7B 6L8. If you were married outside the province, refer to Appendix 2 for a list of addresses to write to for your copy. This copy no longer needs to be certified.

The cost of this copy of registration in Ontario is currently $15*. Send a certified cheque, or money order, payable to the Minister of Finance with a letter including the following particulars:

(a) Full name of wife (maiden name)

(b) Full name of husband

(c) Date of marriage

(d) Place of marriage

b. FOREIGN MARRIAGES

If you were married in a country other than Canada, the United States, or a Commonwealth country, you will be required to prove the validity of your marriage certificate. This is usually done by having the document translated under oath by a translator and by having that translator's certificate attached.

A lawyer or legal aid office will be able to supply the name of a translator who is accustomed to providing this service. In

---

Note that all fees are subject to change without notice. Please check all fees with the court or appropriate government office before submitting funds.

most cases, a motion concerning the admissibility of the affidavit must also be made.

If you are at all uncertain of what to do in this slightly complicated situation, I suggest that you consult a lawyer for this purpose only. Don't forget to get a quotation for the fee. It should cost about $100.

c. PREPARATION OF JOINT PETITION

The Petition shown in Sample #3 is a Joint Petition and is to be used when *both* spouses jointly seek a Divorce Judgment. It is important to note that a Joint Petition can be used *only* under section 8(2)(a) of the Divorce Act (i.e., one-year separation). If you want to proceed under section 8(2)(b) (i.e., adultery or cruelty), you must file as a sole petitioner. Also, a Joint Petition can be used only when a divorce is sought on consent of both parties. That means if you and your spouse disagree on any issue, such as custody, access, or support, you must not use a Joint Petition.

In a Joint Petition, the parties are simply referred to as "husband" and "wife." All claims must be agreed to by both spouses. The divorce will be granted to both spouses.

If you purchased the set of forms available from the publisher (see page xii), you should make a copy of the Joint Petition. Use one copy for rough work and the other for the final copy. You should then photocopy the completed petition *before signing*. You and your spouse should then sign two copies, so that you have two originals. These two signed copies will be taken to the court to issue the Petition. The court keeps one of the copies and returns an issued Petition to you. Both you and your spouse should retain a photocopy of the issued Petition for your own records. You will also require an additional photocopy of the issued Petition when you set the matter down for hearing.

Refer to Sample #3 while drafting your own Joint Petition. Make certain that your name and your spouse's name are *exactly* as set out in the marriage certificate or marriage registration. If a woman elected to retain her maiden name, this will be noted on the marriage documents and should be used on the Petition. If you or your spouse are known by any other name, set out the names as follows:

John Que Public,
also known as
John Que Private

1. Explanatory notes for completing a Joint Petition

Complete all relevant sections of the Petition as briefly and concisely as possible. Refer to examples that set out the basic pleadings for particulars of your grounds for divorce. The following sections correspond to the sections in the Petition for Divorce.

Paragraph 1 — Joint Petition

Set out exactly the relief you are seeking. If you are asking the court to ratify other orders such as custody or support or the division of property that you and your spouse have agreed to on consent, you may set out these other terms in subparagraph 1(b).

Under subparagraph 1(c), or under the Family Law Act, you may also ask the court to recognize consent arrangements to custody, access, and support. It is wise to list these things under 1(b) and under 1(c). Should the court then not grant your divorce for some reason, you will still be entitled to an order granting the other relief.

You must consider exactly what relief you want the court to grant, and ask for it. As you can see on the sample, your Petition first claims that you and your spouse should be divorced from each other. Other common orders sought in a Joint Petition are the following:

(a) Custody of the infant child(ren) of the marriage with reasonable access to the spouse. If custody is claimed, you may claim "reasonable access," or if access is to be specified, you must set out in paragraph 24 the actual access agreed upon. For example:

> The husband and wife have agreed that the husband shall have access to the children on alternate weekends, one week during the Christmas holidays, and one month during the summer vacation.

Note: The terms of access will be included in the Divorce Judgment.

(b) Reasonable access to the infant child(ren).

(c) Support for the husband/wife and the said infant child(ren) in the amount of $_____.

Be absolutely certain whether or not you wish to claim support or division of property for yourself before issuing the Petition. If no order for support for you (exclusive of payments for the children) or division of property is set out in the Judgment, you will not later be able to apply for such relief in the divorce action. However, you may still have property or support rights under the Family Law Act. If you intend to pursue these rights in separate proceedings after your divorce has been finalized, you would be well advised to consult a lawyer prior to getting a divorce judgment.

Paragraph 2 — Grounds for divorce — Separation

In paragraph 2, fill in the appropriate date indicating when your separation began. Also indicate with dates the beginning and end of any periods during which you and your spouse resumed cohabitation.

Paragraphs 3 and 4 — Reconciliation

If no efforts have been made to reconcile, simply indicate this with the words "there have been no attempts at reconciliation" or "none."

If reconciliation has been attempted, indicate this concisely. Here is an example:

> The parties hereto went to a marriage counsellor in July 20—, but were not able to effect a reconciliation.

Paragraphs 5 to 17 — Details of marriage

Remember, Petitions will not normally be accepted for filing unless your marriage certificate or a copy of the registration of your marriage is filed as well. The registrar has the discretion to accept the Petition, however, if there is a valid reason for your inability to file a certificate or copy of registration and that reason is stated in paragraph 17(b).

Paragraphs 18 to 21 — Residence

If either you or your spouse has been ordinarily resident in Ontario for at least one year before the Petition is issued, the court has the jurisdiction to grant a divorce.

Paragraphs 22 to 28 — Children

All children who are under 16 years of age or those over 16 but dependent on either spouse due to illness, disability, because they are still attending school (generally up to the age of 22), or other cause should be listed in the Petition with their places and dates of birth.

If there are children of your marriage, the court must be satisfied that proper support arrangements have been made before a divorce is granted. Remember, if you and your spouse disagree about child custody or financial arrangements, you *cannot* use the Joint Petition procedure.

In paragraph 23, fill in the particulars of the request of your custody order to agree with your claim under paragraph 1 of the Petition. If you had a child, the terms of the order might read:

> Custody to the wife. Reasonable access to the husband.

If there is a child or children, paragraph 25 would be completed with wording such as:

(i) Since the child's birth, the husband and wife have shared responsibility for his care.

(ii) The father's occupation as a long-distance bus driver requires him to travel frequently.

(iii) The wife is in a better position to meet the day-to-day needs of the child.

(iv) The child has a close relationship with both parents.

Paragraph 27 must be completed if there is a claim for support. The court must be satisfied that reasonable arrangements have been made for the support of any children before a divorce will be granted, and you must set out financial particulars in sufficient detail to allow the court to reach this conclusion.

Paragraph 29 — Other court proceedings

This section includes matters such as family court support hearings or actions for judicial separation, custody, or annulment. If you were involved in any such proceedings, indicate when the matter was heard, and the results. If there is a previous action still not completed, consult a lawyer so that it can be disposed of.

Paragraph 30 — Domestic contracts and financial arrangements

Set out the date of any pertinent agreements, either written or verbal, such as a marriage contract as defined by the Family Law Act, a separation agreement, or a financial arrangement.

Paragraph 31 — No collusion

If you are guilty of collusion (see Glossary for a definition of this term), your divorce will be refused. If you feel you may have a problem complying with this requirement, you should consult a lawyer.

Paragraph 32 — Declaration of spouses

This paragraph calls for a declaration of spouses; simply sign where indicated. Since both parties sign the Petition, obviously the document need not be served. To complete your Petition, date the document and complete the document back.

2. Preparing the other documents

Once you have completed the Petition, you must prepare these other documents:

(a) Notice of Motion (see Sample #5) (This document sets out the evidence to be relied on)

(b) Joint Affidavit (see Sample #6)

(c) Financial Statement (see Sample #12) (if child or spousal support is to be paid)
or
Waiver of Financial Statements (see Sample #7) (if no support of any kind is to be paid)

(d) Support Deduction Order (Sample #14) (where child and/or spousal support is being paid)

(e) Support Deduction Order Information Form (Sample #15) (where child and/or spousal support is being paid)

(f) Case Information Statement (Sample #16) (only if you are filing for divorce in Toronto Region, District of Algoma, or Essex County)

(g) Divorce Judgment (see Sample #8)

(h) Certificate of Divorce (see Sample #9)

(i) Affidavit (re no appeal) (see Sample #10)

The Joint Affidavit (see Sample #6) must be sworn before a lawyer, notary public, or a commissioner for taking oaths.

3. The Motion Record

Once you have completed these documents, you are ready to form your Motion Record and file your documents with the court. The Motion Record is a collection, in booklet form, of all the documents that have to be filed in the registrar's office. They are put together in chronological order so that the court officials and the judge can refer to them quickly and easily.

The Record must contain typed copies or photocopies of the originals. Photocopies will be allowed only if they are clear and true duplicates. Your record must contain the following documents in the order listed:

(a) A table of contents or index, describing each document by its name and date. This should also give the page number (or tab number if you separate the documents by tabs) of each document in the Record (therefore, you must number all the pages in the Motion Record; see Sample #4).

(b) The Notice of Motion

(c) A *copy* of the Petition for Divorce (You must keep the Petition with the original signatures separated from the bound Record.)

(d) The Waiver of Financial Statements (or Financial Statement if applicable)

(e) The Joint Affidavit

(f) A Record Back (the same as shown in Sample #2 but typed on light blue cardboard or stiff paper that can be purchased at a stationery store or with the set of forms available from the publisher)

Staple the Record together (three staples down the left side of the bundle) to form a neat package (like a book), number the pages consecutively, and list the titles and page numbers of the documents on the contents page. Make an extra copy of the Record, typed or photocopied, to keep for yourself.

4. Filing your documents

After your Motion Record is prepared, take it to your nearest court office along with the original Petition for Divorce, your marriage certificate, four copies of your Divorce Judgment (see Sample #8), and two self-addressed, stamped envelopes: one addressed to you and one addressed to your spouse. These are for the use of the court when it mails the Divorce Judgment to you and your spouse.

If you are not certain that your Record and other documents are in order, ask one of the clerks in the divorce section of the court office to check them over for you. There may be slight differences in the procedure for filing from office to office, but the clerks will be able to assist you and inform you if anything is missing. (Both spouses do *not* have to do this; only one spouse need file the Petition.)

Locate the nearest *Ontario* Superior Court of Justice courthouse by referring to the blue pages of your telephone book under Governments, Ontario, Attorney General or by phoning your nearest court building.

You will be required to pay the following fees when you file your forms:*

(a) $170 for a Clearance Certificate (for your marriage certificate "search" by the ministry; the court will provide an individual petitioner with the form to complete for a Clearance Certificate) and for issuing the Petition — cash or by money order made payable to the Minister of Finance.

(b) $195 to "set a joint or uncontested matter down" — cash or by money order made payable to the Minister of Finance.

(c) $19 for your Certificate of Divorce payable to the Minister of Finance.

Pay the filing fee to the cashier. He or she will stamp the date on all copies and "seal" the original Petition. A court clerk will also stamp a number on the upper right-hand corner and will retain the Record for the court file.

5. Application for judgment

If you have filed a Joint Petition for divorce, you and your spouse are applying and are eligible for judgment in the court office *immediately* after the Petition is accepted by the court (i.e., the process described above is completed).

Remember that the court will not give you a Divorce Judgment unless you and your spouse have lived separate and apart for at least one year, but you can process the paperwork ahead of time. The Divorce Judgment will be signed by a judge once you have filed the above documents.

After 31 days from the date the Judgment is signed, you can make application to the registry where the Petition was filed to obtain a Certificate of Divorce. You do this by completing the draft Certificate of Divorce (see Sample #9) and the Affidavit (see Sample #10). Take these court documents to the court office for signing with your $19 fee (cash or money order made payable to the Minister of Finance). The Certificate is confirmation that your divorce is final.

d. PREPARATION OF SOLE PETITION

You will note from Sample #11 that when you are applying for a divorce as a sole petitioner, there is a standard Petition for Divorce which can be obtained from the store where you bought this book or from other department, book, and stationery stores. You may also obtain the forms from the publisher by sending in the coupon at the front of this book. Alternatively, you can type the whole Petition yourself.

Refer to Sample #11 when filling out your Petition. Make certain that your name, as petitioner, and your spouse's name, as respondent, are exactly as shown in the marriage certificate. If you or your spouse is known by any other name, show the names as follows:

John Que Public,
otherwise known as
John Que Private

1. Explanatory notes for completing a Sole Petition

Complete all relevant sections of the Petition as briefly and concisely as possible. Refer to the examples that state the best pleadings for your grounds for divorce.

You will note that on the first page of the Petition for Divorce the number of days the other party is allowed to file a defence (called an Answer) must be shown. Your spouse may also counter-petition you or sue you for certain relief. This is called an Answer and Counter-Petition. If your spouse is served in Ontario, he or she is allowed 20 days in which to answer; if your spouse is served in another province or state, he or she is allowed 40 days in which to answer; if he or she is served elsewhere, 60 days are allowed.

When you have completed your Petition, but before you sign it, make one photocopy. Then sign both the original and the copy.

Paragraph 1 — Claim

You must ask the judge for what you want from the court. This "relief" will be in the form of "orders" given by the judge. If you propose to include provisions of a separation agreement in the Divorce Judgment, you should refer to the specific provisions to be included.

The following is a list of the most commonly sought orders:

(a) A divorce

(b) Custody of the infant children of the marriage

(c) Support for the petitioner and the infant children

(d) Costs against the respondent spouse (You should always insert this even though you may have no reasonable expectations of getting it.)

Remember, you must consider exactly what relief you want the court to grant, and ask for it. The court will not, in most circumstances, allow you to add requests for relief at the trial of your divorce action without ordering that the documents be re-served on the respondent.

Paragraph 2 — Grounds

Refer to the section of the act under which you intend to proceed. Make certain you have the full and accurate Divorce Act section number. Check with the section numbers that I have supplied; say exactly what has happened to give rise to this Petition. Additional examples are as follows.

Adultery

The respondent spouse has committed adultery. Particulars are as follows:

Since the date of the marriage, the husband has engaged in adulterous sexual intercourse with one Jane Private on or about the 15th day of April, 20__, at 425 Wellington Avenue, in the city of London, in the Province of Ontario.

or

Since the date of the marriage, the husband has engaged in adulterous sexual intercourse, and in particular, has committed adultery with one Janis Lane and is presently cohabiting with the said Janis Lane as husband and wife at 925 Wellington Avenue in the City of London, in the Province of Ontario. As a result of the aforementioned relationship, the husband has fathered a child, bearing the name Jake Public, born on the 18th day of December, 20__.

Note: You will, of course, have to alter the details of these examples to fit your specific set of facts.

Cruelty

The respondent has treated the petitioner with physical or mental cruelty of such a kind as to render intolerable the continued cohabitation of the spouses. Particulars are as follows:

(a) The husband has been guilty of numerous acts of violence against me, and in particular, assaulted me during the last week of March 20__ and the first week of April 20__. The husband has, for the past five years, been a heavy drinker and has continually come home drunk and has physically and verbally abused me causing me serious emotional upset which required a doctor's treatment;

(b) The husband has on frequent occasions threatened to kill me and the infant children;

(c) The husband has an irrational explosive temper and during his outbursts has destroyed my clothing, thrown meals on the floor, ruined our furniture, and hurled ash-trays at me;

(d) Due to the husband's conduct, I have received medical treatment for injuries suffered and am in fear of ever having to live with the husband again.

Note: The above details about the cruelty are only examples of acts of cruelty which may well constitute grounds for divorce. Obviously, there will be other details that you may wish to include. I suggest that you keep it as brief as possible and that you include only those acts of cruelty that are the most obvious.

Paragraphs 3 and 4 — Reconciliation

If no efforts have been made to reconcile, simply indicate this with the word "none." The clause in the sample Petition (Sample #11) under the heading "Reconciliation" shows one of the more common steps taken by parties attempting reconciliation.

Paragraphs 5 to 17 — Details of marriage

Make sure the information you put in this section conforms exactly to the statistics in the copy of your marriage registration, which by now you will have received from the Registrar of Vital Statistics.

If you are not certain of your spouse's place and date of birth, indicate as specifically as possible the information you do have (e.g., Poland, March 1950).

Paragraphs 18 to 21 — Residence

Residence means the province where you now live (not necessarily permanently). The court says that you must have resided a certain length of time in a province before you are entitled to proceed with a divorce action. This residence time is 12 months and you must have actually lived in Ontario for 12 months immediately preceding the start of your divorce action.

Paragraphs 22 to 28 — Children

All children who are under 16 years of age, or those over 16 but dependent on either spouse due to illness, disability, or other cause, must be listed in the Petition with their places and dates of birth. See the examples of the proposed custody of the children in Sample #11. Refer also to the section on custody in chapter 3.

Paragraph 29 — Other court proceedings

All Petitions for Divorce filed in the *Ontario Superior Court of Justice* must contain a paragraph concerning the "joinder of causes" or other proceedings involved. Virtually everyone involved in a do-it-yourself divorce will indicate that this paragraph is "Not Applicable."

However, those of you who are bringing a claim against your spouse for a portion of his or her separate property or business assets should briefly state the nature of your claim here, and if you have already had a hearing on the matter, you should also indicate the result of your claim. If the claim was to be joined (heard at the same time) with your Petition, then all of the extra documents in support of this claim will also have to be filed.

In any event, if you are advancing a claim against your spouse's property under the Family Law Act, it is highly unlikely that you are acting without legal representation. You certainly should have such representation.

This section also includes matters such as family court support hearings, previous divorce actions, custody actions, or actions for annulment. If you were involved in any such proceedings, simply indicate when the matter was heard and the result. If there is a previous action still not completed, consult a lawyer so that it can be disposed of.

Paragraph 30 — Domestic contracts and financial arrangements

Simply state the date of any pertinent agreements, either written or oral.

Paragraph 31 and 32 — Collusion, condonation, and connivance

If you are guilty of collusion, your divorce will be refused. If you are guilty of condonation or connivance, your Petition will be dismissed unless the judge feels it would be in the public interest to grant the divorce.

Collusion is an agreement to manufacture, fabricate, or suppress evidence in order to deceive the court and secure a divorce.

Condonation means that you forgave your spouse for the acts that you are now using as grounds for divorce. Condonation actually arises if you continue to live with your spouse or return to live with him or her after learning of his or her misconduct. Remember, however, if you have lived with your spouse for a period or periods not more than 90 days after learning of his or her misconduct in an attempt to effect a reconciliation, you will not be guilty of condonation.

Connivance means that you either encouraged your spouse's conduct or stood idly by and did nothing about it.

If you feel you may have a problem complying with these requirements, you should consult a lawyer.

Paragraph 32 concerning condonation and connivance is not relevant if the divorce is sought on the ground of separation only.

Paragraph 33 — Matters other than divorce and custody

Here you set out the details in support of claims other than for the divorce itself and custody of any children. As shown in the sample, these details would normally relate to a claim for support.

Paragraph 34 — Trial

If your divorce action will be going to trial, you will appear before a judge.

2. Financial statement

If you are asking for child or spousal support or division of assets, both spouses will have to file a Financial Statement, as shown in Sample #12. You must attach to the Financial Statement a copy of your most recent tax return and tax assessment notice.

To get your spouse to fill out the appropriate form, send a Notice to File Financial Statement (see Sample #13). Your spouse must file this form within the same time limits for filing an Answer to the Petition. (The time limits are noted on the first page of the Petition.)

3. Support Deduction Order and Support Deduction Order Information Form

Under the Family Responsibility and Support Arrears Enforcement Act, all matters involving custody and/or support must include a Support Deduction Order and a Support Deduction Order Information Form. You should file these with your Petition (see Samples #14 and #15).

The Support Deduction Order and the Information Form are reviewed and signed by a judge. The employer is then ordered to deduct monthly support payments from the payor spouse's wages. These payments are forwarded to the Family Support Plan and then to the recipient.

Follow these steps to fill out the Support Deduction Order:

(a) Fill in the name of court as *"Ontario Superior Court of Justice"* and give the address of the courthouse where you are filing the petition, e.g., "393 University Avenue, Toronto."

(b) Fill in the court file number and names of petitioner and respondent. Do not fill in the date; the court will insert this information.

(c) In paragraph 1, fill in the name of the person who will be paying support.

(d) File the Support Deduction Order with your Motion Record after serving your spouse with the Petition.

Follow these steps to fill out the Support Deduction Order Information Form:

(a) Fill in the name of court as *"Ontario Superior Court of Justice"* and give the address of the courthouse where you are filing the Petition.

(b) Under "TYPE OF SUPPORT ORDER," put an X in the box next to "FINAL."

(c) Fill in the court file number.

(d) Fill in which Family Support Plan Regional Office you fall under (see the blue pages of your phone book) and your case number, if you know it.

(e) Complete sections 1. and 2. Check off "Additional income source…" if the payor has more than one source of income, i.e., two jobs. Check off "Payor not receiving…" if the payor is self-employed or is otherwise not capable of paying through payroll deduction because there is no employer/employee relationship. Check off "Recipient does not know" if you do not know the payor's place of employment.

(f) Complete section 3., leaving shaded areas blank.

(g) Fill in your name next to "Prepared by."

(h) File the Support Deduction Order Information Form with your Motion Record after serving your spouse with the Petition.

When an order for support is made, the order or judgment is automatically sent to the Family Responsibility Office by the court, along with the Support Deduction Order. If both parties agree, it is now possible to withdraw from the Family Responsibility Office. Both parties must write to the Family Responsibility Office to say that they want to withdraw from the program. Both parties can sign and send one letter or each party can send a separate letter.

4. Case Information Statement

You must complete the Case Information Statement only if you are filing for divorce in the Toronto Region, Algoma District, or Essex County (see Sample #16). Case management is a system employed by the courts whereby a judge is assigned to monitor your case to ensure that it is resolved efficiently. This means that one judge is appointed to hear all matters on the case arising from the litigation until trial. This should not be a concern for you if you are expecting to obtain an uncontested divorce. You will receive a Case Management Timetable when you issue your Petition, which will set deadlines for filing of materials. Follow the deadlines given and you will have no difficulty.

Follow these steps to fill out the Case Information Statement:

(a) Fill in the court office address and the title of the case, e.g., "Public v. Public."

(b) Under "THIS FORM FILED BY," put an X in the box next to "applicant/petitioner/plaintiff."

(c) Under "ORDER SOUGHT...," put an X in the box next to "divorce" and indicate any other orders you are seeking.

(d) Complete "PERSON FILING THIS FORM," "OTHER SPOUSE," and "CHILDREN" sections with the information requested.

(e) Under "THIS PERSON'S LAWYER," provide your own name, address, and telephone number. Fill in the date.

(f) File the Case Information Statement along with your Petition.

5. Filing the documents

As was stated at the start of this chapter, the documents we are discussing are suitable for filing in the *Ontario* Superior Court of Justice (Chapter 6 deals with areas under the jurisdiction of the *Ontario* Superior Court of Justice Family Court Branch). However, if custody and/or access of the children is involved, the trial (if one is necessary) must take place in the county or district where the child resides.

Take your filing fee, your marriage certificate (or copy of your marriage certificate), and your documents (including your original Petition and the signed copy) to the *Ontario* Superior Court of Justice. Have the official in charge of divorce matters look through your documents to see that they are in order.

Pay the filing fee to the cashier; he or she will stamp the date on the file copy and process a copy through the cash register. This indicates to the court officials that you have, in fact, paid the necessary fee. (Currently, the fee is $170 which must be made in cash or money order payable to the Minister of Finance. This includes $135 for issuing the Petition and $10 for the clearance certificate. Personal cheques are not accepted.)

Return the documents to the official at the divorce counter. He or she will date and sign the Petition for Divorce, assign a number to your action, and then stamp the *Ontario* Superior Court of Justice seal on the original Petition. The registrar retains the copy with the cash register stamp and you receive back the original. You must then photocopy the required number of copies for service on the respondent and the co-respondent (if applicable).

You will need the original Petition for Divorce, plus an additional copy for each party to be served (usually only the respondent husband/wife), and a copy for yourself.

You are now ready to have the Petition (and Financial Statement and Notice to File Financial Statement, if applicable) served on the appropriate parties. If you are issuing the Petition in the Toronto Region, Algoma District, or Essex County, you must also serve the Warning/Timetable provided to you by the Court, as well as the Case Information Statement.

6. Family Information Session Program

If you are commencing your divorce in Toronto and are claiming relief other than a divorce, costs, and the incorporation of the terms of a separation agreement or prior court order, you and your spouse will be required to attend a Family Information Session. The program is designed to provide information about separation and the legal process and may include topics such as:

(a) options available for resolving differences, including alternatives to a court proceeding;

(b) the impact that the separation of parents has on children; and

(c) resources available to deal with problems arising from separation.

When you issue the Petition, the court provides a date for each spouse to attend the program, no later than 45 days from the date the Petition is issued. The spouses do not attend this program together. A Notice of Family Information Session is to be served on your spouse when the Petition for Divorce is served. When you attend the program, you take the Notice with you and a court official signs it as proof of your attendance. Similarly, your spouse must also attend and obtain a Certificate of Attendance. The Certificates of Attendance must be filed with the court before the divorce can proceed. Attendance at a Family Information Session is not required if you are only claiming a divorce.

7. Serving the documents

You must serve the documents within six months of issuing them with the registrar. Unless there is a court order to the contrary, you must have the Petition for Divorce served on your spouse and on any other person named in the divorce proceedings either in the Title of Proceedings or in the body of the Petition. If you are basing your Petition on adultery, the person against whom adultery is alleged need be served only if he or she is named in the Petition. If you have been given a Case Management Timetable by the court, this must also be served on the respondent.

The Notice to File the Financial Statement and your Financial Statement must also be served on your spouse, if Financial Statements are necessary. Service of Financial Statements is required if the Petition contains a claim for support or division of property. In response to the claim, the respondent must serve and file Financial Statements. Automatic filing of Financial Statements where a claim for custody is made is no longer required.

You can serve the respondent by mail with an Acknowledgment of Receipt Card (see Sample #17) by personal service, or through your spouse's lawyer if the lawyer agrees to accept service. You can also enlist the services of the sheriff of the county in which your spouse resides. This method is useful if you expect your spouse to be uncooperative.

The following is a more detailed description of methods of service, beginning with the easiest.

(a) Service by mail

The Petition for Divorce can be served on your spouse and any other person by mailing the appropriate documents to the last known address of the person to be served. But service by mail is effective only if the Acknowledgment of Receipt Card (see Sample #17) or a post office receipt bearing the signature of the person served is received by the sender.

Once the card is sent back, the sender must produce an affidavit of service for the court, attaching the card that verifies receipt by the respondent. The affidavit is filed when you go to set the divorce down at court. The affidavit should indicate the date the card was sent, to which address it was sent, and when it was received back. Attach the card to the affidavit.

If your spouse is unco-operative, and you think he or she will refuse to sign the Acknowledgment of Receipt Card, you shouldn't use this method to serve your documents.

(b) Service on a lawyer

Service on someone who has a lawyer may be made by leaving a copy of the document with the lawyer or an employee in the lawyer's office. But service in this way is effective only if the lawyer endorses on the documents (or a copy of them) an acceptance of service and the date of acceptance.

(c) Personal service

Your spouse can be personally served by having someone leave a copy of the document with him or her and having your spouse sign the Acknowledgment of Service on the backing sheet of the Petition for Divorce (see Sample #18). Please note that you personally cannot serve any person who may be named in the Petition for Divorce. Some other person must effect personal service. The person who serves your spouse must also prepare an Affidavit of Service (see Sample #19).

(d) Service by sheriff

It may be that you cannot serve your spouse by mail and your spouse does not have a lawyer. It may also be that you do not know anyone who can serve your spouse personally. In this case, the documents can be served by the sheriff of the county in which your spouse resides. If your spouse is located in some isolated area, the sheriff, whose office is also located in the courthouse, will instruct you on how best to serve him or her.

You must take all your documents and copies to the sheriff. In addition, you should make sure you have some money with you so that you are in a position to give a deposit against the sheriff's fees.

The sheriff serving the documents must swear an affidavit to confirm to the court that those persons with an actual interest in the proceedings have been notified that you are proceeding with an action for divorce.

The standard Affidavit of Service simply says that a certain person served the documents on the spouse and party with whom adultery has been alleged (if applicable) at a certain time and place (see Sample #19). A separate Affidavit of Service must be completed for each person served.

If you think your spouse will avoid service, be prepared to supply the sheriff with as much information as possible regarding his or her habits, place of work, etc.

If possible, the endorsement on the Petition backing sheet should be properly signed and witnessed. If it is not, the Affidavit of Service should provide an explanation.

A copy of the Petition is attached to the sheriff's affidavit and marked as "Exhibit A."

(e) Service by sheriff outside your county

If the party or parties to be served live outside your county, the sheriff in the county where the parties live may serve the documents. If this is your case, follow these steps:

(a) Obtain the address of the appropriate sheriff's office from your local sheriff.

(b) Go in person to the sheriff's office. If this is not possible, prepare a letter of instruction for the sheriff that lists the addresses of the parties to be served (preferably both home and business); your spouse's (and the co-respondent's) telephone number, if available; and a picture of your spouse and the other person to be served (if possible).

(c) Enclose two or three copies of the Petition for Divorce (as the case may be): one copy for the respondent, one copy for the other person (if applicable), and one copy for the sheriff to affix to the Affidavit of Service.

(d) Enclose copies of the Financial Statement and Notice to File Financial Statement.

The sheriff may wish his or her fee secured, and the terms must be satisfied (e.g., prepayment or deposit). I suggest that you prepare a letter similar to the one shown in Sample #20 if you intend to instruct the sheriff by letter.

If you do not have a photograph of your spouse, instruct the sheriff to establish identification by the best means available. In some cases, the respondent and/or the person with whom adultery has been alleged will permit the serving officer to take a photograph. In other cases, the sheriff's officer will be able to obtain sufficient information, along with the signature acknowledging receipt of the documents, to satisfy the court requirements for identification. In some cases, the party (or parties) will give the sheriff's officer a photograph to be used in the Affidavit of Service.

If you require the sheriff's officer to serve any other party named in the Petition, you must supply the address of that person's residence, place of business, etc. A picture of the other party may also be helpful.

It is important to remember that the sheriff's office will prepare the Affidavit of Service as part of its service and will give you the affidavit once the amount is paid.

It will cost a minimum of $25 to have the documents served by a sheriff's officer. This varies, of course, according to the distance the officer has to travel and how many trips he or she must make to serve the documents. However, if you send a deposit in the amount of $20 or $25 along with your letter enclosing the documents, any unused portion of your deposit will be refunded when the Affidavit of Service is sent to you.

(f) Service by process server

If you do not have a picture of your spouse, I suggest you hire a private process server who may wish to establish identity by taking a picture of your spouse at the time of service. The process server will require the same documents and information as the sheriff. Once the documents have been served, the server will provide you with his or her Affidavit of Service.

If you do engage a process server, you will have to prepare the Affidavit of Service to be sworn by him or her. The process server will provide you with the particulars of service and, when the affidavit is prepared, will take it to a notary public or a commissioner for taking affidavits and have it sworn. This affidavit should be included in the fee.

(g) Service by substitution

If you do not know the whereabouts of your spouse, you will require what is known as an "Order for Substituted Service." In other words, if your spouse cannot be served personally with the Petition for Divorce, the court must order that you be allowed to serve the Petition in some other manner, such as publishing a notice in a newspaper or posting documents in an appropriate registry.

In many cases, the petitioner simply does not know where the spouse is, either because they have been separated for a considerable length of time, or because the spouse is effectively covering his or her tracks to avoid creditors or certain financial obligations to the family.

In such circumstances, the petitioner is obviously going to have difficulty serving the documents. As a court appearance and preparation of fairly complicated documentation is required to obtain an order for substitutional service; you should retain a lawyer for this purpose only. However, you can still save a good deal in lawyer's fees if you are prepared to extend the following efforts to locate your spouse. (If you don't do these things, you will have to pay a lawyer to do them.)

(a) If you have been separated from your spouse for a long time, write to his or her relatives requesting information about his or her whereabouts. (If you have lost track of your spouse, you might also check the central Divorce Registry in case he or she has already arranged a divorce.)

(b) Place an advertisement in a newspaper published and circulated in the last place your spouse is known to have lived requesting information about his or her whereabouts. Keep in mind that the fees for legal advertisements in newspapers are often very expensive; they can be more than $250.

(c) It may be possible, if your spouse has had difficulties with the law, to contact the police department in the area where he or she was last known to be, requesting any information they can give about his or her whereabouts. You may find, however, that in most instances, the police department does not wish to become involved in civil matters.

(d) Contact friends and acquaintances of your spouse who might be able to give you information about when and where they last saw him or her.

(e) You may also use the services of a credit bureau or collection agency that can do a "skip trace" on your spouse and perhaps uncover his or her whereabouts.

8. Dispensing with service on a person named in the Petition

If you are not able to have your documents served because you have not been able to locate your spouse and/or anyone else named in the Petition, you can obtain a court order dispensing with service on that person. Again, if such an order is necessary, you should retain the services of a lawyer for this purpose only.

9. Role of the Office of the Children's Lawyer

The Office of the Children's Lawyer — formerly the Official Guardian — is charged with the responsibility of protecting the interests of children involved in matrimonial proceedings. The definition of a child is someone under the age of 16 or over the age of 16 who is still dependent on the parents. The only time the Office of the Children's Lawyer becomes involved in a divorce proceeding is when there is a dispute and the court orders that a Children's Lawyer be appointed, or if, during a motion of interim relief, the court considers that a report from the Children's Lawyer would be beneficial. If a Children's Lawyer is appointed in your case, it would be wise for you to consult a lawyer.

10. How the action is set down for trial

After you have served everyone with all the documents, you must wait the prescribed amount of time shown on the Petition for Divorce (i.e., 20 days if served in Ontario, 40 days if served in another province or state, 60 days if served elsewhere in the world). If you filed for divorce in the Toronto Region, Algoma District, or Essex County, the court issues a Warning/Timetable when you issue the Petition. You must set the matter down for hearing within 230 days from the date the proceeding was begun, or the court will dismiss your proceedings. When the time has expired, you will be required to file the following documents with the court clerk:

(a) The original Petition for Divorce (and original Financial Statement, Notice to File Financial Statement, if appropriate, and Warning/Timetable, a Case Information Statement if you are filing for divorce in the Toronto Region, Algoma District, or Essex County, and a Notice of Family Information Session, if required, for Toronto) and Affidavit of Service

(b) A Motion Record

(c) Two self-addressed, stamped envelopes — one addressed to you and one addressed to the respondent — for the use of the court when it mails the Divorce Judgment to you and the respondent

(d) Support Deduction Order (Sample #14) (where child and/or spousal support is being paid)

(e) Support Deduction Order Information Form (Sample #15) (where child and/or spousal support is being paid)

(f) Four copies of the Divorce Judgment (see Sample #22)

(g) Certificate of Attendance (required if you commence your divorce in Toronto and were provided with a Notice of Family Information Session)

(a) Petition for Divorce

You will file the original Petition for Divorce with the Affidavit of Service attached. When the Petition for Divorce is served, whoever serves it will ask the respondent to sign the Petition backing sheet in the space provided (see Sample #18). The respondent is not required to sign the Petition.

Whoever serves the Divorce Petition will then provide the Affidavit of Service (discussed earlier) that states that the respondent was asked to sign the back of the Petition and

either signed it or refused to sign and that a copy was left with the respondent at his or her address or place of business.

(b) The Motion Record

The Motion Record is a collection, in booklet form, of all the documents that have to be filed in the registrar's office. They are put together in chronological order so that the court officials and the judge can refer to them quickly and easily. As noted above, the Motion Record is filed at the end of the time allocated on the Petition for Divorce for an Answer (i.e., 20 days if served in Ontario)

The Record must contain typed copies or photocopies of the originals. Photocopies will be allowed only if they are clear duplicates. Your record must contain the following documents in the order listed:

(a) A table of contents or index, describing each document by its name and date. This should also give the page number (or tab number if you separate the documents by tabs) of each document in the Record (therefore, you must number all the pages in the Motion Record; see Sample #4).

(b) The Requisition/Notice of Motion (see Sample #23). (This document sets out the evidence to be relied on and should also set out whether or not the petitioner intends to present oral evidence at the hearing, otherwise the matter will proceed by way of affidavit evidence.)

(c) A *copy* of the Petition for Divorce (You must keep the Petition with the original signatures separated from the bound Record.)

(d) The Financial Statement, if applicable

(e) If you have obtained an Order for Substituted Service, a copy of that Order

(f) If you have an Order dispensing with service on a person named in the Petition, a copy of that Order

(g) A copy of any other Order regarding the hearing of the divorce

(h) The Affidavit of the petitioner

(i) The Affidavit of the respondent (if you have one)

(j) Record Back (the same as Sample #2 but typed on light blue cardboard or stiff paper that can be purchased at a stationery store or included with the set of forms available from the publisher)

Staple the Record together (three staples down the left side of the bundle) to form a neat package (like a book), number the pages consecutively, and list the titles and page numbers of the documents on the contents page. Make an extra copy of the Record, typed or photocopied, to keep for yourself.

If you have not already filed the Support Deduction Order and the Support Deduction Order Information Form, you can do so with the Motion.

Wait about three to four weeks for your Record to be processed. You may then phone the registrar's office to ask for the timing on your Divorce Judgment or your trial date. In cases where the evidence presented by Affidavit does not comply with the rules, is insufficient, or is incorrect, the trial judge may require a court hearing. Claims for custody, support, or division of assets, other than on consent, will also, in all likelihood, be sent to trial.

(c) Affidavit evidence

You must file affidavits to be used as evidence. You should file a Petitioner's Affidavit (see Sample #24) and a Respondent's Affidavit (see Samples #25 and #26) or any affidavit of corroborating evidence. If the grounds for your divorce is a one year separation, your affidavit alone, setting out the evidence, is usually all that is required by the court.

Sample #24 shows a Petitioner's Affidavit in a simple divorce. Use the following checklist to ensure you include all necessary information on your affidavit. Besides filling out clauses 1 and 2, the Petitioner's Affidavit must do the following:

(a) Refer to the certificate or registration of marriage by title, date, and place of issue and the name and office of the person who issued it and state that it contains the correct particulars of the marriage. (If no certificate or registration of marriage has been filed, you must state what efforts have been made to obtain a certificate and why it is impossible, the date and place of marriage, and sufficient particulars to prove the marriage.)

(b) Set out the particulars of the grounds for divorce.

(c) State that there has been no agreement, conspiracy, understanding, or arrangement to which you are a party for the purpose of subverting the administration of justice, fabricating or suppressing evidence, or deceiving the court.

(d) If you are relying on the respondent's adultery or cruelty, state that you have not condoned or connived the act or conduct complained of, or if there has been condonation or connivance, state why it would be in the public interest to grant the divorce.

(e) Provide particulars of the present and proposed custody and access arrangements for each child of the marriage if different than that stated in the Petition.

(f) If you are claiming support, attach your most current income tax return to your affidavit, along with the respondent's current income tax return. Confirm both of your incomes in your affidavit. Indicate whether support is in accordance with a separation agreement or court order. State how much support is payable from the table of Child Support Guidelines. Give as much detail as you can about your particular circumstances (see Sample #34, section 10).

(g) If you do not claim a division of property, state this and that you are aware that a claim may be barred after the divorce.

(h) If you wish to include in the judgment provisions of a consent, settlement, separation agreement, or previous court order, refer to the document as an exhibit and refer to the specific provisions included.

(i) If you are claiming costs, set out the facts to enable the court to decide whether they should be awarded.

(j) If you wish your divorce to take effect earlier than 31 days after the Divorce Judgment is granted, set out the special circumstances to justify why.

(k) Provide the respondent's last known address and state the means by which the address is known.

(d) Divorce Judgment

You must file four copies of a draft Divorce Judgment (see Sample #22) together with stamped, addressed envelopes for each of the parties and the Children's Lawyer, if one is involved. If you, as the Petitioner, chose to appear before a judge to present evidence, rather than presenting affidavit evidence, you should insert the clause "and on hearing the evidence presented by the petitioner" to the last line of the Divorce Judgment.

If the Judgment is granted according to the draft filed, the registrar signs and enters the Judgment and mails a copy of it in the envelopes provided. If the Judgment is to be granted, but not in accordance with the draft filed, the judge will make an endorsement on the Record and will grant the Judgment as of the date when the draft is

corrected to conform to the judge's endorsement and filed with the registrar. The registrar will then sign and enter the Judgment and mail it. (The 31-day period for the granting of the Certificate of Divorce begins to run only after the Judgment is granted. A defective draft Judgment will, therefore, delay the finality of the divorce.)

When you have all of these documents in order, you take them to the courthouse. The clerk will search the file and determine whether an Answer has been filed by the respondent. If the respondent has not contested the divorce, the clerk will take your documents. The charge for filing these documents, a process called "setting the matter down," is currently $195, which must be paid in cash or by money order made payable to the Minister of Finance. If an Answer has been filed, then you are going to have a contested divorce that will require a hearing before a judge. This will cost $293 to set down and you should consult a lawyer immediately.

If you are not certain that your Record and other documents are in order, ask one of the clerks in the divorce section of the registrar's office to check them over for you. There may be slight differences in the procedure for filing from office to office, but the clerks will be able to assist you and inform you if anything is missing.

After your documents have been accepted by the clerk, it will take approximately three to four weeks for you to hear anything. The documents are given to a judge to look over and if all the documents are in order, the judge will sign the Divorce Judgment. You will receive a copy in the self-addressed, stamped envelope you provided to the clerk. The respondent will also receive a copy. If the judge finds anything wrong in the documents you submitted, the clerk will call you and let you know what the problem is so that you can correct it.

For enforcement purposes, the Divorce Judgment may be registered with any court in a province and enforced in the same manner as if it were an order of that court.

Under the registration section, in Ontario, an order from another province may be registered by filing a certified copy with the local registrar at Toronto; the order will then be entered as an order of the Ontario court. A certified copy of the order may be filed by simply mailing it with a written request that registration is sought pursuant to section 20(3)(a) of the Divorce Act.

e. CERTIFICATE OF DIVORCE

After you have received your Divorce Judgment back from the court, wait 31 days. Then fill in the Certificate of Divorce (Sample #9) and the Affidavit (re no appeal) (Sample #27), which tells the court that there has been no appeal from the Judgment. Take these two documents to the courthouse where the clerk will issue your Certificate of Divorce for a fee of $19 payable to the Minister of Finance.

A Certificate of Divorce is legal throughout Canada. Should you ever wish to remarry, you must provide an original copy of the Certificate of Divorce to obtain a marriage licence.

f. UNDERTAKING NOT TO APPEAL

The effective date of the final Divorce Judgment can be shortened if there are special circumstances and the spouses agree and undertake that no appeal from the Judgment will be made (see Sample #28). The details demonstrating the special circumstances in support of an expedited Certificate of Divorce should be set out in an affidavit and in your Divorce Judgment. Examples of such circumstances would be an impending remarriage of one party or the birth of a child.

Therefore, at the same time as the action is set down for trial, you can file the Notice of Motion for Judgment, draft Divorce Judgment, Undertaking Not to Appeal, and Certificate of Divorce.

g. CONDUCT OF THE TRIAL (if one is necessary)

Most uncontested divorces are done over the counter without parties appearing in court. If a trial is required, the results of your work (good or bad) will come under the critical eye of the judge.

My experience has indicated that in cases where the work has been done carefully and thoroughly, the judge will co-operate to the fullest and "take you by the hand" through the proceedings. However, when the judge detects mistakes, omissions, or general sloppy work, he or she will be less helpful. IT IS THEREFORE CRUCIAL THAT ALL YOUR DOCUMENTS BE IN PROPER ORDER AND THAT YOU COMPLETE PROPERLY ALL THE STEPS LEADING UP TO TRIAL.

As mentioned previously, the court appearance is understandably the most difficult part for the layperson. Consider the possibility of retaining a lawyer just to handle your case in court. This could cost you approximately $600. For this fee, a lawyer will also prepare and file the Divorce Judgment. The choice is up to you.

For those who have the confidence and feel they can represent themselves as well as a lawyer can, or for those who simply cannot afford to retain a lawyer, the following detailed explanation of the courtroom procedure will guide you.

The important thing here (besides having your documents in good order) is to watch a session or two of uncontested divorce cases, preferably before the same judge who will be handling your case. From this, you will see what information the judge wants and in what order he or she wants it. Take notes and modify the general explanation set out below to suit your own circumstances.

When you appear before the judge, take your reference notes so that you don't forget anything. If you want to use this book as an aid, it is probably wiser to tear out the applicable pages rather than take the whole book in with you. Judges seem to have an aversion to watching people read their case out of a book or from a printed sheet of instructions. The best procedure is to use notes; but use them just to remind you what the next point is and then state the point in your own language.

A better technique is to point out to a judge at the start of the trial that you are representing yourself and request that he or she lead you through the proceedings. Fortunately, your chances of getting co-operation are good if you have prepared your documents correctly.

Because lawyers are called in order of seniority, your case will be put at the bottom of the list and will usually be the last of the day. Therefore, there will be only the judge, you, the clerk, and whatever witnesses you have in the court. This makes it a more informal hearing.

1. Your testimony

Always address the judge as "Your Honour" before a judge of the *Ontario* Superior Court of Justice. If the judge is a woman, ask the court beforehand how she is to be addressed: usually she will be referred to as "Your Honour."

When the judge calls your case, you will step up to the front of the courtroom, introduce yourself, and state that you are acting on your own behalf. In most cases, the judge will lead you through the proceedings. You will be asked to take the stand and give the court the following information orally.

Reconciliation

Is there any possibility of reconciliation? If your answer is no, you may also be asked, "Why not?"

Particulars of marriage

Be prepared to relate the particulars of the marriage. For example —

(a) I was married at Toronto, Ontario, on July 29, 1977.

(b) My surname before marriage was Public; *or* my wife's surname before marriage was Smith.

(c) My surname at birth was Smith.

(d) At the time of the marriage I had never been married before.

(e) At the time of the marriage my husband/wife had never been married before. (Reference will also be made to your marriage registration certificate. Simply state that it is a true copy of the registration of the marriage and that the facts given on it are correct.)

Residence

(a) I reside at (give your address).

(b) I have resided in Ontario since (give date) and I regard the province as my permanent home.

(c) During the 12 months before starting this action, I lived at (give address).

Grounds for divorce

(a) I am seeking divorce from my (husband/wife) on the grounds of marriage breakdown based on (give here the section as set out in your Petition).

(b) My (wife/husband) and I separated on (give date).

(c) I have not lived with my (wife/husband) since that time; *or* I lived with my (wife/husband) for two months after the separation in an effort to reconcile.

(d) The particulars of my grounds for divorce are (give details of your allegations of adultery or cruelty).

Children

If there are children of the marriage, identify them by giving their full names and dates of birth. If there are no children of the marriage, clearly state this.

Tell the court who has custody of the children, who they are being supported by, what schools they attend, and what you propose regarding future custody and upbringing. If you are asking for custody, you should mention whether or not you wish your spouse to have visiting rights. If your spouse has custody of the children, you should say whether or not you wish access to the children.

Other proceedings

If there have been no other petitions or proceedings with reference to the marriage, simply say so. If there have been other proceedings, simply state the nature of these proceedings, and the outcome.

Separation agreements and financial arrangements

If there are no such agreements, say so. If you have an informal (oral) agreement for the respondent to pay support to you, state the amount received each month. If you have a formal separation agreement, have your copy of the agreement with you and hand it to the judge.

Collusion, connivance, and condonation

Be sure you know the meaning of these words before you go into court! (See the Glossary at the end of this book.) Make the following statements.

(a) There is no collusion or connivance between my (wife/husband) and me with regard to these proceedings.

(b) I have not forgiven my (wife/husband) for the adultery and/or cruelty.

(c) I have not stood idly by and encouraged the adultery or cruelty.

In conclusion, simply tell the court that you want a Divorce Judgment and any of the following that are applicable:

(a) Custody of the children

(b) Support

(c) Costs

(d) Anything else applicable to your case

2. Your witnesses' testimony

In most cases, witnesses are required to corroborate testimony. If you have a witness, you should have him or her called to the witness box and sworn in by the clerk after you have completed your own testimony. Then do the following:

(a) Ask the witness whether he or she knows your spouse.

(b) Ask your witness to tell the court of his or her personal knowledge of the allegation of cruelty or adultery, or the period of separation contained in your Petition.

You should always know what your witness is going to say. Interview him or her before the court appearance to ensure that there will be no surprises in the testimony.

In most cases, your witnesses will be either personal friends or acquaintances who will not present too great a problem. If your case is going to be based on the testimony of a hostile or unfriendly witness, you must retain a lawyer to conduct the court hearing. In addition, the witness should be subpoenaed to ensure his or her presence at the trial. If everything goes all right at your trial, the judge should grant your Divorce Judgment along with any other orders such as custody and support. Take careful note of what the judge says because it is up to you (or your lawyer if you decide to hire one for the trial only) to prepare the Divorce Judgment. If you are representing yourself and you miss what the judge says (which is very easy to do), ask if you can see your Trial Record following the trial. The judge will have written down the order on the back of the Record. This may be obtained from the clerk immediately following the trial or from the registrar of the court.

If the judge reserves judgment, it may mean that he or she is not satisfied about some point and wants to consider it further or that he or she is giving you a chance to correct a defect and appear at a later date. Usually, the judge will also instruct you to see a lawyer. If so, you will have no alternative but to do so.

You then proceed to draft the Divorce Judgment according to what the judge has ordered, present it to the court clerk who will check it against the Record to make sure that it is exactly in accordance with the judge's order. The court clerk will send it out to all parties. (Remember, you must provide stamped, addressed envelopes.)

The Certificate of Divorce can be obtained 31 days after the date of the Divorce Judgment.

h. WHAT NAME CAN A WIFE USE?

When a woman marries, she is entitled to continue to use her maiden name or, at her option, may legally use her husband's name. Even if she adopts her husband's name, she cannot legally be prevented from reverting to her maiden name at any time. These rights evolve from the principle that a person may use whatever name he or she chooses, as long as it is not for fraudulent purposes.

Practically, however, it is usually difficult for a wife to convince appropriate authorities (e.g., passport office, motor vehicle licence bureau) to change her official documents to her maiden name without either a court order or a Divorce Judgment. Once you have obtained your Divorce Judgment, simply show this document to the appropriate authorities.

Court file no._____

ONTARIO SUPERIOR COURT OF JUSTICE

John Que Public   HUSBAND

(Court seal)

and

Joan Que Public   WIFE

JOINT PETITION FOR DIVORCE

Date_____Issued by_____

Local registrar

Address of court office
393 University Avenue
Toronto, Ontario
M5G 1E6

JOINT PETITION

State precisely everything you want the court to include in the judgment. Everything you want to include must have been agreed to by both spouses. If you want to include provisions of a separation agreement in the judgment, refer to the specific provisions to be included.

1.   The husband and wife jointly seek:

(a)   a divorce;

(b)   under the Divorce Act,

(i)

SAMPLE #3 — Continued

If relief is
claimed on con-
sent under any
other Act, refer to
the Act in the
claim.

~~(c)   under the Family Law Act,~~

(i)

GROUNDS FOR DIVORCE — SEPARATION

2.   The spouses have lived separate and apart since June 1, 200-_____.

   Date

The spouses have resumed cohabitation during the following periods in an unsuccessful attempt at reconciliation:

Date(s) of cohabitation

If none, state
"none."

None

RECONCILIATION

3. There is no possibility of reconciliation of the spouses.

State details. Where no efforts have been made, state "none."

4. The following efforts to reconcile have been made:

   None

DETAILS OF MARRIAGE

Where possible, copy the information from the marriage certificate.

5. Date of marriage: December 27, 1984

6. Place of marriage: Toronto, Ontario
   (City, town, or municipality, province or state, country)

7. Wife's surname immediately before marriage: Jones

8. Wife's surname at birth: Jones

9. Husband's surname immediately before marriage: Public

10. Husband's surname at birth: Public

11. Marital status of husband at time of marriage: Never married
    (Never married, divorced, or widower)

12. Marital status of wife at time of marriage: Never married
    (Never married, divorced, or widow)

13. Wife's birthplace: Toronto, Ontario
    (City, town, or municipality, province or state, country)

14. Wife's birthdate: April 11, 1955

15. Husband's birthplace: Calgary, Alberta
    (City, town, or municipality, province or state, country)

16. Husband's birthdate: May 12, 1954

Check one of (a), (b), or (c) and complete as required.

17. (a) [X] A certificate of [ ] the marriage [X] the registration of the marriage of the spouses has been filed with the court

   (b) [ ] It is impossible to obtain a certificate of the marriage or its registration because:

   (c) [ ] A certificate of the marriage or its registration will be filed before this action is set down for trial or a motion is made for judgment.

SELF-COUNSEL PRESS-DIVONT-JOINT(100-3)00

RESIDENCE

18. The wife has resided in: Toronto, Ontario
    (City, town, or municipality, province or state, country)
    since birth
    (Date)

19. The husband has resided in: Toronto, Ontario
    (City, town, or municipality, province or state, country)
    since December, 1982
    (Date)

20. The husband's current address is: 1000 Yonge Street, Toronto, Ontario

    The wife's current address is: 322 Lakeshore Road, Toronto, Ontario

Check appropriate box or boxes.

21. The [x] husband [X] wife has habitually resided in Ontario for at least one year immediately preceding the commencement of this proceeding.

CHILDREN

22. The following are all the living children of the marriage as defined by the Divorce Act:

Full name	Birthdate	School and grade or year	Person with whom child lives and length of time child has lived there

There are no children of the marriage.

The children ordinarily reside in:_____
(City, town, or municipality, province or state, country)

Be sure that this paragraph agrees with the claim under 1. above.

23. (a) The spouses seek an order on consent for custody or joint custody of the following children on the following terms:

Name of child	Terms of the order

Not applicable

Check appropriate box. Strike out if not applicable.

(b) ~~The spouses are not seeking an order for custody and~~

☐ are content that a previous order for custody remain in force

☐ are attempting to obtain an order for custody in another proceeding full particulars of which are as follows:

State name of court, court file number, and particulars of the order or proceeding.

Be sure that this paragraph agrees with the claim under 1. above or strike out if inapplicable.

~~7(c) - The spouses seek an order on consent for access (visiting arrangements) to the following children on the following terms:~~

Name of child   Terms of the order

SELF-COUNSEL PRESS-DIVONT-JOINT(100-5)00

State details such as days of the week, hours of visit, and place of access.

24. ~~(a) The following are the existing visiting arrangements (access) for the spouse who does not have the children living~~ with him or ~~her:~~

SELF-COUNSEL PRESS-DIVONT-JOINT(100-6)00

Check appropriate box.

(b) The existing visiting arrangements (access) are: ☐ satisfactory   ☐ not satisfactory

If not satisfactory, give reasons and describe how the arrangements should be changed.

25. The order sought in paragraph 23 is in the best interests of the children for the following reasons:

26. The following material changes in the circumstances of the spouses are expected to affect the children, their custody, and the visiting arrangements (access) in the future:

SELF-COUNSEL PRESS-DIVONT-JOINT(100-7)00

48

SAMPLE #3 — Continued

27. (a) ~~The existing arrangements between the spouses for support for the children are as follows:~~

Amount paid	Time period (Weekly, monthly, etc.)	Paid by (Husband or wife)	Paid for (Name of child)

Check appropriate box.

If not being honoured, specify how much is unpaid and for how long. If you agree on an order for payment of part or all of the unpaid amount, be sure to include it

(b) ~~The existing support arrangements ☐ are being honoured ☐ are not being honoured.~~

Be sure that this paragraph agrees with the claim under 1. above.

(c) ~~The spouses propose that the support arrangements for the children should be as follows:~~

Amount to be paid	Time period (Weekly, monthly, etc.)	To be paid by (Husband or wife)	To be paid for (Name of child)

Check appropriate box.

If not being met, state particulars.

28. The education needs of the children ☐ are being met ☐ are not being met.

SELF-COUNSEL PRESS-DIVONT-JOINT(100-8)00

OTHER COURT PROCEEDINGS

State the name of the court, the court file number, the kind of order the court was asked to make, and what order, if any, the court made. If the proceeding is not yet completed, state its current status.

29. The following are all other court proceedings with reference to the marriage or any child of the marriage:

None

DOMESTIC CONTRACTS AND FINANCIAL ARRANGEMENTS

Indicate whether the contract or arrangement is now in effect, and if support payments are not being paid in full, state the amount that has not been paid.

30. The spouses have entered into the following domestic contracts and other written or oral financial arrangements:

Date	Nature of contract or arrangement	Status
None		

NO COLLUSION

31. There has been no collusion in relation to this divorce proceeding.

SELF-COUNSEL PRESS-DIVONT-JOINT(100-9)00

DECLARATION OF SPOUSES

32.

(a) I have read and understand this petition for divorce. The statements in it are true, to the best of my knowledge, information, and belief.

(b) I understand that I have the right to seek independent legal advice concerning this proceeding and to retain my own separate counsel.

(c) I understand that I may lose my right to make a claim for division of property after the divorce if I do not make the claim at this time.

Date _May 2, 200-_ _____ _John Q. Public_ _____
(Signature of husband)

Date _May 2, 200-_ _____ _Joan Public_ _____
(Signature of wife)

SELF-COUNSEL PRESS-DIVONT-JOINT(100-10)00

Court File No.

ONTARIO SUPERIOR COURT OF JUSTICE

BETWEEN:

JOAN PUBLIC

Petitioner (Wife)

-and-

JOHN QUE PUBLIC

Respondent (Husband)

_____

MOTION RECORD

_____

Date: , 200-

JOAN PUBLIC
322 Lakeshore Road
Toronto, Ontario

Court File No.

ONTARIO SUPERIOR COURT OF JUSTICE

BETWEEN:

JOAN PUBLIC

Petitioner (Wife)

-and-

JOHN QUE PUBLIC

Respondent (Husband)

INDEX

TAB

1. Requisition to Note Default and Notice of Motion for Judgment dated August 2, 200-.

2. Petition for Divorce, dated May 2, 200-.

3. Affidavit of the Petitioner, sworn May 2, 200-.

Court file no._____

ONTARIO SUPERIOR COURT OF JUSTICE

BETWEEN:

John Que Public   HUSBAND

- and -

Joan Public   WIFE

NOTICE OF MOTION

The motion is for default judgment in accordance with the petition.

The grounds for the motion are that the spouses jointly petitioned for divorce.

The following documentary evidence will be relied on:

1. the petition

2. the certificate of marriage or the registration of marriage filed in this action

3. the affidavits of the husband and wife petitioner dated _July 2, 200-_____

(List any other)

~~The petitioners intend to present oral evidence at the hearing of the motion.~~

(Delete if not applicable)

Date _August 2, 200-_____

Names, addresses, and telephone numbers of petitioners.

John Que Public   Joan Public
1000 Yonge Street   322 Lakeshore Road
Toronto, Ontario   Toronto, Ontario
555-1111   555-5666

SELF-COUNSEL PRESS-DIVONT-JOINT(101-1)00

Court file no. _____

ONTARIO SUPERIOR COURT OF JUSTICE

BETWEEN:

Type in name of husband.

JOHN QUE PUBLIC   (HUSBAND)

- and -

Type in name of wife.

JOAN PUBLIC   (WIFE)

JOINT AFFIDAVIT

Name of husband

We, John Que Public _____ (Husband), of

City, town Municipality or county
Name of wife

the _City of Toronto_____ in the_Municipality of_____

Metropolitan Toronto_____ and _____Joan Public_____ (Wife),

City, town Municipality or county

of the _City of Toronto_____, in the_Municipality of_____
Metropolitan Toronto_____ , MAKE OATH AND SAY AS FOLLOWS:

1. We are the husband and wife described above and as such have knowledge of the matters to which we hereinafter depose.

2. We are jointly petitioning for divorce on the grounds that we have lived separate and apart since the ___1st_____ day of ___June_____ , 200-_____ .

3. There is no possibility of our reconciliation. The following efforts to reconcile have taken place: None

Set out particulars. If no efforts to reconcile have been made, state "None"

4. The particulars of our marriage as contained in the Certificate of Marriage are true. Attached hereto and marked as Exhibit "A" is a true copy of the Marriage Certificate.

SELF-COUNSEL PRESS-DIVONT-JOINT(102-1)00

5. All the information as set out in the Joint Petition for Divorce, filed, that relates to details of the marriage and separation is correct.

Insert the number of children. If there are no children, type in "no."

6. We have _____ no _____ child(ren).

Their names and dates of birth are as follows:

Name   Birthdate

Not applicable

Type in "mother" or "father."

We are the parents of the child(ren). The child(ren) have lived with the _____ since birth and we agree that they should continue to do so.

The child(ren) are currently residing at _____
                                                                              (address)

Type in "mother" or "father" as appropriate.

7. We are in agreement that there should be joint custody where the _____ has access to the child(ren) during the following times:

Set out in detail all access arrangements, exactly as described in Petition.

Not applicable

8. This arrangement is in the best interests of the child(ren) for the following reasons:

Not applicable

9. The arrangements we have made for support are as follows:

Amount paid	Time period (weekly, monthly)	Paid by (husband or wife)	Paid for (name of child)

Not applicable

Type in "father" or 'mother" as appropriate.
Type in "father" or 'mother" as appropriate.

10. We have agreed that the support arrangements for the child(ren) should be as set out above based on the financial statements, filed, and the budgets of the children. We agree that the child(ren) cost approximately $_____ per month and, based on our earnings, we agree that the _____ should pay $_____ to the _____.

11. The educational needs of the children are being met.

12. The following are all other court proceedings with reference to the marriage or any child(ren) of the marriage:

Set out particulars. If none, state "None."

Not applicable

13. We have entered into the following domestic contracts and other written or oral financial arrangements:

Set out particulars. If none, state "None."

Date	Nature of contract or arrangement	Status

None

SELF-COUNSEL PRESS-DIVONT-JOINT(102-3)00

14. There has been no agreement, conspiracy, understanding or arrangement to which we are directly or indirectly a party for the purpose of subverting the administration of justice, fabricating or suppressing evidence, or deceiving the Court.

15. We have agreed that the issues of property and spousal support have been settled. We do not claim a division of property at this time and we are aware that a claim for a division of property may be barred after the divorce.

16. Neither the husband nor the wife intends to appeal the Divorce Judgment.

17. The present address for the husband is: ___1000 Yonge Street, Toronto, Ontario___

   The means by which this is known are: ___personal knowledge___

18. The present address for the wife is: ___322 Lakeshore Road, Toronto, Ontario___

   This means by which this is known are: ___personal knowledge___

SEVERALLY SWORN BEFORE ME at the)
___City of Toronto___)
in the ___Municipality of___)
___Metropolitan Toronto___) _John Q. Public_
this ___2nd___ day of ___July___) John Que Public
200-_____.)
)
)
) _Joan Public_
) Joan Public

___I. C. Ewe___
A Commissioner for taking Affidavits.

SELF-COUNSEL PRESS-DIVONT-JOINT(102-4)00

Court file no._____

ONTARIO SUPERIOR COURT OF JUSTICE

BETWEEN:

John Que Public   HUSBAND

- and -

Joan Public   WIFE

WAIVER OF FINANCIAL STATEMENTS

The husband and the wife waive financial statements in respect of claims made in this action for support under the Divorce Act.

Date:___July 2, 200-_____   Date:___July 2, 200-_____

_____*Joan Public*_____   _____*John Q. Public*_____
Signature of wife   Signature of husband

Wife's name___Joan Public_____   Husband's name___John Que Public___

Address:__322 Lakeshore Road___   Address:__1000 Yonge Street____
___Toronto, Ontario_____   ___Toronto, Ontario_____

__Z1P 0G0_____   __Z1P 0G0_____

Tel. No:__555-5666_____   Tel. No:_555-1111_____

SELF-COUNSEL PRESS-DIVONT-JOINT(103-1)00

Court file no._____

ONTARIO SUPERIOR COURT OF JUSTICE

THE HONOURABLE   JUSTIN J. JUDGE   Monday, August 2 **200-**

(day and date judgment given)

BETWEEN:

JOHN QUE PUBLIC   HUSBAND,

- and -

(Court seal)

JOAN PUBLIC

                                                                   WIFE

DIVORCE JUDGMENT

THIS MOTION made jointly by the spouses for judgment for divorce was heard this day at ___Toronto, Ontario_____

(place)

The spouses jointly petitioned for divorce.

ON READING the petition, the notice of motion for judgment, the affidavit dated ___July 2, 200-_____ of the husband and the wife

(date)

filed in support of the motion and

(add any other material filed)

1. THIS COURT ORDERS AND ADJUDGES THAT ___John Que Public___
(names of spouses)

and ___Joan Public___
who were married at ___Toronto, Ontario___
(place)

on ___December 27, 199-___
(date)

are divorced and that the divorce takes effect on ___August 9, 200-___
(date)

2. THIS COURT ORDERS AND ADJUDGES

~~This judgment bears interest at the rate of _____ percent per year commencing on _____~~
(date)

(This clause required in a judgment for the payment of money on which postjudgment interest is payable. Delete if inapplicable.)

If you are claiming support, add the Family Support Plan paragraph here.

Justin J. Judge

(In a judgment that provides for payment of support, set out the last known address of the support creditor and debtor.)

THE SPOUSES ARE NOT FREE TO REMARRY UNTIL THIS JUDGMENT TAKES EFFECT, AT WHICH TIME A CERTIFICATE OF DIVORCE MAY BE OBTAINED FROM THIS COURT. IF AN APPEAL IS TAKEN IT MAY DELAY THE DATE WHEN THIS JUDGMENT TAKES EFFECT.

SELF-COUNSEL PRESS-DIVONT-JOINT(104-2)00

Court file no._____

ONTARIO SUPERIOR COURT OF JUSTICE

(Court seal)

CERTIFICATE OF DIVORCE

This is to certify that the marriage of

John Que Public

and

Joan Public

which was solemnized at ___Toronto, Ontario_____

on ___December 27, 1984_____

was dissolved by a judgment of this court which became effective on ___August 9, 200-___
(date)

Date:___August 15, 200-_____   Issued by:_____
Local registrar

at

SELF-COUNSEL PRESS-DIVONT-JOINT(105-1)00

Court file no. _____

ONTARIO SUPERIOR COURT OF JUSTICE

BETWEEN:

John Que Public   **HUSBAND**
(   )

-and-

Joan Que Public   **WIFE**
(   )

AFFIDAVIT

I, __John Que Public_____ , of the __City of Toronto_____

in the __Municipality of Metropolitan Toronto_____

MAKE OATH AND SAY (or AFFIRM):

1. I am the Husband/Wife herein and as such have knowledge of the matters hereinafter deposed to.
2. No appeal from the divorce is pending.
3. No order has been made extending the time for appealing from the divorce.

SWORN BEFORE ME at the _____)
)
of _____ in the   )
)
_____) _____
)
this ____ day of _____ 200-____)

_____
A Commissioner for taking Affidavits, etc.

SELF-COUNSEL PRESS-DIVONT-JOINT(106-1)00

Court file no._____

ONTARIO SUPERIOR COURT OF JUSTICE

BETWEEN:

The parties should be identified in the title of the proceeding as "husband" and "wife" in addition to their designation as "petitioner" and "respondent." The parties may then be referred to in the body of the document as "husband" and "wife."

PETITIONER

(Wife   )

(Court seal)   Joan Que Public

and

John Que Public

RESPONDENT

(Husband   )

PETITION FOR DIVORCE

TO THE RESPONDENT

A LEGAL PROCEEDING FOR DIVORCE HAS BEEN COMMENCED AGAINST YOU by the petitioner. The claim made against you appears on the following pages.

IF YOU WISH TO DEFEND THIS PROCEEDING, you or an Ontario lawyer acting for you must prepare an answer in Form 69D prescribed by the Rules of Civil Procedure, serve it on the petitioner's lawyer(s) or, where the petitioner does not have a lawyer, serve it on the petitioner, and file it, with proof of service, in this court office, WITHIN TWENTY DAYS after this petition is served on you, if you are served in Ontario.

If you are served in another province or territory of Canada or in the United States of America, the period for serving and filing your answer is forty days. If you are served outside Canada and the United States of America, the period is sixty days.

Instead of serving and filing an answer, you may serve and file a notice of intent to defend in Form 69J prescribed by the Rules of Civil Procedure. This will entitle you to ten more days within which to serve and file your answer.

If this petition for divorce contains a claim for support or division of property, you must serve and file a financial statement in Form 69K prescribed by the Rules of Civil Procedure within the time set out above for serving and filing your answer, whether or not you wish to defend this proceeding. If you serve and file an answer, your financial statement must accompany your answer.

IF YOU FAIL TO SERVE AND FILE AN ANSWER, A DIVORCE MAY BE GRANTED IN YOUR ABSENCE AND WITHOUT FURTHER NOTICE TO YOU, JUDGMENT MAY BE GRANTED AGAINST YOU ON ANY OTHER CLAIM IN THIS PETITION AND YOU MAY LOSE YOUR RIGHT TO SUPPORT OR DIVISION OF PROPERTY. IF YOU WISH TO DEFEND THIS PROCEEDING BUT ARE UNABLE TO PAY LEGAL FEES, LEGAL AID MAY BE AVAILABLE TO YOU BY CONTACTING A LOCAL LEGAL AID OFFICE.

Name and address of each respondent.

NEITHER SPOUSE IS FREE TO REMARRY until a divorce has been granted and has taken effect. Once a divorce has taken effect, you may obtain a certificate of divorce from this court office.

Date _____Issued by_____

Local registrar

To: John Que Public
    1000 Yonge Street
    Toronto, ON ZIP 0G0

Address of court office
393 University Ave.
Toronto, ON M5G 1E6

SELF-COUNSEL PRESS-DIVONT-SOLE(107-1)00

CLAIM

1. The petitioner claims:

(a) a divorce;

(b) Under the Divorce Act,
  (i) interim and permanent custody of the child of the marriage, Robert John Public, born June 1, 1985
  (ii) interim and permanent support for the child, Robert John Public, in the amount of $500 per month
  (iii) costs, including interim disbursements

(c) Under the Family Law Act,
  (i) interim and permanent custody (or joint custody) of the child of the marriage, Robert John Public, born June 1, 1985
  (ii) an Order that all support payments be increased annually on the anniversary date of the Order by the percentage change in the Consumer Price Index for Canada for all prices of all items since the same month of the previous year as published by Statistics Canada pursuant to section 34(5) and (6) of the Act
  (iii) an Order requiring the respondent to pay proportionately to income the cost of post-secondary education for the child of the marriage
  (iv) equalization of all family property pursuant to section 5 of the Act

  (v) interim and permanent exclusive possession of the matrimonial home at 322 Lakeshore Road, Toronto, Ontario
  (vi) costs, including interim disbursements

(d) Under the Children's Law Reform Act,
  (i) interim and permanent custody of the child of the marriage, Robert John Public, born June 1, 1985
  (ii) an Order restraining the Respondent from removing the child from the province of Ontario without the consent in writing of the Petitioner, or further Court Order

(e) Under the Change of Name Act,
  (i) an Order that neither party shall change the surname of the child

(f) Under the Courts of Justice Act,
  (i) pre-judgment and post-judgment interest pursuant to sections 138 and 139 of the Act

(g) Costs

GROUNDS FOR DIVORCE — SEPARATION

2. (a) The spouses have lived separate and apart since June 1, 200-
                                                                    (Date)

The spouses have resumed cohabitation during the following periods in an unsuccessful attempt at reconciliation:

Date(s) of cohabitation

None

GROUNDS FOR DIVORCE — ADULTERY

2. (b) The respondent spouse has committed adultery. Particulars are as follows:

GROUNDS FOR DIVORCE — CRUELTY

2. (c) The respondent has treated the petitioner with physical or mental cruelty of such a kind as to render intolerable the continued cohabitation of the spouses. Particulars are as follows:

SELF-COUNSEL PRESS-DIVONT-SOLE(107-3)00

66

RECONCILIATION

3. There is no possibility of reconciliation of the spouses.

4. The following efforts to reconcile have been made:

State details. If no efforts have been made, state "none."

The parties made an effort to reconcile by attending family counselling at the Clarke Institute during the months of February, March, and April, 200-.

DETAILS OF MARRIAGE

If possible, copy this information from the marriage certificate.

5. Date of marriage: December 27, 1984

6. Place of marriage: Toronto, Ontario
   (City, town, or municipality, province or state, country)

7. Wife's surname immediately before marriage: Jones

8. Wife's surname at birth: Jones

9. Husband's surname immediately before marriage: Public

10. Husband's surname at birth: Public

11. Marital status of husband at time of marriage: Never married
    (Never married, divorced, or widower)

12. Marital status of wife at time of marriage: Never married
    (Never married, divorced, or widow)

13. Wife's birthplace: Toronto, Ontario
    City, town, or municipality, province or state, country)

14. Wife's birthdate: April 11, 1985

15. Husband's birthplace: Calgary, Alberta
    (City, town, or municipality, province or state, country)

16. Husband's birthdate: May 12, 1954

Check one of (a), (b), or (c) and complete.

17. (a) ☒ A certificate of ☐ the marriage ☒ the registration of the marriage of the spouses has been filed with the court.

    (b) ☐ It is impossible to obtain a certificate of the marriage or its registration because:

    (c) ☐ A certificate of the marriage or its registration will be filed before this action is set down for trial or a motion is made for judgment.

SELF-COUNSEL PRESS-DIVONT-SOLE(107-4)00

RESIDENCE

18. The petitioner has resided in __Toronto, Ontario__
    (City, town, or municipality, and province, state or country)
    since __April 11, 1955__
    (Date)

19. The respondent has resided in __Toronto, Ontario__
    (City, town, or municipality, and province, state or country)
    since __December, 1982__
    (Date)

20. The respondent's current address is __1000 Yonge Street__

Check appropriate box or boxes

21. The [x] petitioner   [x] respondent   has habitually resided in Ontario for at least one year immediately preceding the commencement of this proceeding.

CHILDREN

22. The following are all the living children of the marriage as defined by the Divorce Act:

Full name	Birthdate	School and grade or year	Person with whom child lives and length of time child has lived there.
Robert John Public	June 1, 199-	The Great School Grade 4	The child has lived with husband and wife since his birth.

The children ordinarily reside in: __Toronto, Ontario__
(City, town, or municipality, and province, state or country)

Make sure that this paragraph agrees with the claim under 1. above.

23. (a) The petitioner seeks an order for custody or joint custody of the following children on the following terms:

Name of child	Terms of the order
Robert John Public	Custody to the wife; liberal and generous access to the husband

Check appropriate box.

The respondent [ ] agrees   [X] does not agree with the above terms.

SELF-COUNSEL PRESS-DIVONT-SOLE(107-5)00

68

Strike out if not applicable.

Check appropriate box.

(b) The petitioner is not seeking an order for custody and

☐ is content that a previous order for custody remain in force

☐ is attempting to obtain an order for custody in another proceeding full particulars of which are as follows:

State name of court, court file number and particulars of the order or proceeding.

Strike out if not applicable.

(c) The petitioner seeks an order for access (visiting arrangements) and is content that the respondent have an order for custody of the following children on the following terms:

Name of child	Terms of the order

Check appropriate box.

The respondent ☐ agrees ☐ does not agree with the above terms.

SELF-COUNSEL PRESS-DIVONT-SOLE(107-6)00

24. (a) The following are the existing visiting arrangements (access) for the spouse who does not have the children living with him or her:

State details such as days of the week, hours of visits, and place of access.

Both spouses continue to occupy the matrimonial home. The wife has, since the date of the separation, assumed the day-to-day care of the child.

SELF-COUNSEL PRESS-DIVONT-SOLE(107-7)00

Check appropriate box.

(b) The existing visiting arrangements (access) are ☐ satisfactory ☒ not satisfactory.

The husband has not committed himself to any specific access schedule which makes it difficult for the wife to maintain continuity in her own life as well as that of the child. Although the husband travels a great deal with his profession, he is capable of providing a monthly flight schedule around which access can be arranged.

If not satisfactory, state reasons and describe how the arrangements should be changed.

25. The order sought in paragraph 23 is in the best interests of the children for the following reasons:

(i) The wife is self-employed as an accountant and works out of the matrimonial home

(ii) Since the child's birth, the wife has been primarily responsible for his care

(iii) The husband's employment as a pilot necessitates him travelling extensively

(iv) The wife and child have a close relationship and it is in the child's best interests to sustain their close bond

(v) The wife is in a better position to meet the day-to-day needs of the child

26. The following material changes in the circumstances of the spouses are expected to affect the children, their custody and the visiting arrangements (access) in the future:

The wife is claiming exclusive possession of the matrimonial home and the circumstances for the child will not change materially. The wife proposes that the husband have visiting arrangements as his time and schedule permit and is in the best interests of the child.

SELF-COUNSEL PRESS-DIVONT-SOLE(107-8)00

27. (a) The existing arrangements between the spouses for support of the children are as follows:

Amount paid	Time period (Weekly, monthly, etc.)	Paid by (Husband or wife)	Paid for (Name of child)

There are no existing arrangements between the spouses for the support of the child.

Check appropriate box.

If not being honoured, specify how much is unpaid and for how long. If you seek an order for payment of part or all of the unpaid amount, be sure to include it in the claim under 1. above.

(b) The existing support arrangements ☐ are being honoured ☐ are not being honoured.

Not applicable

Be sure that this paragraph agrees with the claim under 1. above.

(c) The petitioner proposes that the support arrangements for the children should be as follows:

Amount to be paid	Time period (Weekly, monthly, etc.)	To be paid by (Husband or wife)	To be paid for (Name of child)
Interim $500	monthly	husband	Robert John Public
Permanent $700	monthly	husband	Robert John Public

Check appropriate box.

If not being met, state particulars.

28. The educational needs of the children ☒ are being met ☐ are not being met.

SELF-COUNSEL PRESS-DIVONT-SOLE(107-9)00

OTHER COURT PROCEEDINGS

State the name of the court, the court file number, the kind of order the court was asked to make, and what order, if any, the court made. If the proceeding is not yet completed, state its current status.

29. The following are all other court proceedings with reference to the marriage or any child of the marriage:

There have been no other court proceedings with reference to

the marriage.

DOMESTIC CONTRACTS AND FINANCIAL ARRANGEMENTS

Indicate whether the contract or arrangement is now in effect, and if support payments are not being paid in full, state the amount that has not been paid.

30. The spouses have entered into the following domestic contracts and other written or oral financial arrangements:

Date	Nature of contract or arrangement	Status

There have been no domestic contracts or financial arrangements

between the husband and wife.

COLLUSION, CONDONATION, AND CONNIVANCE

31. There has been no collusion in relation to this divorce proceeding.

32. ~~There has been no condonation of or connivance at the grounds for divorce in this proceeding.~~

Strike out paragraph 32 if the divorce is sought on the ground of separation only.

Where there has been condonation or connivance, strike out the previous sentence. State details and set out the facts relied on to justify a divorce in the circumstances

SELF-COUNSEL PRESS-DIVONT-SOLE(107-10)00

MATTERS OTHER THAN DIVORCE AND CUSTODY

Set out in separate, consecutively numbered paragraphs the material facts relied on to substantiate the claims.

33. The grounds for the relief sought in paragraph 1, other than a divorce or custody, are as follows:

(i)   The wife has filed her Financial Statement along with her Petition for Divorce

(ii) The wife requires support in the amount of $500.00 per month to meet the needs of the child

(iii) The husband earns $35,000 a year and is capable of assisting financially in meeting the day-to-day needs of the child

Exclusive Possession of the Matrimonial Home

(i)   The child has resided in the matrimonial home since his birth

(ii) The wife carries on business out of the matrimonial home

(iii) The child's school is within walking distance of the matrimonial home

(iv) The child has established close contacts with the neighbours and has friends with whom he associates daily

Accounting

(i)   The husband and wife own joint and separate assets that require valuation and accounting for the purposes of calculating their net family property

(ii) The wife claims an equalization of Net Family Property according to section 5 of the Family Law Act

SELF-COUNSEL PRESS-DIVONT-SOLE(107-11)00

TRIAL

Where a claim is made for custody of a child who ordinarily resides in Ontario, the place of trial must be in the county where he or she ordinarily resides.

34. The petitioner proposes that if there is a trial in this action, it be held at:

Toronto, Ontario

DECLARATION OF PETITIONER

35. I have read and understand this petition for divorce. The statements in it are true, to the best of my knowledge, information, and belief.

Date_____May 2, 200-_____   *Joan Public*_____
                                                           (Signature of petitioner)

                                                  (Name, address, and telephone number of petitioner)

                                                  Joan Public
                                                  322 Lakeshore Road
                                                  Toronto, Ontario Z1P 0G0
                                                  (416) 555-5666

SELF-COUNSEL PRESS-DIVONT-SOLE(107-12)00

SAMPLE #12
FINANCIAL STATEMENT

Court file no. _____

ONTARIO SUPERIOR COURT OF JUSTICE

BETWEEN:

Joan Public   PETITIONER, (Wife   )

- and -

John Que Public   RESPONDENT (Husband   )

FINANCIAL STATEMENT

I, __Joan Public__ of the __City__
     (full name of deponent)   *(city, town, etc.)*

of __Toronto__ in the __Municipality__

of __Metropolitan Toronto__ make oath and say:
                        (county, municipality, etc.)
                          /affirm:

    1. Particulars of my financial situation and of all my property are accurately set out below, to the best of my knowledge, information, and belief.

ALL INCOME AND MONEY RECEIVED

(Include all income and other money received from all sources, whether taxable or not. Show gross amount here and show deductions on pages 2, 3, 4 & 5. Give current actual amount where known or ascertainable. Where amount cannot be ascertained, give your best estimate. Use weekly, monthly or yearly column as appropriate.)

Category	Weekly	Monthly	Yearly
1. Salary or wages			$35,000.00
2. Bonuses			
3. Fees			
4. Commissions			
5. Family allowance		$33.93	
6. Unemployment insurance			
7. Workers' compensation			
8. Public assistance			
9. Pension			
10. Dividends			
11. Interest			
12. Rental income			
13. Allowances and support from others			
14. Other (Specify)			
TOTAL	$	(A)$ 33.93	$35,000.00

Weekly total $_____ × 4.33 = (B)$_____ monthly

Yearly total $ __35,000.00__ ÷ 12 = (C)$ __2916.66__ monthly

GROSS MONTHLY INCOME (A) + (B) + (C) = (D)$ __2950.59__

SELF-COUNSEL PRESS-DIVONT-SOLE(108-1)00

76

OTHER BENEFITS

(Show all non-monetary benefits from all sources, such as use of a vehicle or room and board, and include such items as insurance or dental plans or other expenses paid on your behalf. Give your best estimate where you cannot ascertain the actual value.)

Item	Particulars	Monthly Market Value

TOTAL (E) $2,950.59

GROSS MONTHLY INCOME AND BENEFITS (D) + (E) = $_____

ACTUAL AND PROPOSED BUDGETS

	ACTUAL BUDGET for twelve month period from June 1 _____, 200-___ to June 1 _____, 200-___ Show actual expenses, or your best estimate where you cannot ascertain actual amount.			PROPOSED BUDGET Show your proposed budget, giving your best estimate where you cannot ascertain actual amount.		
CATEGORY	Weekly	Monthly	Yearly	Weekly	Monthly	Yearly
Housing 1. Rent		$1,000		1.		
2. Real property taxes				2.		$1,200
3. Mortgage				3.	$1,000	
4. Common expense charges				4.		
5. Water		$15		5.	$15	
6. Electricity		$20		6	$20	
7. Natural gas		$100		7.	$100	
8. Fuel oil				8.		
9. Telephone		$25		9.	$25	
10. Cable T.V.		$20		10.	$20	
11. Home insurance			$600	11.		$600
12. Repairs and maintenance			$100	12.		$100
13. Gardening and snow removal				13.		
14. Other (Specify)				14.		
Food, Toiletries and Sundries 15. Groceries	$50			15. $75		
16. Meals outside home	$10			16. $20		
17. Toiletries and sundries	$20			17. $25		
18. Grooming	$20			18. $30		

SELF-COUNSEL PRESS-DIVONT-SOLE(108-2)00

CATEGORY	ACTUAL BUDGET			PROPOSED BUDGET		
Food Toiletries and Sundries–cont'd.	Weekly	Monthly	Yearly	Weekly	Monthly	Yearly
19. General household supplies	$20			19. $25		
20. Laundry, dry cleaning	$10			20. $20		
21. Other (Specify)				21.		
Clothing 22. Children		$100		22.	$200	
23. Self		$100		23.	$200	
Transportation 24. Public transit		$150		24.	$150	
25. Taxis, car pools	$10			25. $20		
26. Car Insurance			$450	26.		$450
27. Licence			$70	27.		$70
28. Car maintenance			$500	28.		$500
29. Gasoline, oil	$20			29.		
30. Parking	$5			30.		
31. Other (Specify)				31.		
Health and Medical 32. Doctors, chiropractors				32.		
33. Dentist (regular care)			$120	33.		$200
34. Orthodontist or special dental care				34.		$1,000
35. Insurance premiums			$720	35.		$720
36. Drugs				36.		
37. Other (Specify)				37.		
Deductions from Income 38. Income tax		$500		38.	$500	
39. Canada Pension Plan		$30		39.	$30	
40. Unemployment insurance		$30		40.	$30	
41. Employer pension				41.		
42. Union or other dues				42.		

CATEGORY	ACTUAL BUDGET			PROPOSED BUDGET		
Deductions from Income–cont'd.	Weekly	Monthly	Yearly	Weekly	Monthly	Yearly
43. Group insurance				43.		
44. Credit union loan				44.		
45. Credit union savings				45.		
46. Other (Specify)				46.		
Miscellaneous						
47. Life insurance premiums			$200	47.		$200
48. Tuition fees, books, etc.				48.		
49. Entertainment	$10			49. $20		
50. Recreation	$10			50. $20		
51. Vacation			0	51.		$500
52. Gifts			0	52.		$500
53. Babysitting, day care	$50			53. $75		
54. Children's allowances				54.		
55. Children's activities	$10			55. $20		
56. Support payments				56.		
57. Newspapers, periodicals		$10		57.	$10	
58. Alcohol, tobacco		$50		58.	$75	
59. Charities				59.		
60. Income tax (not deducted at source)				60.		
61. Other (Specify)				61.		
Loan Payments						
62. Banks				62.		
63. Finance companies				63.		
64. Credit unions				64.		
65. Department stores				65.		
66. Other (Specify)				66.		

CATEGORY	ACTUAL BUDGET			PROPOSED BUDGET		
	Weekly	Monthly	Yearly	Weekly	Monthly	Yearly
Savings						
67. R.R.S.P.				67.		
68. Other (Specify)				68.		
	$	$	$	$	$	$

TOTALS OF ACTUAL BUDGET

Monthly Total $ 2,150.00

Weekly Total $ 245 × 4.33 = $ 1,060.85

Yearly Total $ 2,760.00 ÷ 12 = $ 230.00

MONTHLY ACTUAL BUDGET   = (F) $ 3,440.85

TOTALS OF PROPOSED BUDGET

Monthly Total $ 2,375.00

Weekly Total $ 380.00 × 4.33 = $ 1,645.00

Yearly Total $ 6,040.00 ÷ 12 = $ 503.55

MONTHLY PROPOSED BUDGET   = (G) $ 4,523.95

SUMMARY OF INCOME AND EXPENSES

Actual

Gross monthly income
(Amount D from page 1) $ 2,950.59

Subtract Monthly actual budget
(Amount F from page 5)   − $ 3,440.85

ACTUAL MONTHLY SURPLUS / DEFICIT $ 490.26

Proposed

Gross monthly income
(Amount D from page 1) $ 2,950.59

Subtract Proposed monthly budget
(Amount G from page 5)   − $ 4,523.95

PROPOSED MONTHLY SURPLUS / DEFICIT $ 1,573.36

SELF-COUNSEL PRESS-DIVONT-SOLE(108-5)00

80

SAMPLE #12 — Continued

LAND

(Include any interest in land owned on the valuation date, including leasehold interests and mortgages, whether or not you are registered as owner. Include claims to an interest in land, but do not include claims that you are making against your spouse in this or a related proceeding. Show estimated market value of your interest without deducting encumbrances or costs of disposition, and show encumbrances and costs of disposition under Debts and Other Liabilities on page 9.)

Nature and Type of Ownership State percentage interest where relevant.	Nature and Address of Property	Estimated Market Value of Your Interest as of: See instructions above.		
		Date of Marriage	Valuation Date	Date of Statement
Joint tenancy 50%	Matrimonial home, 322 Lakeshore Road Toronto, Ontario	125,000.00	135,000.000	$140,000.00
	TOTAL $	62,500.00	(H) 67,500.00	$70,000.00

GENERAL HOUSEHOLD ITEMS AND VEHICLES

(Show estimated market value, not cost of replacement for these items owned on the valuation date. Do not deduct encumbrances here, but show encumbrances under Debts and Other Liabilities on page 9.)

Item	Particulars	Estimated Market Value of Your Interest as of: See instructions above.		
		Date of Marriage	Valuation Date	Date of Statement
General household contents excluding special items (a) at matrimonial home(s)	Refrigerator, stove, washer, dryer, furniture, etc.	$10,000.00	8,000.00	5,000.00
(b) elsewhere Jewellery	Diamond ring (gift)		1,200.00	1,400.00
Works of art Vehicles and boats	1984 Station wagon	15,000.00	13,000.00	10,000.00
Other special items				
	TOTAL $	25,000.00	(I) 22,200.00	16,400.00

SELF-COUNSEL PRESS-DIVONT-SOLE(108-6)00

SAMPLE #12 — Continued

SAVINGS AND SAVINGS PLANS

(Show items owned on the valuation date by category. Include cash, accounts in financial institutions, registered retirement or other savings plans, deposit receipts, pensions and any other savings.)

Category	Institution	Account Number	Amount as of:		
			Date of Marriage	Valuation Date	Date of Statement
None					
		TOTAL $		(J)	

SECURITIES

(Show items owned on the valuation date by category. Include shares, bonds, warrants, options, debentures, notes and any other securities. Give your best estimate of market value if the items were to be sold on an open market.)

Category	Number	Description	Estimated Market Value as of:		
			Date of Marriage	Valuation Date	Date of Statement
None					
		TOTAL $		(K)	

LIFE AND DISABILITY INSURANCE

(List all policies owned on the valuation date.)

Company and Policy No.	Kind of Policy	Owner	Beneficiary	Face Amount	Cash Surrender Value as of:		
					Date of Marriage	Valuation Date	Date of Statement
INS Co.	Life	Self	Child	$100,000	no cash surrender value		
				TOTAL $		(L)	

SELF-COUNSEL PRESS-DIVONT-SOLE(108-7)00

ACCOUNTS RECEIVABLE

(Give particulars of all debts owing to you on the valuation date, whether arising from business or from personal dealings.)

Particulars	Amount as of:		
	Date of Marriage	Valuation Date	Date of Statement
None			
TOTAL $		(M)	

BUSINESS INTERESTS

(Show any interest in an unincorporated business owned on the valuation date. A controlling interest in an incorporated business may be shown here or under Securities on page 7. Give your best estimate of market value if the business were to be sold on an open market.)

Name of Firm or Company	Interest	Estimated Market Value as of:		
		Date of Marriage	Valuation Date	Date of Statement
None				
	TOTAL $		(N)	

OTHER PROPERTY

(Show other property owned on the valuation date by categories. Include property of any kind not shown above. Give your best estimate of market value.)

Category	Particulars	Estimated Market Value as of:		
		Date of Marriage	Valuation Date	Date of Statement
None				
	TOTAL $		(O)	

SELF-COUNSEL PRESS-DIVONT-SOLE(108-8)00

SAMPLE #12 — Continued

DEBTS AND OTHER LIABILITIES

(Show your debts and other liabilities on the valuation date, whether arising from personal or business dealings, by category such as mortgages, charges, liens, notes, credit cards and accounts payable. Include contingent liabilities such as guarantees and indicate they are contingent.)

| Category | Particulars | Amount as of: | | |
		Date of Marriage	Valuation Date	Date of Statement
None				
	TOTAL $		(P)	

PROPERTY, DEBTS AND OTHER LIABILITIES ON DATE OF MARRIAGE

(Show by category the value of your property and your debts and other liabilities calculated as of the date of your marriage. Do not include the value of a matrimonial home that you owned at the date of marriage.)

| Category | Particulars | Value as of date of marriage | |
		Assets	Liabilities
None			
	TOTAL $	(Q) $	(R) $

NET VALUE OF PROPERTY OWNED ON DATE OF MARRIAGE (Amount Q Subtract Amount R) = (S) $_____

SELF-COUNSEL PRESS-DIVONT-SOLE(108-9)00

EXCLUDED PROPERTY

(Show the value by category of property owned on the valuation date that is excluded from the definition of "net family property".)

Category	Particulars	Value on Valuation Date
Gift	Diamond ring	$1,200.00
	TOTAL	(T) $1,200.00

DISPOSAL OF PROPERTY

(Show the value by category of all property that you disposed of during the two years immediately preceding the making of this statement, or during the marriage, whichever period is shorter.)

Category	Particulars	Value
	TOTAL	(U) $

SELF-COUNSEL PRESS-DIVONT-SOLE(108-10)00

SAMPLE #12 — Continued

CALCULATION OF NET FAMILY PROPERTY

Value of all property owned on valuation date (Amounts H,I,J,K,L,M,N and O from pages 6 to 8) $ 89,700.00

Subtract value of all deductions (Amounts P and S from page 9) — $

Subtract value of all excluded property (Amount T from page 10) — $ 1,200.00

NET FAMILY PROPERTY $ 88,500.00

2. The name(s) and address(es) of my employer(s) are:

3. Attached to this affidavit are a copy of my income tax return filed with the Department of National Revenue for the last taxation year, together with all material filed with it, and a copy of any notice of assessment or reassessment that I have received from the Department for that year.

4. I do not anticipate any material changes in the information set out above.

(Delete inapplicable paragraph 4)

4. I anticipate the following material changes in the information set out above:

(Give particulars:)

Sworn before me at the City of Toronto
Affirmed

in the Municipality of Metropolitan Toronto

Joan Public

on   July 2,   200-

Signature of deponent

Commissioner for Taking Affidavits, etc.

SELF-COUNSEL PRESS-DIVONT-SOLE(108-11)00

Court file no._____

ONTARIO SUPERIOR COURT OF JUSTICE

BETWEEN:

Joan Que Public

- and -

John Que Public

PETITIONER
(Wife   )

RESPONDENT
(Husband   )

(Court Seal)

NOTICE TO FILE FINANCIAL STATEMENT

TO:

☐n this proceeding a claim has been made against you for_____support_____

_____

YOU ARE REQUIRED, WHETHER OR NOT YOU DEFEND THIS PROCEEDING, to serve and file a financial statement in Form 69K prescribed by the Rules of Civil Procedure. Your financial statement must accompany your responding document if you defend this proceeding and must be served and filed in any event within the time for delivering your responding document after the original process in this proceeding was served on you.

If you fail to file a financial statement as required, an order may be made without further notice to compel you to file a financial statement.

Date_____

Joan Public

322 Lakeshore Road

Toronto, Ontario   Z1P 0G0

555-5666

Petitioner appearing in person

To:
 John Que Public

 1000 Yonge Street

 Toronto, Ontario   Z1P 0G0

_____

SELF-COUNSEL PRESS-DIVONT-SOLE(109-1)00

SAMPLE #14
SUPPORT DEDUCTION ORDER

Name of Court _Ontario Superior Court of Justice_

Nom du tribunal

Location _393 University Avenue, Toronto, ON_

Lieu

SUPPORT DEDUCTION ORDER
ORDONNANCE DE RETENUE DES ALIMENTS

Family Responsibility and Support Arrears Enforcement Act, 1996
Loi de 1996 sur les obligations familiales et l'execution des arriérés d'aliments

Form/Formule 1

Court file no./N° de dossier du tribunal

_____
Judge/*Juge*

_____
Date

Between:/*Entre:*

Joan Public

and / *et*

John Que Public

Applicant/Petitioner/Plaintiff
Requérant/Demandeur

Respondent/Defendant
Intimé/Défendeur

SUPPORT DEDUCTION ORDER / ***ORDONNANCE DE RETENUE DES ALIMENTS***

Upon making an order this day which provides for payment of support on a periodic basis at regular intervals

Après avoir rendu une ordonnance ce jour qui prévoit le versement d'aliments sur une base périodique à intervalles réguliers

and on making the necessary inquiries required by section 3.1(3) of the Family Responsibility and Support Arrears Enforcement Act, 1996:

et après avoir fait les recherches nécessaires visées au paragraphe 3.1(3) de la Loi de 1996 sur les obligations familiales et l'execution des arriérés d'aliments:

1.　THIS COURT ORDERS THAT___ John Que Public ___ pay support as set out in
　　LE TRIBUNAL ORDONNE que　　　　　　　　　　　　　　　verse les aliments tel qu'il

　　the attached information form.
　　est énoncé dans la formule de renseignements ci-jointe.

2.　THIS COURT ORDERS that any income source that receives notice of this support deduction
　　LE TRIBUNAL ORDONNE que toute source de revenu qui reçoit avis de la présente ordonnance

　　order make payments to the Director of the Family Responsibility Office in respect of the
　　fasse des versements au directeur du Régime des obligations alimentaires envers la famille

　　payor out of money owed by the income source to the payor.
　　à l'égard du payeur à même l'argent que la source de revenu doit au payeur.

_____
Signature of Judge, Registrar, or Clerk of the Court
Signature du juge, ou du greffier du tribunal

SELF-COUNSEL PRESS-DIVONT-BOTH(110-1)00

88

SAMPLE #15
SUPPORT DEDUCTION ORDER INFORMATION FORM

Name of Court _Ontario Superior Court_ of Justice
Location _393 University Avenue, Toronto_

**SUPPORT DEDUCTION ORDER
INFORMATION FORM**
Family Responsibility and Support Arrears Enforcement Act

*Note: Please print.
Leave shaded areas blank,
the court will fill them in.*

Type of Support Order
Interim ☐ Final ☐

Form 2

Court file no.

FAMILY RESPONSIBILITY OFFICE (F.R.O.) FILE INFORMATION
Family Support Plan Regional Office _____ F.R.O. Case Number (if known) |__|__|__|__|__|__|__|

1. **INFORMATION ON PARTIES**
   Payor name _John Que Public_ Birthdate |1|2|0|5|5|4| Sex ☑ M ☐ F
   Day Month Year

   Payor address _1000 Yonge Street, Toronto, ON Z1P 0G0_
   Street and Number   Town/City   Province   Postal code
   Recipient name _Joan Public_ Birthdate |1|0|0|4|5|5| Sex ☐ M ☒ F
   Day Month Year

   Payor address _322 Lakeshore Road, Toronto, Ontario Z1P 0G0_
   Street and Number   Town/City   Province   Postal code

2. **INFORMATION ON PAYOR'S EMPLOYER(S) AND OTHER INCOME SOURCE(S)**
   Employer/Income source name _FlyBy Airline Co._ Telephone _555-2343_
   Payroll office address _100 Airport Road, Malton, Ontario   Z1P 0G0_
   Street and number   Town/City   Province   Postal code

   ☐ Additional income source information attached.
   ☐ Payor not receiving periodic payments as explained in the Family Support Plan Act.
   ☐ Recipient does not know.

3. **SUPPORT ORDER INFORMATION**
   The attached support deduction order relates to a support order which says that:
   _____ is required to pay support for the following persons:
   Payor name
   (Court will change this list if necessary)

Name	Birthdate Day month year	Amount payable	Frequency of payments	Payments to begin Day month year
Spouse a.	/ /	$		/ /
Other Dependants b Robert John	01 /06 /9–	$		/ /
c.	/ /	$		/ /
d.	/ /	$		/ /
e.	/ /	$		/ /

   Is the support order a variation of a previous support order? ☐ Yes ☐ No

4. **COST OF LIVING ADJUSTMENTS**   ☐ **None provided**
   Support is indexed in accordance with ☐ s.34(5) of the _Family Law Act_ OR ☐ as per attached
   Or ☐ as follows_____

5. **ARREARS** (Complete if applicable)
   Arrears are fixed at $_____ as of the_____ day of_____ 20____
   To be paid as follows (if applicable):_____

6. **TERMINATION OF SUPPORT** (Complete if previously ordered support is terminated _by this order_)
   Support is terminated for the following persons
   for_____ on the_____ day of_____ 20____
   for_____ on the_____ day of_____ 20____

SELF-COUNSEL PRESS-DIVONT-BOTH(111-1)00

SAMPLE #16
CASE INFORMATION STATEMENT

Form 1   COURT FILE NO: _____

<u>Courts of Justice Act</u>

ONTARIO SUPERIOR COURT OF JUSTICE

SHORT TITLE OF CASE   Public   -and-   Public

CASE INFORMATION STATEMENT

THIS FORM FILED BY

[X] applicant/petitioner/plaintiff
[ ] respondent/defendant - give name

[ ] other - specify kind and party and give name

ORDER SOUGHT BY PERSON FILING THIS FORM

<u>Divorce Act</u>
[X] divorce
[X] child support
[ ] spousal support
[X] custody
[ ] access
[ ] other - specify

<u>Family Law Act</u>
[X] child support
[ ] spousal support
[X] property - equalize
[X] excl. possession
[ ] restraining order
[ ] other - specify

<u>Children's Law Reform Act</u>
[X] custody
[ ] access
[ ] paternity declaration
[ ] other - specify

Other
[ ] constructive/resulting trust
[ ] partition/sale
[ ] annulment
[ ] other - specify

PERSON FILING THIS FORM

[X] married - date Dec. 27, 1984   Separated - date   June 1, 200-
[ ] not married -
   cohabited from - date   Separated - date

Birth date April 11, 1958   Social Insurance Number 441 321 337
Employer's name,
address and
telephone

OTHER SPOUSE

Birth date May 12, 1954   Social Insurance Number   441 532 182
Employer's name,
address and   Airline Company, 1 Main Street
telephone   Toronto, ON Z1P 0G0
                (416) 555-4444

CHILDREN   Name and birth date   Name and birth date

Robert John Public, Born June 1, 199-   ....

....

THIS PERSON'S LAWYER (if no lawyer, give person's name, address for service, telephone and fax numbers)

Name and firm   Joan Public
Address   322 Lakeshore Road, Toronto, ON Z1P 0G0
Telephone   Fax   Date
   (416) 555-5666   January 29, 200-

Court file no. _____

ONTARIO SUPERIOR COURT OF JUSTICE

BETWEEN:

JOAN PUBLIC   PETITIONER
                    (Wife   )

- and -

(Court seal)

JOHN QUE PUBLIC   RESPONDENT
                    (Husband   )

ACKNOWLEDGMENT OF RECEIPT CARD

TO:

You are served by mail with the document enclosed with this card in accordance with the Rules of Civil Procedure.

You are requested to sign the acknowledgment below and mail this card immediately after you receive it. If you fail to do so, the documents may be served on you in another manner and you may have to pay the costs of service.

ACKNOWLEDGMENT OF RECEIPT

I ACKNOWLEDGE that I have received a copy of the following documents:

Petition

Case Information Statement

Timetable/warning

Dated _August 3, 200-_____ at _Toronto, Ontario_____

_____

Signature of person served

SELF-COUNSEL PRESS-DIVONT-SOLE(113-1)00

91

RESPONDENT ( )

Court file no._____

ONTARIO SUPERIOR COURT
OF JUSTICE

Proceedings commenced at

Petition for
Divorce

Name, address, and telephone number of petitioner.

Petitioner appearing in person

and

PETITIONER ( )

(Short title of proceeding)

ACKNOWLEDGMENT OF SERVICE

I,

am the respondent named in this petition. I acknowledge receipt of a copy of this petition. My address for service of documents in this divorce proceeding is

Date_____

_____
Signature of respondent

_____
Signature of witness

I,

served this petition personally on the respondent.
☐ The respondent completed and signed the acknowledgment of service above in my presence and I signed it as witness.
or
☐ The respondent declined to complete and sign the acknowledgment of service.

_____
Signature

Court file no._____

ONTARIO SUPERIOR COURT OF JUSTICE

BETWEEN:

Joan Public   PETITIONER,

(Wife)

- and -

John Que Public   RESPONDENT

(Husband)

AFFIDAVIT OF SERVICE

I, __Fred F. Friend_____ of the City

of __Toronto_____, in the Municipality

of __Metropolitan Toronto_____ MAKE OATH AND SAY (or AFFIRM):

1. On __June 10, 200-_____, I served the respondent,

__John Que Public_____ with the __Petition for Divorce__

by leaving a copy with him/~~her at~~ __1000 Yonge Street, Toronto, Ontario__.

2. I was able to identify the person by means of __his oral confirmation that he was__
__the person to be served._____.

3. I requested the respondent to sign the back of the __Petition for Divorce__

and the respondent did ~~(or did not)~~ comply with my request.

SWORN BEFORE ME at the City of   )

__Toronto_____)

in the Municipality of   )

__Metropolitan Toronto_____)

this __3rd__ day of __July, 200-__)   *Fred F. Friend*

)   *(name)*

S M Commissioner

A Commissioner for taking Affidavits, etc.

SELF-COUNSEL PRESS-DIVONT-SOLE(114-1)00

Joan Public
322 Lakeshore Road
Toronto, Ontario
Z1P 0G0

June 15, 200-

The Sheriff
The Courthouse
Toronto, Ontario

Dear Sheriff:

Public v. Public — Divorce Proceedings

I am acting on my own behalf in divorce proceedings against my husband. I enclose two [or three] copies of the Petition for Divorce with the request that you serve the documents on my spouse [and on the co-respondent]. Also enclosed is a picture of my husband [and of the other party] to assist your identifying the person[s] to be served.

The following particulars may be of assistance to you.

Name of spouse:	John Que Public
Residence:	1000 Yonge Street, Toronto, Ontario
Place of business:	Ontario Hydro, Toronto, Ontario
Telephone numbers:	555-0000 (home) 555-1111 (business)

I also enclose my cheque for $25 as a deposit against your fees for this service. The balance, if any, of your fees will be remitted immediately upon receipt of your account.

Should you require any further information, please contact me by telephone at 555-6666.

Yours very truly,

Joan Public

Joan Public

Court file no._____

ONTARIO SUPERIOR COURT OF JUSTICE

BETWEEN:

PETITIONER,

Joan Public   (Wife   )

- and -

RESPONDENT

John Public   (Husband   )

AFFIDAVIT OF SERVICE (By mail)

I, _____ Joan Public _____ of the

City _____ of _ Toronto _____ in the _Municipality_

Metropolitan Toronto _____ MAKE OATH AND SAY (or AFFIRM):

1. On _ January 1, 200– _____ , I sent to
the Respondent by regular letter (or registered mail) to _1000 Yonge Street,_
Toronto _____a copy of the Petition for Divorce, and

2. On _ January 15, 200– _____, I received the attached acknowledgment
of receipt card (or post office receipt) bearing a signature that purports to
be the signature of _____ John Public _____.

SWORN BEFORE ME at the _____)

of _____)

in the _____)

_____)

this ____ day of_____)

_____)   _____

)   *(name)*

_____

A Commissioner for taking Affidavits, etc.   SELF-COUNSEL PRESS-DIVONT-SOLE(115-1)00

Court file no._____

ONTARIO SUPERIOR COURT OF JUSTICE

THE HONOURABLE   Justine J. Judge, Mon, Aug. 2, 200-   _____

(day and date judgment given)

BETWEEN:

Joan Petitioner

PETITIONER,

(Wife   )

- and -

(Court seal)   John Que Public

RESPONDENT

(Husband   )

DIVORCE JUDGMENT

THIS MOTION made by the petitioner for judgment for divorce was heard this day at___Toronto, Ontario_____

(place)

The respondent did not defend this action although properly served with the petition as appears from the affidavit of service filed.

ON READING the petition, the notice of motion for judgment, the affidavit dated _May 2, 200-_____of the petitioner filed in support of the motion.

(date)

(Add any other material filed.)

SELF-COUNSEL PRESS-DIVONT-SOLE(116-1)00

96

1. THIS COURT ORDERS AND ADJUDGES THAT __Joan Public_____

   (names of spouses)

   and ___John Que Public_____

   who were married at _Toronto, Ontario_____

   (place)

   on _December 27, 1984_____

   (date)

   are divorced and that the divorce takes effect on ___August 9, 200–_____

   (date)

2. THIS COURT ORDERS AND ADJUDGES

   Under the Divorce Act that:

   1. Custody of the child of the marriage, Robert John Public, born June 1, 199-, be granted to the Petitioner, Joan Public, with reasonable access by the Respondent, John Que Public.
   2. Support to the child of the marriage, Robert John Public, in the amount of $500 per month to be paid by the Respondent, John Que Public, to the Petitioner, Joan Public.

   Unde the Family Law Act that:

   3. The Petitioner, Joan Public, be granted exclusive possession of the matrimonial home until 200- when the matrimonial home will be sold and the proceeds distributed equally between the Petitioner and the Respondent.
   4. $_____ shall be paid to the Petitioner as equalization of all Net Family Property.
   5. Costs as between the Petitioner and the Respondent, fixed at $_____.

   *THIS COURT ORDERS AND ADJUDGES THAT unless the support order is withdrawn from the Office of the Director of the Family Responsibility Office, it shall be enforced by the Director and amounts owing under the support order shall be paid to the Director, who shall pay them to the person to whom they are owed.

   This judgment bears interest at the rate of _____ percent per year on any payment or payments in respect of which there is a default from the date of default.

   (This clause required in a judgment for the payment of money on which postjudgment interest is payable. Delete if inapplicable.)

If you are claiming support, add the Family Support Plan paragraph here.

Justin J. Judge
_____

(In a judgment that provides for payment of support, set out the last known address of the support creditor and debtor.)

THE SPOUSES ARE NOT FREE TO REMARRY UNTIL THIS JUDGMENT TAKES EFFECT, AT WHICH TIME A CERTIFICATE OF DIVORCE MAY BE OBTAINED FROM THIS COURT. IF AN APPEAL IS TAKEN IT MAY DELAY THE DATE WHEN THIS JUDGMENT TAKES EFFECT.

SELF-COUNSEL PRESS-DIVONT-SOLE(116-2)00

*Include this paragraph if you are claiming support.
**If you are claiming support, attach a sheet with the names and addresses of both parties (creditor and debtor).

Court file no._____

ONTARIO SUPERIOR COURT OF JUSTICE

BETWEEN:

Joan Public

PETITIONER

(Wife   )

- and -

(Court seal)

John Que Public

RESPONDENT

(Husband   )

REQUISITION

TO THE REGISTRAR:

I require you to note the respondent ___John Que Public_____
(name)

in default in this action on the ground that he/she has not filed an answer within the prescribed time. The petition has been filed with proof of service.

NOTICE OF MOTION

The motion is for default judgment in accordance with the petition.

The grounds for the motion are that the respondent has not filed an answer and has been noted in default.

The following documentary evidence will be relied on:

1. the petition

2. the certificate of marriage or of the registration of marriage filed in this action

3. the affidavit of the petitioner dated ___May 2, 200-_____

   (List any other)

4. The Affidavit of the Respondent dated May 2, 200-

~~The petitioner intends to present oral evidence at the hearing of the motion.~~
(Delete if not applicable)

Date ___July 15, 200-_____

Name, address and telephone number of petitioner.

Joan Public

322 Lakeshore Road
Toronto, Ontario Z1P 0G0
555-5666

SELF-COUNSEL PRESS-DIVONT-SOLE(117-1)00

Court file no._____

ONTARIO SUPERIOR COURT OF JUSTICE

BETWEEN:

Joan Public   **PETITIONER**

(Wife   )

- and -

(Court seal)

John Que Public   **RESPONDENT**

(Husband   )

AFFIDAVIT

I,_____Joan Public_____

of the ____City_____ of ____Toronto_____ , in

the ___Municipality___*City, town* of ___Metropolitan Toronto_____ ,

_____*County, Regional Municipality*_____

the petitioner in this action,

MAKE OATH/AFFIRM AND SAY:

1. There is no possibility of the reconciliation of the spouses because: *(Give particulars)*

OR

1. It would clearly not be appropriate in the circumstances for the court to consider the possibility of the reconciliation of the spouses because: *(Give particulars)*

the respondent and I have been living separate and apart since

June 1, 200-

SELF-COUNSEL PRESS-DIVONT-SOLE(118-1)00

2. All the information in the petition in this action is correct, with the following exceptions:
(Give particulars. If no exceptions, state "None.")

3. The certificate of marriage No. 210101 issued December 27, 1984 at Toronto, Ontario and signed by John Doe of the United Church of Canada contains the correct particulars of the marriage.

4. The ground for divorce as stated in the Petition for Divorce is marriage breakdown evidenced by a separation of more than one year.

5. There has been no agreement, conspiracy, understanding, or arrangement to which I am either directly or indirectly a party for the purpose of subverting the administration of justice, fabricating or suppressing evidence or deceiving the court.

6. I do not claim a division of property at this time and I am aware that a claim for a division of property may be barred after the divorce.

7. The Respondent's last known address, as evidenced by the Affidavit of Service, is 1000 Yonge Street, Toronto, Ontario Z1P 0G0.

SWORN BEFORE ME AT
the City of Toronto   )
)
in the Municipality of   )
Metropolitan Toronto   )
this _2nd_ day of _May_   200-   ) _Joan Public_
& M Commissioner   Petitioner's signature
A Commissioner for taking Affidavits, etc.

SELF-COUNSEL PRESS-DIVONT-SOLE(118-2)00

Court file no._____

ONTARIO SUPERIOR COURT OF JUSTICE

BETWEEN:

Joan Public   PETITIONER

(Wife   )

- and -

(Court seal)

John Que Public   RESPONDENT

(Husband   )

AFFIDAVIT

I,_____John Que Public_____

of the _____City_____ of ____Toronto_____ , in
          City, town

the __Municipality_____ of __Metropolitan Toronto_____ ,
        County, Regional Municipality

the petitioner in this action,

MAKE OATH/AFFIRM AND SAY:

1. There is no possibility of the reconciliation of the spouses because: *(Give particulars)*

OR

1. It would clearly not be appropriate in the circumstances for the court to consider the possibility of the reconciliation of the spouses because: *(Give particulars)*

   The Petitioner and I have been living separate and apart since
   June 1, 200-

2. All the information in the petition in this action is correct, with the following exceptions:
   (Give particulars. If no exceptions, state "None.")

   None

SWORN BEFORE ME AT
the City of Toronto
_____   )

in the Municipality of   )
Metropolitan Toronto   )
_____   )

this __2nd__ day of __May__ 200-   ) _John Que Public_____
__Ǫ M Commissioner__   ) ~~Petitioner's signature~~
A Commissioner for taking Affidavits, etc.   Respondent's signature

Court file no._____

ONTARIO SUPERIOR COURT OF JUSTICE

BETWEEN:

Joan Public

PETITIONER

(Wife)

- and -

(Court seal)

John Que Public

RESPONDENT

(Husband)

AFFIDAVIT

I,___John Que Public_____

of the ___City_____ of ___Toronto_____ , in
        City, town

the ___Municipality_____ of ___Metropolitan Toronto_____ ,
    County, Regional Municipality

the petitioner in this action,

MAKE OATH/AFFIRM AND SAY:

1. There is no possibility of the reconciliation of the spouses because: *(Give particulars)*

    :

    OR

1. It would clearly not be appropriate in the circumstances for the court to consider the possibility of the reconciliation of the spouses because: *(Give particulars)*

The Petitioner and I have been living separate and apart since
June 1, 200-

2. All the information in the petition in this action is correct, with the following exceptions: (*Give particulars. If no exceptions, state "None."*)

None

3. I am aware that I am not obliged to give evidence that I have committed adultery. I am willing to give that evidence.

SWORN BEFORE ME AT
The City of Toronto   )
)
in the Municipality of   )
Metropolitan Toronto   )
)
this 2nd day of   May   200-   )   *John Que Public*
J M Commissioner   ~~Petitioner's signature~~
A Commissioner for taking Affidavits, etc.   Respondent's signature

Court file no. _____

ONTARIO SUPERIOR COURT OF JUSTICE

BETWEEN:

Joan Public

PETITIONER

(Wife   )

-and-

John Que Public

RESPONDENT

(Husband   )

AFFIDAVIT

I, _____Joan Public_____ , of the _City of Toronto_____

in the _Municipality of Toronto_____

MAKE OATH AND SAY (or AFFIRM):

1.   I am the Petitioner herein and as such have knowledge of the matters hereinafter deposed to.

2.   No appeal from the divorce is pending.

3.   No order has been made extending the time for appealing from the divorce.

SWORN BEFORE ME at the _____)

)

of _____ in the)

)

_____)   _____

)

this ___ day of _____ 200-____)

_____

A Commissioner for taking Affidavits, etc.

SELF-COUNSEL PRESS-DIVONT-SOLE(119-1)00

Court file no._____

ONTARIO SUPERIOR COURT OF JUSTICE

BETWEEN:

Joan Public

PETITIONER

(Wife)

- and -

(Court seal)

John Que Public

RESPONDENT

(Husband)

UNDERTAKING NOT TO APPEAL

We, the undersigned, do hereby agree, in the event that the Divorce Judgment is granted by this Honourable Court, to the granting of a Divorce Judgment forthwith and do hereby undertake that no appeal will be taken from the said Divorce Judgment. We understand that if the Divorce Judgment is made final at trial neither of us will thereafter be able to make application for a division of the family assets under the Family Law Act and that we will be forever barred from doing so.

Dated at Toronto, this __3rd__ day of ___July, 200-_____

WITNESS:

I C Ewe
_____

J M Witness
_____

Joan Public
_____

John Que Public
_____

6

ONTARIO SUPERIOR COURT OF JUSTICE
FAMILY COURT BRANCH

If you and/or your spouse live in any of the areas listed below, you are in an area under the jurisdiction of the *Ontario* Superior Court of Justice Family Court, formerly the Ontario Court (General Division), or formerly the Unified Family Court. If you do not live in any of the areas listed below, see Chapter 5.

The Family Law Rules apply to the following jurisdictions:

- County of Frontenac
- County of Haliburton
- County of Lanark
- County of Lennox and Addington
- County of Northumberland
- County of Peterborough
- County of Simcoe
- County of Victoria
- Regional Municipality of Durham
- Regional Municipality of Hamilton-Wentworth
- the part of the Regional Municipality of Niagara that was the County of Lincoln as it existed on December 31, 1969
- Regional Municipality of Ottawa-Carleton
- Regional Municipality of York
- Territorial District of Muskoka
- United Counties of Leeds and Grenville
- United Counties of Stormont, Dundas, and Glengarry
- United Counties of Prescott and Russell

The forms required to process an uncontested divorce in Family Court are different, some say simpler, than those required in all other jurisdictions. A husband and wife, on consent of each other, may be joint applicants. This will eliminate the requirement for service of the documents. After the application is issued by the court office, you may proceed to prepare a Continuing Record described below.

The forms required for Family Court are the following:

(a) Application (General) Form 8 or Application (Divorce) Form 8A (see Samples #29 and #30)

(b) Financial Statement Form 13 (see Sample #31)

(c) Acknowledgment of Service Form 6 (see Sample #32)

(d) Affidavit of Service Form 6B (see Sample #33)

(e) Affidavit for Divorce Form 36 (see Sample #34)

(f) Continuing Record (see Sample #35)

(g) Certificate of Clerk (Divorce) Form 36A (see sample 36)

(h) Divorce Order Form 25A (see Sample #37)

(i) Certificate of Divorce Form 36B (see Sample #38)

(j) Support Deduction Order (see Sample #14)

(k) Support Deduction Order Information Form (see Sample #15)

(Note: The Support Deduction Order and the Support Deduction Order Information Form are the same for both the *Ontario* Superior Court of Justice Family Court and the *Ontario* Superior Court of Justice.)

If you live in one of these cities, you can still file for divorce in the *Ontario* Superior Court of Justice in a different judicial district unless there are children involved. If children are involved, the papers must be filed in the area where the children live. As well, if a trial is necessary, it must be held in the jurisdiction where you or your spouse live. In summary, if you live in one of the jurisdictions listed earlier in this Chapter and wish to file for divorce, you are likely to be required to complete the forms set out here.

Although the forms differ from those presented in Chapter 5, the concepts of obtaining an uncontested divorce in the Family Court are similar to those in other jurisdictions. I therefore recommend that you follow the outline provided here, substituting the Family Court forms for the *Ontario* Superior Court of Justice forms where applicable. In reading the material about the *Ontario* Superior Court of Justice, please note that the person beginning the proceeding is referred to as the "Petitioner," whereas in the Family Court, that person is referred to as the "Applicant."

The courts also differ slightly in their procedures, such as how they wish the court documents to be filed. At the time you issue your originating documents, you may wish to check with the court clerk in your own jurisdiction to confirm the particular procedures and to make sure there have not been any changes. This is a new court, and it is still in its initial stages, so it is conceivable that changes will occur to its procedures.

If you are filing in Family Court, you will still need to read the rest of this book so that you have an understanding of the process. However, keep the following in mind.

First, the Application replaces the Petition for Divorce. As you read the Application (see Samples #29 and #30), you will notice that you are required to complete and file a Financial Statement like the one shown in Sample #31 and file it with the Application if you are claiming child or spousal support, or have any other monetary claims.

When you go to court to issue the Application you should take a copy of your Financial Statement with you, if monetary claims are being made. These documents form part of the Continuing Record, which will be discussed later in the chapter. The court registrar will provide you with the date of hearing and complete the "First Court Date" on the Application at that time.

The cost to issue the Application is $150*, which is payable to the Minister of Finance by cash, money order, or certified cheque. At this point, if you have your original marriage certificate, you should file it with the court.

The Application and Financial Statement (if applicable), must then be served on the respondent after the documents are issued. The manner of serving the documents under the Family Law Rules is referred to as special service and is the same as set out in section d.7 of Chapter 5 *Serving the documents.*

Once the documents are served, the recipient of the documents may either acknowledge service by completing and signing the Acknowledgment of Service (Form 6 — Sample #32), or the process server may complete an Affidavit of Service (Form 6B — Sample #33).

If your spouse has not filed any responding documents by the prescribed time shown on the Application (i.e., 30 days if served in Canada or the United States, 60 days if served elsewhere in the world), you can proceed for an uncontested divorce.

The date of the hearing provided by the court should have been far enough in advance that it will not have expired by the time you get to this step. If the date is approaching and you are not yet ready to proceed, you can simply fax a letter to the court requesting that it extend the date of the hearing; provide a reason why it should do so. This way, you avoid an unnecessary court appearance.

Before the return court date, if your spouse has not contested the Application, you can set the matter down for hearing. You will need to pay the court $280*. Again, a certified cheque or money order must be made payable to the Minister of Finance. The court will also accept cash.

In order to set the matter down, you need to also file the documents with the court in what is called a Continuing Record (see Sample #35). It will consist of a red cover page entitled Continuing Record, followed by three tabs labelled Contents, Endorsements, and Documents. The Contents section provides an index of the documents in the Continuing Record), the Endorsements section contains ten pages simply entitled Endorsement Page for the Judge to write his or her decisions, followed by the original documents: Application (Form 8 — Sample #29 or Form 8A — Sample #30), Financial Statement (if required) (Form 13 — Sample #31), Affidavit of Service (Form 6B — Sample #33), and Affidavit for Divorce (Form 36 — Sample #34) (unless you wish to attend on the hearing date and give oral evidence). All the documents in the Record are to be listed on the Contents page. The documents should be bound by simply inserting a brass round fastener in the top left-hand corner of the documents. This procedure may vary from court to court and you may want to inquire with the court you are specifically dealing with.

You will also file (separate from the Record) three copies of the Divorce Order, and if a claim for support is being made, one extra copy of the Divorce Order and two copies each of a Support Deduction Order (see Sample #14) and a Support Deduction Order Information Form (see Sample #15). You also need to supply two stamped self-addressed envelopes, one envelope addressed to you, one addressed to your spouse.

You do not need to appear in court if you set out your evidence in an Affidavit for Divorce and file it with the court as part of the Continuing Record. You can, however, appear before a judge to give your evidence in person on the trial date set by the court.

The sample of the Divorce Order shown (Sample #37) is for a divorce only. If additional claims have been made, further clauses must also be added. See the sample of the Divorce Judgment (Sample #22) in Chapter 5 for clauses for support and custody.

Once you receive the issued Divorce Order in the mail from the court, you may apply for a Certificate of Divorce 31 days after the date of Order. To do this, take a copy of your Divorce Order and a completed Certificate of Divorce (see Sample #38) to the court, along with a further $18.* The clerk at the court will then issue the Certificate.

---

* Note that all fees are subject to change without notice. Please check all fees with the court or appropriate government office before submitting funds.

SAMPLE #29
FORM 8 — APPLICATION (GENERAL)

SUPERIOR COURT OF JUSTICE FAMILY COURT

(Name of court)

Court File Number

SEAL

at _____

Court office address

Form 8: Application
(General)

Applicant(s)

Full legal name & address for service — street and number, municipality, postal code, telephone & fax numbers and e-mail address (if any).	Lawyer's name & address — street and number, municipality, postal code, telephone & fax numbers and e-mail address (if any).
Joan Public 322 Lakeshore Road London, ON L5N 3N2 (519) 123-4567	

Respondent(s)

Full legal name & address for service — street and number, municipality, postal code, telephone & fax numbers and e-mail address (if any).	Lawyer's name & address — street and number, municipality, postal code, telephone & fax numbers and e-mail address (if any).
John Que Public 1000 Yonge Street London, ON L5N 3N1 (519) 765-4321	

TO THE RESPONDENT(S):

A COURT CASE HAS BEEN STARTED AGAINST YOU IN THIS COURT. THE DETAILS ARE SET OUT ON THE ATTACHED PAGES.

☐ THE FIRST COURT DATE IS *(date)* . . . .
. . . . AT . . . .
a.m./p.m. or as soon as possible after that time, at: *(address)*

NOTE: *If this is a divorce case, no date will be set unless an Answer is filed.*

If you have also been served with a notice of motion, there may be an earlier court date and you or your lawyer should come to court for the motion.
☐ **THIS CASE IS ON THE FAST TRACK OF THE CASE MANAGEMENT SYSTEM.** A case management judge will be assigned by the time this case first comes before a judge.

☐ **THIS CASE IS ON THE STANDARD TRACK OF THE CASE MANAGEMENT SYSTEM. No court date has been set for this case** but, if you have been served with a notice of motion, it has a court date and you or your lawyer should come to court for the motion. A case management judge will not be assigned until one of the parties asks the clerk of the court to schedule a case conference or until a notice of motion under subrule 14(5) is served before a case conference has been held. If, after 200 days, the case has not been scheduled for trial, the clerk of the court will send out a warning that the case will be dismissed in 30 days unless the parties file proof that the case has been settled or one of the parties asks for a case conference or a settlement conference.

IF YOU WANT TO OPPOSE ANY CLAIM IN THIS CASE, you or your lawyer must prepare an *Answer* (Form 10 — a blank copy should be attached), serve a copy on the applicant(s) and file a copy in the court office with an *Affidavit of Service* (Form 6B). **YOU HAVE ONLY 30 DAYS AFTER THIS APPLICATION IS SERVED ON YOU (60 DAYS IF THIS APPLICATION IS SERVED ON YOU OUTSIDE CANADA OR THE UNITED STATES) TO SERVE AND FILE AN ANSWER. IF YOU DO NOT, THE CASE WILL GO AHEAD WITHOUT YOU AND THE COURT MAY MAKE AN ORDER AND ENFORCE IT AGAINST YOU.**

Check this box ☐ if this paragraph applies.   This case includes a claim for support or for property. You **MUST** fill out a *Financial Statement* (Form 13 — a blank copy attached), serve a copy on the applicant(s) and file a copy in the court office with an *Affidavit of Service* even if you do not answer this case.

If you want to make a claim of your own, you or your lawyer must fill out the claim portion in the *Answer*, serve a copy on the applicant(s) and file a copy in the court office with an *Affidavit of Service.*

You should get legal advice about this case right away. If you cannot afford a lawyer, you may be able to get help from your local Legal Aid office. *(See your telephone directory under LEGAL AID).*

_____
Date of issue

_____
Clerk of the court

Continued on the next page.

SELF-COUNSEL PRESS-DIVONT-FAM(200-1)00

110

Form 8: Application (General) (page 2)   Court file number . . . .

FAMILY HISTORY

APPLICANT: Age: . .34. . . Birthdate: . May 12, 1964 . . . .

Resident in *(municipality & province)* . County of Middlesex, Ontario . . . .

since *(date)* . .birth . . . .

Surname at birth: . .Jones . . . .   Surname just before marriage: Jones . . . .

Divorced before? [X] No.   [] Yes. *(Place and date of previous divorce)* . . . .

RESPONDENT: Age: .45. . . . Birthdate: May. 12,. 1954 . . . .

Resident in *(municipality & province)* . .County. of. Middlesex . . . .

since *(date)* . . . .birth . . . .

Surname at birth: . . .Public. . . . .   Surname just before marriage: . .Public. . . . .

Divorced before? [X] No.   [] Yes. *(Place and date of previous divorce)* . . . .

RELATIONSHIP DATES:

[] Married on *(date)* December 27, 1984 [] Started living together on *(date)*

[] Separated on *(date)* June 1, 1995   [] Never lived together.   [] Still living together.

THE CHILD(REN):

List all children involved in this case, even if no claim is made for these children.

Full Legal Name	Age	Birthdate	Resident in *(municipality & province)*	Now Living with *(name of person and relationship to child)*
Robert John Public	14	June 1, 1985	County of Middlesex ON	Applicant since separation

PREVIOUS CASES OR AGREEMENTS

Have the parties or the children been in a court case before?

[X] No.   [] Yes. *(Attach a summary of court cases — Form 8E.)*

Have the parties made a written agreement dealing with any matter involved in this case?

[X] No.   [] Yes. *(Give date of agreement. Indicate which of its terms are in dispute. Attach an additional page if you need more space.)*

Continued on next the sheet.

SELF-COUNSEL PRESS-DIVONT-FAM(200-2)00

111

Form 8: Application (General) (page 3)   Court file number . . . .

CLAIM BY APPLICANT

I ASK THE COURT FOR THE FOLLOWING:
(Claims below include claims for temporary orders.)

Claims under the *Divorce Act* Check boxes in this column only if you are asking for a divorce.)	Claims under the *Family Law Act* or *Children's Law Reform Act*	Claims relating to property
00 ☒ a divorce	10 [] support for me	20 [] equalization of net family properties
01 [] support for me	11 ☒ support for child(ren)	21 [] exclusive possession of matrimonial home
02 ☒ support for child(ren)	12 ☒ custody of child(ren)	22 [] exclusive possession of contents of matrimonial home
03 ☒ custody of child(ren)	13 [] access to child(ren)	23 [] freezing assets
04 [] access to child(ren)	14 [] restraining/non-harassment order	24 [] sale of family property
	15 [] indexing spousal support	**Other claims**
	16 [] declaration of parentage	30 [] costs
	17 [] guardianship over child's property	31 [] annulment of marriage
		32 [] prejudgment interest

50 []   *(Other; specify.)*

Give details of the order that you want the court to make. *(Include any amounts of support (if known) and the names of the children for whom support, custody or access is claimed.)*

Custody: The child of the marriage resides with the wife/applicant and has resided with her since the parties separated. The husband/respondent has liberal and generous access to the child, and exercises access every second weekend from Friday night until Sunday night. The wife is in a better position to meet the childs day-to day needs, and has been the childs primary caretaker since birth. The child is happy and well adjusted in the present circumstances, is doing well in school, and it would be in his best interests that the present situation does not change.

Child Support: The husband earns $50,000.00 per year. In accordance with the Child Support Guidelines he is required to pay $414.00 per month child support, not taxable to either party.

Continued on the next page.

SELF-COUNSEL PRESS-DIVONT-FAM(200-3)00

Form 8: Application (General) (page 4)   Court file number . . . .

IMPORTANT FACTS SUPPORTING MY CLAIM FOR DIVORCE

☐ **Separation:** The spouses have lived separate and apart since *(date)* June 1, 1995 . . . .   and
    ☐ have not lived together again since that date in an unsuccessful attempt to reconcile.
    ☐ have lived together again during the following period(s) in an unsuccessful attempt to reconcile: *(Give dates.)*

☐ **Adultery:** The respondent has committed adultery. *(Give details. It is not necessary to name any other person involved but, if you do name the other person, then you must serve this application on the other person.)*

   Not applicable

☐ **Cruelty:** The respondent has treated the applicant with physical or mental cruelty of such a kind as to make continued cohabitation intolerable. *(Give details.)*

   Not applicable

IMPORTANT FACTS SUPPORTING MY OTHER CLAIM(S)
(Set out below the facts that form the legal basis for your other claim(s). Attach an additional page if you need more space.)

Put a line through any blank space left on this page

Joan Public   June 1, 20 -
_____   _____
Applicant's signature   Date of signature

For divorce cases only   **LAWYER'S CERTIFICATE**

My name is:
and I am the applicant's lawyer in this divorce case. I certify that I have complied with the requirements of section 9 of the *Divorce Act.*

_____   _____
Lawyer's signature   Date of signature

SELF-COUNSEL PRESS-DIVONT-FAM(200-4)00

SAMPLE #30
FORM 8A — APPLICATION (DIVORCE)

SUPERIOR COURT OF JUSTICE FAMILY COURT

(Name of court)

Court File Number

....

SEAL

at _____

Court office address

Form 8A: Application
(divorce) ☐ Joint
         ☐ Simple

Applicant

Full legal name & address for service — street and number, municipality, postal code, telephone & fax numbers and e-mail address (if any).	Lawyer's name & address — street and number, municipality, postal code, telephone & fax numbers and e-mail address (if any).
Joan Public 322 Lakeshore Road London, ON L5N 3N2 (519) 123-4567	

Respondent(s)

Full legal name & address for service — street and number, municipality, postal code, telephone & fax numbers and e-mail address (if any).	Lawyer's name & address — street and number, municipality, postal code, telephone & fax numbers and e-mail address (if any).
John Que Public 1000 Yonge Street London, ON L5N 3N1 (519) 765-4321	

☐ **THIS CASE IS A JOINT APPLICATION FOR DIVORCE. THE DETAILS ARE SET OUT ON THE ATTACHED PAGES.** The application and affidavits in support of the application will be presented to a judge when the materials have been checked for completeness.

☐ IN THIS CASE, THE APPLICANT IS CLAIMING DIVORCE ONLY.

TO THE RESPONDENT(S): A COURT CASE FOR DIVORCE HAS BEEN STARTED AGAINST YOU IN THIS COURT. THE DETAILS ARE SET OUT ON THE ATTACHED PAGES.

THIS CASE IS ON THE STANDARD TRACK OF THE CASE MANAGEMENT SYSTEM. **No court date has been set for this case** but, if you have been served with a notice of motion, it has a court date and you or your lawyer should come to court for the motion. A case management judge will not be assigned until one of the parties asks the clerk of the court to schedule a case conference or until a notice of motion under subrule 14(5) is served before a case conference has been held. If, after 200 days, the case has not been scheduled for trial, the clerk of the court will send out a warning that the case will be dismissed in 30 days unless the parties file proof that the case has been settled or one of the parties asks for a case conference or a settlement conference.

IF YOU WANT TO OPPOSE ANY CLAIM IN THIS CASE, you or your lawyer must prepare an answer (Form 10 — a blank copy should be attached), serve a copy on the applicant and file a copy in the court office with an affidavit of service (Form 6B).

YOU HAVE ONLY 30 DAYS AFTER THIS APPLICATION IS SERVED ON YOU (60 DAYS IF THIS APPLICATION IS SERVED ON YOU OUTSIDE CANADA OR THE UNITED STATES) TO SERVE AND FILE AN ANSWER. IF YOU DO NOT, THE CASE WILL GO AHEAD WITHOUT YOU AND THE COURT MAY MAKE AN ORDER AND ENFORCE IT AGAINST YOU.

If you want to make a claim of your own, you or your lawyer must fill out the claim portion in the answer, serve a copy on the applicant and file a copy in the court office with an affidavit of service.

You should get legal advice about this case right away. If you cannot afford a lawyer, you may be able to get help from your local Legal Aid office. *(See your telephone directory under LEGAL AID).*

_____
Date of issue

_____
Clerk of the court

Continued on the next page.

SELF-COUNSEL PRESS-DIVONT-FAM(201-1)00

Form 8A: Application (divorce) (page 2)   Court file number . . . .

FAMILY HISTORY

HUSBAND: Age: . . .45. . Birthdate: May 12, 1954 . . . .

Resident in *(municipality & province)* County of Middlesex, Ontario . . . .

since *(date)* . .since birth . . . .

Surname at birth: . . . .Public . . . . Surname just before marriage: Public . . . .

Divorced before?   ⊠ No.   [] Yes. *(Place and date of previous divorce)* . . . .

WIFE: Age: . .34. . . . . Birthdate: April 11, 1954 . . . .

Resident in *(municipality & province)* County of Middlesex, Ontario . . . .

since *(date)* . . .birth . . . .

Surname at birth: . . .Jones . . . . Surname just before marriage: .Jones . . . .

Divorced before?   ⊠ No.   [] Yes. *(Place and date of previous divorce)* . . . .

RELATIONSHIP DATES:

[] X Married on *(date)* December 27, 1984 [] Started living together on *(date)*

[] Separated on *(date)* June 1, 1995   [] Never lived together.

THE CHILD(REN):

List all children involved in this case, even if no claim is made for these children.

Full Legal Name	Age	Birthdate	Resident in *(municipality & province)*	Now Living with *(name of person and relationship to child)*
Robert John Public	14	June 1, 1985	County of Middlesex ON	Applicant

PREVIOUS CASES OR AGREEMENTS

Have the parties or the children been in a court case before?

  [] No.   [] Yes. *(Attach a summary of court cases — Form 8E.)*

Have the parties made a written agreement dealing with any matter involved in this case?

  [] No.   [] Yes. *(Give date of agreement. Indicate which of its terms are in dispute. Attach an additional page if you need more space.)*

Continued on next sheet.

SELF-COUNSEL PRESS-DIVONT-FAM(201-2)00

Form 8A: Application (divorce) (page 3)   Court file number . . . .

CLAIMS

USE THIS FRAME ONLY IF THIS CASE IS A JOINT APPLICATION FOR DIVORCE.

WE JOINTLY ASK THE COURT FOR THE FOLLOWING:

Claims under the *Divorce Act*

- 00 ▣ a divorce
- 01 [] spousal support
- 02 [] support for child(ren)
- 03 [] custody of child(ren)
- 04 [] access to child(ren)

Claims under the *Family Law Act* or *Children's Law Reform Act*

- 10 [] spousal support
- 11 [] support for child(ren)
- 12 [] custody of child(ren)
- 13 [] access to child(ren)
- 14 [] restraining/non-harassment order
- 15 [] indexing spousal support
- 16 [] declaration of parentage
- 17 [] guardianship over child's property

Claims relating to property

- 20 [] equalization of net family properties
- 21 [] exclusive possession of matrimonial home
- 22 [] exclusive possession of contents of matrimonial home
- 23 [] freezing assets
- 24 [] sale of family property

Other claims

- 30 [] costs
- 31 [] annulment of marriage
- 32 [] prejudgment interest
- 50 [] *(Other; specify.)*

USE THIS FRAME ONLY IF THE APPLICANT'S ONLY CLAIM IN THIS CASE IS FOR DIVORCE.

I ASK THE COURT FOR: *(Check if applicable.)*

- 00 ▣ a divorce   30 [] costs

IMPORTANT FACTS SUPPORTING THE CLAIM FOR DIVORCE

[] **Separation:** The spouses have lived separate and apart since *(date)* June 1, 1995 . . . . and

     [] have not lived together again since that date in an unsuccessful attempt to reconcile.

     [] have lived together again during the following period(s) in an unsuccessful attempt to reconcile: *(Give dates.)*

[] **Adultery:** *(Name of spouse)* . . . . Not applicable . . . . has committed adultery. *(Give details. It is not necessary to name any other person involved but, if you do name the other person, then you must serve this application on the other person.)*

[] **Cruelty:** *(Name of spouse)* . . . Not applicable . . . . has treated *(name of spouse)* . . . . with physical or mental cruelty of such a kind as to make continued cohabitation intolerable. *(Give details.)*

SELF-COUNSEL PRESS-DIVONT-FAM(201-3)00

SAMPLE #30 — Continued

Form 8A: Application (divorce) (page 4)   Court file number . . . .

USE THIS FRAME ONLY IF THIS CASE IS A JOINT APPLICATION FOR DIVORCE.

The details of the other order(s) that we jointly ask the court to make are as follows: *(Include any amounts of support and the names of the children for whom support, custody or access is to be ordered.)*

IMPORTANT FACTS SUPPORTING OUR CLAIM(S)
(Set out below the facts that form the legal basis for your claim(s). Attach an additional page if you need more space.)

Put a line through any blank space left on this page

In a joint application for divorce, there will be two signatures — one for each spouse. But in an application where the applicant's only claim is for divorce, you and your lawyer are the only ones who will sign and you should strike out the inappropriate zone for your spouse's signature and corresponding date.

_____   _____
Signature of applicant husband   Date of signature

_____   _____
Signature of applicant wife   Date of signature

LAWYER'S CERTIFICATE

My name is:
and I am the lawyer for *(name)* . . . . in this divorce case. I certify that I have complied with the requirements of section 9 of the *Divorce Act*.

_____   _____
Lawyer's signature   Date of signature

SELF-COUNSEL PRESS-DIVONT-FAM(201-4)00

SAMPLE #31
FORM 13 — FINANCIAL STATEMENT

SUPERIOR COURT OF JUSTICE FAMILY COURT
_____
(Name of court)

Court File Number

....

Form 13: Financial Statement dated

....

at _____
Court office address

Applicant(s)

Full legal name & address for service — street and number, municipality, postal code, telephone & fax numbers and e-mail address *(if any)*. Joan Public 322 Lakeshore Road London, Ontario L5N 3N2 (519) 123-4567	Lawyer's name and address — street and number, municipality, postal code, telephone & fax numbers and e-mail address *(if any)*.

Respondent(s)

Full legal name and address for service — street and number, municipality, postal code, telephone & fax numbers and e-mail address *(if any)*. John Que Public 1000 Yonge Street London, Ontario L5N 3N1 (519) 765-4321	Lawyer's name and address — street and number, municipality, postal code, telephone & fax numbers and e-mail address *(if any)*.

My name is *(full legal name)*

I live in *(municipality & province)*

and I swear/affirm that the following is true:

1. My financial statement set out on the following pages is accurate to the best of my knowledge and belief and sets out the financial situation as of *(give date for which information is accurate)* .... for

Check one or more boxes as circumstances require.
- ☐ me
- ☐ the children listed in Part 1 of this statement
- ☐ the following person(s): *[Give name(s) and relationship to you.]*

2. I attach to this statement:

See the instructions in the note on the back of this sheet.
- ☐ Parts 1 to 6 of this Form and the documents mentioned in Part 2 (items 9 to 12).
- ☐ Part 7 of this Form.
- ☑ Parts ☐ 8 to 10 of this Form.
- ☐ 11 to 16 of this Form.

Sworn/Affirmed before me at ....
municipality

in ....
province, state or country

on ....
date

_____
Commissioner for taking affidavits
(Type or print name below if signature is illegible.)

_____
Signature
(This form is to be signed in front of a lawyer, justice of the peace, notary public or commissioner for taking affidavits.)

Continued on other side. ➡

SELF-COUNSEL PRESS-DIVONT-FAM(202-1)00

Form 13: Financial Statement (page 2)   Court file number . . . .

HOW TO FILL OUT THIS FORM

You must fill out and attach Parts 1 to 6 of this Form if this case includes:
- ■ a claim for support;
- ■ a claim for a change in support;
- ■ an enforcement of a support order or of the support provisions of a domestic contract or paternity agreement;
- ■ a claim for custody or access where the court has ordered the filing of a financial statement
- ■ a claim for exclusive possession of the matrimonial home and its contents; or
- ■ a property dispute that does not involve equalization of net family property under Part I of the *Family Law Act*.

You must also fill out and attach Part 7, **BUT ONLY IF THIS CASE INCLUDES A CLAIM FOR CHILD SUPPORT THAT IS DIFFERENT FROM THE TABLE AMOUNT IN THE CHILD SUPPORT GUIDELINES** (a claim for add-ons for special or extraordinary expenses for the child(ren); a child 18 years of age or more; a claim for undue hardship; a support claim in a case of split or shared custody; or a case where a party's annual income is over $150,000).

Finally, you must also give information about your property and your debts. **YOU MUST FILL OUT AND ATTACH:**
- (a)   **PARTS 8 TO 10** if this case includes one or more of the matters mentioned above, BUT NOT a claim for equalization of net family property under Part I of the *Family Law Act;*

OR
- (b)   **PARTS 11 TO 16** if this case deals **includes** a claim for equalization of net family property under Part I of the *Family Law Act*, even if it also includes one or more of the matters mentioned above..

For example, if this case is only about the equalization of family property under Part I of the *Family Law Act*, you would skip Parts 1 to 7 and only fill out and attach Parts 11 to 16.

FURTHER IMPORTANT NOTE

As soon as you find out that:
- (a)   the information in this financial statement is incorrect or incomplete; or
- (b)   there is a material change in your circumstances that affects or will affect the information in this financial statement,

you **MUST** serve on every other party to this case and file with the court,
- (c)   the correct or complete information; or
- (d)   a new financial statement with updated information,

together with any documents that back up that information.

DECLARATION
This declaration is to be filled out only if your income is tax exempt because of your Indian status.

My name is *(full legal name)*

I live in *(municipality & province)*

and I declare that the following is true:

1.   I am an Indian within the meaning of the *Indian Act* of Canada.

2.   Because of my status, my income is tax exempt and I am not required to file an income tax return.

3.   I have therefore not filed an income tax return for the past three years.

Declared before me at . . . .
                                                        municipality

in . . . .
                              province, state or country

on . . . .
          date

Commissioner for taking affidavits
(Type or print name below if signature is illegible.)

Signature
(This form is to be signed in front of a lawyer, justice of the peace, notary public or commissioner for taking affidavits.)

Continued on next sheet. ➡

SELF-COUNSEL PRESS-DIVONT-FAM(202-2)00

Form 13: Financial Statement (page 3)   Court file number . . . .

PARTS 1 TO 6 MUST BE FILLED OUT AND ATTACHED TO THIS FINANCIAL STATEMENT if this case includes:
- ■ a claim for support;
- ■ a claim for a change in support;
- ■ an enforcement of a support order or of the support provisions of a domestic contract or paternity agreement;
- ■ a claim for custody or access where the court has ordered the filing of a financial statement
- ■ a claim for exclusive possession of the matrimonial home and its contents; or
- ■ a property dispute that does not involve equalization of net family property under Part I of the *Family Law Act*.

You would skip this part if this case deals only with equalization of net family property.

PART 1: NAMES AND BIRTHDATES OF CHILD(REN)

Part 1 must be filled out if this case involves a claim by you or by another party:
- *(a)   for child support;*
- *(b)   for the enforcement of child support; or*
- *(c)   for custody of or access to a child, but only where a court has ordered each party to serve and file a financial statement;*
- *(d)   for any combination of the above.*

You still have to fill out this Part, even if you have decided not to oppose another party's claim for custody or child support. Part 1 does not apply if this case contains no claim regarding children.

	CHILD'S FULL LEGAL NAME	BIRTHDATE (d,m,y)	SEX
1.			
2.			
3.			
4.			
5.			
6.			
7.			

PART 2: INCOME

for the 12 months from *(date)* . . . . to *(date)* . . . .

Include all income and other money that you get from all sources, whether taxable or not. Show the gross amount here and show your deductions in Part 5. Give the current actual amount if you know it or can find out. If you can't find out, give your best estimate. To get a monthly figure for items 13 to 28, you must multiply any weekly income by 4.33 or divide any yearly sum by 12.

9. I am   □   employed by *(name and address of employer)*

        □   self-employed, carrying on business under the name of *(name and address of business)*

        □   unemployed since *(date when last employed)*

10. I attach to this form:
- □ a copy of my income tax returns that were filed with the Department of National Revenue for the past 3 taxation years, together with a copy of all material filed with the returns and a copy of any notices of assessment or re-assessment that I have received from the Department for those years.
- □ a statement from the Department of National Revenue that I have not filed any income tax returns for the past 3 years.
- □ a declaration that I am not required to file an income tax return because of the *Indian Act* (Canada). *[Use the declaration at the bottom of page 2.]*
- □ a direction in Form 13A signed by me to the Taxation Branch of the Department of National Revenue for the disclosure of my tax returns and assessments for the past 3 years.

IMPORTANT!   *If your case requires you to fill out and attach Parts 1 to 6, the clerk of the court will NOT allow you to file this financial statement unless you have checked one of the boxes in paragraph 10 above and have attached the required document(s).*

Continued on other side. ☛

SELF-COUNSEL PRESS-DIVONT-FAM(202-3)00

Form 13: Financial Statement (page 4)   Court file number . . . .

11. I attach to this statement proof of my current income, including my most recent

☐   pay cheque stub.   ☐   employment insurance stub.   ☐   worker's compensation stub.
☐   pension stub.   ☐   *(Other; specify.)*

12. My total income earned so far this year is $ . . . . and is detailed in items 13 to 28 below.   I attach the following document(s) as proof of this year's earnings: *(Identify the document(s) being attached.)*

	CATEGORY	Monthly
13.	Pay, wages, salary, including overtime *(before deductions)*	
14.	Bonuses, fees, commissions	
15.	Social assistance *(employment assist- ance, basic financial assistance)*	
16.	Employment insurance	
17.	Workers' compensation	
18.	Pensions	
19.	Dividends	
20.	Interest	
21.	Rent, board received	

	CATEGORY	Monthly
22.	Child tax benefit	
23.	Support payments actually received	
24.	Income received by children	
25.	G.S.T. refund	
26.	Income tax refund	
27.	Gifts and loans received	
28.	Other *(income from business, tips, etc. Attach statements or details.)*	
29.	**INCOME FROM ALL SOURCES**	

PART 3: OTHER BENEFITS

Show your non-cash benefits — such as the use of a company car, a club membership or room and board that your employer or someone else provides for you or benefits that are charged through or written off by your business. If you cannot find out the actual value of these benefits, give your best estimate.

ITEM	DETAILS	Monthly Market Value
	30. TOTAL	

31. GROSS MONTHLY INCOME AND BENEFITS (Add: [29] plus [30]) $ . . . .

PART 4: OTHER INCOME EARNERS IN THE HOME

Fill in this part only if you are living with another person. It does not matter whether you are married to this person.

32. I am living with *(full legal name of person)*

33. This person has *(give number)* . . . . child(ren) living in the home.

34. This person ☐   works at *(place of work or business)*

☐   does not work outside the home.

35. This person ☐   earns *(give amount)* $. . . . . per . . . .
☐   does not earn anything.

36. This person ☐   pays for about . . . .% of the household expenses.
☐   contributes no money to the household expenses.

Continued on next sheet. ➡

SELF-COUNSEL PRESS-DIVONT-FAM(202-4)00

Form 13: Financial Statement (page 5)   Court file number . . . .

PART 5: AUTOMATIC DEDUCTIONS FROM INCOME

for the 12 months from *(date)* . . . . to *(date)* . . . .
. . .

Give the current actual amount if you know it or can find out. If you can't find out, give your best estimate. To get a monthly figure, you must multiply any weekly amount by 4.33 or divide any yearly sum by 12.

	TYPE OF EXPENSE	Monthly			TYPE OF EXPENSE	Monthly
37.	Income tax deducted from pay			42.	Group insurance	
38.	Canada Pension Plan			43.	Other *(Specify. If necessary attach an extra sheet.)*	
39.	Other pension plans					
40.	Employment insurance					
41.	Union or association dues			44.	**TOTAL AUTOMATIC DEDUCTIONS**	

45. NET MONTHLY INCOME (Do the subtraction: [31] minus [44]): $ . . . .

PART 6:   TOTAL EXPENSES

for the 12 months from *(date)* . . . . to *(date)* . . . .
. . . . .

NOTE: This part must be completed in all cases. You must set out your TOTAL living expenses, including those expenses involving any children now living in your home. If you cannot find out the actual amount, give your best estimate. As with Part 1, convert weekly figures to monthly ones by multiplying by 4.33 or dividing yearly ones by 12.

	TYPE OF EXPENSE	Monthly			TYPE OF EXPENSE	Monthly
	Housing			59.	General household supplies	
46.	Rent / Mortgage			60.	Hairdresser, barber, toiletries & sundries	
47.	Property taxes & municipal levies			61.	Laundry & dry cleaning	
48.	Condominium fees & common expenses			62.	Other *(Specify. If necessary attach an extra sheet.)*	
49.	Water				**Clothing**	
50.	Electricity			63.	Clothing for me	
51.	Heating fuel (natural gas, fuel oil)			64.	Clothing for children	
52.	Telephone			65.	Other. *(Specify. If necessary, attach an extra sheet.)*	
	Housing				**Transportation**	
53.	Cable television & pay television			66.	Public transit	
54.	Home insurance			67.	Taxis	
55.	Home repairs, maintenance, gardening, snow removal, *etc.*			68.	Car insurance	
56	Other household expenses *(Specify. If necessary, attach an extra sheet.)*			69.	Licence	
	Food, Toiletries & Sundries.			70.	Car loan payments	
57.	Groceries			71.	Car maintenance and repairs	
58.	Meals outside home			72.	Gasoline & oil	

Continued on other side. ➡

Continued on other side. ➡

SELF-COUNSEL PRESS-DIVONT-FAM(202-5)00

Form 13: Financial Statement (page 6)   Court file number . . . .

	TYPE OF EXPENSE	Monthly
73.	Parking	
74.	Other *(Specify. If necessary, attach an extra sheet.)*	
	Health & Medical	
75.	Regular dental care	
76.	Orthodontal or special dental care	
77.	Medicine & drugs	
78.	Eye glasses or contact lenses	
79.	Other *(Specify. If necessary, attach an extra sheet.)*	
	Miscellaneous	
80.	Life or term insurance premiums	
81.	School fees, books, tuition, *etc.*	
82.	School activities *(special projects, field trips, etc.)*	
83.	School lunches	
84.	Religious school	
85.	Entertainment & recreation	
86.	Vacation	
87.	Children's summer camp	
88.	Children's activities *(music lessons, clubs, sports, bicycles)*	
89.	Children's allowances	

	TYPE OF EXPENSE	Monthly
90.	Baby sitting	
91.	Day care	
92.	Books for home use, newspapers, magazines, audio/video tapes & discs	
93.	Gifts	
94.	Charities	
95.	Alcohol & tobacco	
96.	Pet expenses	
97.	Support actually being paid in this case	
98.	Support actually being paid in any other case	
99.	Income tax (not deducted from pay)	
100.	Other *(Specify. If necessary, attach an extra sheet.)*	
	Debt payments *(excluding mortgages)*	
101.	Credit cards *(but not for expenses mentioned elsewhere in this statement.)*	
102.	Other *(Specify. If necessary, attach an extra sheet.)*	
	Savings	
103.	R.r.s.p.	
104.	Other *(Specify. If necessary, attach an extra sheet.)*	
105.	**Total of items [46] to [104]**	

SUMMARY OF INCOME AND EXPENSES

Net monthly income (item [45] above)   = $ . . . .
Subtract actual monthly expenses (item [105] above)   = $ . . . .
ACTUAL MONTHLY SURPLUS/DEFICIT   = $ . . . .

IMPORTANT NOTE ABOUT THE NEXT PART

If this case deals with child support *different* from the table amount in the child support guidelines (a claim for add-ons for special or extraordinary expenses for child(ren); a child is 18 years of age or more; a claim for undue hardship; a support claim in a case of split or shared custody; or a case where the payor's annual income is over $150,000), **THEN YOU MUST NEXT FILL OUT AND ATTACH PART 7.**

If, however, the claim for child support in this case is for the table amount in the child support guidelines or if this cases does not deal with child support at all, omit Part 7 completely and instead go on to fill out and attach:

- Parts 8 to 10; *OR*
- Parts 11 to 16,

but not both. See the instructions at the top of Part 8 or Part 11 about the choice that you must make.

Continued on next sheet. ➡

SELF-COUNSEL PRESS-DIVONT-FAM(202-6)00

Form 13: Financial Statement (page 7)   Court file number . . . .

PART 7: EXPENSES OF THE CHILD(REN)

NOTE: DO NOT FILL OUT PART 7 UNLESS THIS CASE INCLUDES A CLAIM FOR CHILD SUPPORT THAT IS DIFFERENT FROM THE TABLE AMOUNT IN THE CHILD SUPPORT GUIDELINES (a claim for add-ons for special or extraordinary expenses for the child(ren); a child is 18 years of age or more; a claim for undue hardship; a support claim in a case of split or shared custody; or a case where the party's annual income is $150,000 or more).

If Part 7 applies to this case, set out the percentage of your actual total monthly living expenses in Part 6 that relates to any child(ren) now living in the household. If you cannot figure out the actual amount of each child's share of a particular expense item, give your best approximation. If there are more than three children, attach extra sheets.

	TYPE OF EXPENSE	% of expense attributed to child			Monthly Total
		Name: Age:	Name: Age:	Name: Age:	
Housing					
106.	Rent / Mortgage	%	%	%	$
107.	Property taxes & municipal levies				
108.	Condominium fees & common expenses				
109.	Water				
110.	Electricity				
111.	Heating fuel (natural gas, fuel oil)				
112.	Telephone				
113.	Cable television & pay television				
114.	Home insurance				
115.	Home repairs, maintenance, gardening, snow removal, etc.				
Food, Toiletries & Sundries					
116.	Groceries				
117.	Meals outside home				
118.	General household supplies				
119.	Hairdresser, barber, toiletries & sundries				
120.	Laundry & dry cleaning				
121.	Other (Specify. If necessary attach an extra sheet.)				
Clothing					
122.	Clothing for children				
123.	Other (Specify. If necessary, attach an extra sheet.)				
Transportation					
124.	Public transit				

Continued on other side. ➡

SELF-COUNSEL PRESS-DIVONT-FAM(202-7)00

Form 13: Financial Statement (page 8)   Court file number . . . .

	TYPE OF EXPENSE	% of expense attributed to child			Monthly Total
		Name:	Name:	Name:	
		Age:	Age:	Age:	
125.	Taxis				
126.	Car insurance				
127.	Licence				
128.	Car loan payments				
129.	Car maintenance & repairs				
130.	Gasoline & oil				
131.	Parking				
132.	Other *(Specify. If necessary, attach an extra sheet.)*				
Health & Medical					
133.	Regular dental care				
134.	Orthodontal or special dental care				
135.	Medicine & drugs				
136.	Eye glasses or contact lenses				
137.	Other *(Specify. If necessary, attach an extra sheet.)*				
Miscellaneous					
138.	Life or term insurance premiums				
139.	School fees, books, tuition, *etc.*				
140.	School residence				
141.	School activities (special projects, field trips, *etc.*)				
142.	School lunches				
143.	Religious school				
144.	Entertainment & recreation				
145.	Vacation				
146.	Children's summer camp				
147.	Children's activities (music lessons, clubs, sports, bicycles)				
148.	Children's allowances				
149.	Baby sitting				
150.	Day care				

Continued on next sheet. ➡

SELF-COUNSEL PRESS-DIVONT-FAM(202-8)00

Form 13: Financial Statement (page 9)   Court file number . . . .

| TYPE OF EXPENSE | % of expense attributed to child | | | Monthly Total |
| | Name: | Name: | Name: | |
	Age:	Age:	Age:	
151. Books for home use, newspapers, magazines, audio/video tapes and discs				
152. Gifts to child(ren)				
153. Gifts from child(ren) to others				
154. Charities				
155. Pet expenses				
156 Other *(Specify. If necessary, attach an extra sheet.)*				
Debt Payments *(excluding mortgage)*				
157. Credit cards *(but not for expenses mentioned elsewhere in this statement)*				
158. Other *(Specify. If necessary, attach an extra sheet.)*				
Savings				
159. Other *(Specify. If necessary, attach an extra sheet.)*				
160. CHILD(REN)'S MONTHLY EXPENSES — TOTAL OF ITEMS [106] TO [159]				$

IMPORTANT NOTE ABOUT THE NEXT PART

YOU MUST NEXT FILL OUT AND ATTACH:
- Parts 8 to 10; *OR*
- Parts 11 to 16,

but not both. See the instructions at the top of Part 8 or Part 11 about the choice that you must now make.

Continued on next sheet. ➡

SELF-COUNSEL PRESS-DIVONT-FAM(202-9)00

Form 13: Financial Statement (page .....)   Court file number . . . .

IMPORTANT NOTE ABOUT PARTS 8-10

If this case includes a claim for equalization of net family property under Part I of the Family Law Act, skip parts 8 to 10 and go directly to Parts 11 to 16. Fill out Parts 8 to 10 ONLY IF this case involves anything else, such as:

- *a claim for support;*   • *a change in support;*
- *an enforcement of a support order or of the support provisions of a domestic contract or paternity agreement;*
- *a claim for custody or access where the court has ordered the filing of a financial statement; or*
- *exclusive possession of the matrimonial home or any other property dispute (except equalization of net family property).*

PART 8: ASSETS IN AND OUT OF ONTARIO

PART 8(a): LAND

Include any interest in land **owned** as of the date of this statement, including leasehold interests and mortgages. Show estimated market value of your interest, but do not deduct encumbrances or costs of disposition; these encumbrances and costs should be shown under Part 9, "Debts and Liabilities". DO NOT INCLUDE LAND THAT YOU DO NOT OWN, even though you are claiming an interest in it.

For example, if you were including the matrimonial home, you might insert "Joint tenancy" in the first column on the left; and in the next column, you might write "Matrimonial home, 123 Main Street, est. value $400,000 today".

Nature & Type of Ownership *(Give your percentage interest where relevant.)*	Nature, address and estimated TOTAL value today *[This total value may be different from the value of your share (set out in the last column) if the property has two or more owners.]*	Estimated Market value of YOUR interest
161. TOTAL VALUE OF LAND		

PART 8(b): GENERAL HOUSEHOLD ITEMS AND VEHICLES

Show estimated market value, not the cost of replacement for these items owned as of the date of this statement. Do not deduct encumbrances or costs of disposition; these encumbrances and costs should be shown under Part 9, "Debts and Liabilities".

ITEM	DESCRIPTION	Tick off ✔ if NOT in your possession	Estimated Market value of YOUR interest
Household goods & furniture			
Cars, boats, vehicles			

Continued on other side. ➡

SELF-COUNSEL PRESS-DIVONT-FAM(202-10)00

Form 13: Financial Statement (page .....)   Court file number . . . .

PART 8(b): GENERAL HOUSEHOLD ITEMS AND VEHICLES			
Jewellery, art, electronics, tools, sports & hobby equipment			
Other special items			
162. TOTAL VALUE OF GENERAL HOUSEHOLD ITEMS AND VEHICLES			

PART 8(c): BANK ACCOUNTS AND SAVINGS

Show the items owned by category. Include cash, accounts in financial institutions, registered retirement or other savings plans, deposit receipts, pensions and any other savings.

Category	INSTITUTION	Account number	Amount
163. TOTAL VALUE OF ACCOUNTS AND SAVINGS			

PART 8(d): SECURITIES

Show the items owned by category. Include bonds, warrants, options, notes and other securities. Give your best estimate of their market value if the items were to be sold on the open market.

Category	Number	Description	Estimated Market Value
164. TOTAL VALUE OF SECURITIES			

Continued on next sheet.

SELF-COUNSEL PRESS-DIVONT-FAM(202-11)00

Form 13: Financial Statement (page .....)   Court file number . . . .

PART 8(e): LIFE & DISABILITY INSURANCE					
List all policies now in existence.					
Company & Pol- icy No.	Kind of Policy	Owner	Beneficiary	Face Amount	Today's Cash Surrender Value
165. TOTAL CASH SURRENDER VALUE OF INSURANCE POLICIES					

PART 8(f): BUSINESS INTERESTS		
Show any interest in an unincorporated business owned today. A controlling interest in an incorporated business may be shown here or under "SECURITIES" in Part 8(d). Give your best estimate of market value if the business were to be sold on an open market.		
Name of Firm or Company	Interest	Estimated Market value of YOUR interest
166. TOTAL VALUE OF BUSINESS INTERESTS		

PART 8(g): MONEY OWED TO YOU	
Give details of all money that other persons owe to you today, whether because of business or from personal dealings. Include any court judgments in your favour and any estate money owed to you.	
DETAILS	Amount Owed to You
167. TOTAL OF MONEY OWED TO YOU	

Continued on other side. ➡

SELF-COUNSEL PRESS-DIVONT-FAM(202-12)00

Form 13: Financial Statement (page .....)   Court file number . . . .

PART 8(h): OTHER PROPERTY		

Show other property or assets owned by categories. Include property of any kind not listed above. Give your best estimate of market value.

CATEGORY	DETAILS	Estimated Market Value
168. TOTAL VALUE OF OTHER PROPERTY		
169. VALUE OF ALL PROPERTY *Add items* **[161]** *to* **[168]**		

PART 9: DEBTS AND OTHER LIABILITIES		

Show your debts and other liabilities today *from personal and business dealings.* List them by category, such as mortgages, charges, liens, notes, credit cards, and accounts payable. Don't forget to Include:
- any money owed to Revenue Canada;
- contingent liabilities such as guarantees or warranties given by you (but indicate that they are contingent); and
- any unpaid legal or professional bills as a result of this case.

CATEGORY	DETAILS	Amount owing
170. TOTAL OF DEBTS AND OTHER LIABILITIES		

PART 10: SUMMARY OF ASSETS AND LIABILITIES	
	Amounts
TOTAL ASSETS *(from item* **[169]** *above)*	$
Subtract TOTAL DEBTS *(from item* **[170]** *above)*	$
171. NET WORTH	$

NOTE: If you have filled out Parts 8-10, then aside from any other documents that you must attach (such as income tax returns), this is the last page of this Form. Do not fill out or attach Parts 11-16.

SELF-COUNSEL PRESS-DIVONT-FAM(202-13)00

Form 13: Financial Statement (page .....) Court file number . . . .

IMPORTANT NOTE ABOUT PARTS 11-16

Fill out Parts 11 to 16 **ONLY IF** *this case includes a claim for equalization of net family property under Part I of the Family Law Act. If, however, this case deals with:*

- *a claim for support;*   • *a change in support;*
- *an enforcement of a support order or of the support provisions of a domestic contract or paternity agreement;*
- *a claim for custody or access where the court has ordered the filing of a financial statement; or*
- *a claim for exclusive possession of the matrimonial home or any other property dispute (aside from equalization of net family property),*

skip parts 11 to 16 and fill out Parts 8 to 10 instead.

PART 11: ASSETS IN AND OUT OF ONTARIO

PART 11(a): LAND

Include any interest in land **owned** on the valuation date or as of the date of this statement, including leasehold interests and mortgages. Show estimated market value of your interest, but do not deduct encumbrances or costs of disposition; these encumbrances and costs should be shown under Part 12, "Debts and Liabilities". DO NOT INCLUDE LAND THAT YOU DO NOT OWN, even though you are claiming an interest in it.

For example, if you were including the matrimonial home, you might insert "Joint tenancy" in the first column on the left; and in the next column, you might write "Matrimonial home, 123 Main Street, est. value $400,000 today".

The valuation date is: *(give date)* . . . .

Nature & Type of Ownership *(Give your percentage interest where relevant.)*	Nature, address and estimated TOTAL value today *[This total value may be different from the value of your share (set out in the last column) if the property has two or more owners.]*	Estimated Market value of YOUR interest		
		on date of marriage	on valuation date	today
	172. TOTAL VALUE OF LAND	$		

PART 11(b): GENERAL HOUSEHOLD ITEMS AND VEHICLES

Show estimated market value, not the cost of replacement for these items owned on valuation date or as of the date of this statement. Do not deduct encumbrances or costs of disposition; these encumbrances and costs should be shown under Part 12, "Debts and Liabilities".

ITEM	DESCRIPTION	Tick off ✔ if NOT in your posses-sion	Estimated Market value of YOUR interest		
			on date of marriage	on valuation date	today
Household goods & furniture					
Cars, boats, vehicles					

Continued on other side. ➡

SELF-COUNSEL PRESS-DIVONT-FAM(202-14)00

Form 13: Financial Statement (page .....)　　　　　Court file number . . . .

PART 11(b): GENERAL HOUSEHOLD ITEMS AND VEHICLES				
Jewellery, art, electronics, tools, sports & hobby equipment				
Other special items				
173. TOTAL VALUE OF GENERAL HOUSEHOLD ITEMS AND VEHICLES			$	

PART 11(c): BANK ACCOUNTS AND SAVINGS					

Show the items owned on the valuation date by category. Include cash, accounts in financial institutions, registered retirement or other savings plans, deposit receipts, pensions and any other savings.

Category	INSTITUTION	Account number	Amount		
			on date of marriage	on valuation date	today
174. TOTAL VALUE OF ACCOUNTS AND SAVINGS			$		

PART 11(d): SECURITIES					

Show the items owned on the valuation date by category. Include bonds, warrants, options, notes and other securities. Give your best estimate of their market value if the items were to be sold on the open market.

Category	Number	Description	Estimated Market value		
			on date of marriage	on valuation date	today
175. TOTAL VALUE OF SECURITIES			$		

Continued on next sheet. ➡

SELF-COUNSEL PRESS-DIVONT-FAM(202-15)00

Form 13: Financial Statement (page .....)   Court file number . . . .

PART 11(e): LIFE & DISABILITY INSURANCE

List all policies in existence on the valuation date.

Company & Pol- icy No.	Kind of Policy	Owner	Beneficiary	Face Amount	Cash Surrender Value		
					Date of Mar- riage	Valuation Date	Today

176. TOTAL CASH SURRENDER VALUE OF INSURANCE POLICIES	$	

PART 11(f): BUSINESS INTERESTS

Show any interest in an unincorporated business owned on the valuation date. A controlling interest in an incorporated business may be shown here or under "SECURITIES" in Part 11(d). Give your best estimate of market value if the business were to be sold on an open market.

Name of Firm or Company	Interest	Estimated Market value of YOUR interest		
		on date of marriage	on valuation date	today

177. TOTAL VALUE OF BUSINESS INTERESTS	$	

PART 11(g): MONEY OWED TO YOU

Give details of all money that other persons owe to you on the valuation date, whether because of business or from personal dealings. Include any court judgments in your favour and any estate money owed to you.

DETAILS	Amount Owed to You		
	on date of marriage	on valuation date	today

178. TOTAL OF MONEY OWED TO YOU	$	

Continued on other side. ➡

SELF-COUNSEL PRESS-DIVONT-FAM(202-16)00

Form 13: Financial Statement (page .....)   Court file number . . . .

PART 11(h): OTHER PROPERTY				

Show other property or assets owned on the valuation date. Include property of any kind not listed above. Give your best estimate of market value.

CATEGORY	DETAILS	Estimated Market value of YOUR interest		
		on date of marriage	on valuation date	today
179. TOTAL VALUE OF OTHER PROPERTY			$	
180. VALUE OF ALL PROPERTY OWNED ON THE VALUATION DATE *Add items* [172] *to* [179]			$	

PART 12: DEBTS AND OTHER LIABILITIES				

Show your debts and other liabilities on the valuation date *from personal and business dealings.* List them by category such as mortgages, charges, liens, notes, credit cards, and accounts payable. Don't forget to include:
- any money owed to Revenue Canada;
- contingent liabilities such as guarantees or warranties given by you (but indicate that they are contingent); and
- any unpaid legal or professional bills as a result of this case.

CATEGORY	DETAILS	Amount owing		
		on date of marriage	on valuation date	today
181. TOTAL OF DEBTS AND OTHER LIABILITIES			$	

Continued on next sheet. ➡

SELF-COUNSEL PRESS-DIVONT-FAM(202-17)00

SAMPLE #31 — Continued

Form 13: Financial Statement (page .....)　　　　Court file number . . . .

PART 13: PROPERTY, DEBTS AND OTHER LIABILITIES ON DATE OF MARRIAGE		
Show by category the value of your property and your debts and other liabilities *as of the date of your marriage.* DO NOT INCLUDE THE VALUE OF A MATRIMONIAL HOME THAT YOU OWNED ON THE DATE OF MARRIAGE.		

CATEGORY AND DETAILS	Value on date of marriage	
	Assets	Liabilities
Land *(exclude matrimonial home owned on date of marriage, unless sold before date of separation.)*		
General household items & vehicles		
Bank accounts and savings		
Securities		
Life & disability insurance		
Business interests		
Money owed to you		
Other property *(Specify.)*		
Debts and other liabilities *(Specify.)*		
TOTALS	$	$
182. NET VALUE OF PROPERTY OWNED ON DATE OF MARRIAGE *(From the total of the "Assets" column, subtract the total of the "Liabilities" column.)*	$	
183. VALUE OF ALL DEDUCTIONS *(Add items* [181] *and* [182].*)*	$	

PART 14: EXCLUDED PROPERTY		
Show by category the value of property owned on the valuation date that is excluded from the definition of "net family property" (such as gifts or inheritances received after marriage).		

CATEGORY	DETAILS	Value on valuation date
184. TOTAL VALUE OF EXCLUDED PROPERTY		$

Continued on other side. ➡

SELF-COUNSEL PRESS-DIVONT-FAM(202-18)00

Form 13: Financial Statement (page .....)

Court file number . . . .

PART 15: DISPOSED PROPERTY		
Show by category the value of property that you disposed of during the two years immediately before the separation.		
CATEGORY	DETAILS	VALUE
	185. TOTAL VALUE OF DISPOSED PROPERTY	$

PART 16: CALCULATION OF NET FAMILY PROPERTY	Deductions	BALANCE
Value of all property owned on valuation date *(from item [180] above)*		$
Subtract value of all deductions *(from item [183] above)*	$	$
Subtract value of all excluded property *(from item [184] above)*	$	$
186. NET FAMILY PROPERTY		$

SAMPLE #32
FORM 6 — ACKNOWLEDGEMENT OF SERVICE

Court File Number ....

SUPERIOR COURT OF JUSTICE FAMILY COURT

_____
(Name of court)

Form 6: **Acknowledgement of Service**

at _____
Court office address

You are asked to fill out and sign this card and to mail it immediately. If you do not return this card, the document(s) listed below may be personally served on you and you may be ordered to pay the costs of service.

My name is: *(full legal name)* John Que Public

I may be served at: *(address where court documents may be mailed to you)* 1000 Yonge Street London Ontario L5N 3N1

I acknowledge receiving a copy of the following document(s):

x **Application dated** ....

☐ **Blank form of application**

x **Financial statement dated** ....

☐ **Blank form of financial statement**

☐ **Answer dated** ....

☐ **Blank form of answer**

☐ **Affidavit of** *(name)* ....
   dated ....

☐ **Notice of motion dated** ....

☐ **Statement of money owed dated** ....

....
   (Other. Give title and date of document.)

_____   _____
Signature   Date of signature

NOTICE: *The address that you give above will be used in future to serve documents by mail until you inform the other parties and the court office of a new address for service.*

SELF-COUNSEL PRESS-DIVONT-FAM(203-1)00

137

SAMPLE #33
FORM 6B — AFFIDAVIT OF SERVICE

SUPERIOR COURT OF JUSTICE FAMILY COURT
_____
(Name of court)

Court File Number
....

at _____
Court office address

Form 6B: Affidavit of
Service dated

. . . .

Applicant(s)

Full legal name & address for service — street & number, municipality, postal code, telephone & fax and e-mail address (if any).	Lawyer's name & address — street & number, municipality, postal code, telephone & fax numbers and e-mail address (if any).
Joan Public 322 Lakeshore Road London, Ontario L5N 3N2 (519) 123-4567	

Respondent(s)

Full legal name & address for service — street & number, municipality, postal code, telephone & fax numbers and e-mail address (if any).	Lawyer's name & address — street & number, municipality, postal code, telephone & fax numbers and e-mail address (if any).
John Que Public 1000 Yonge Street London, Ontario L5N 3N1 (519) 765-4321	

My name is *(full legal name)* John Smith

I live in *(municipality & province)* County of Middlesex, Ontario

and I swear/affirm that the following is true:

1. On *(date)* . July 1, 1995. . . . ., I served *(name of person to be served)* John Que Public

    with the following document(s) in this case:

	Name of document	Author (if applicable)	Date when document signed, issued, sworn, etc.

List the documents served. Application   Applicant

NOTE: *You can leave out any part of this form that is not applicable.*

---

2. I served the documents mentioned in paragraph 1 by,

Check one box only and go to indicated paragraph.

- **X** special service. *(Go to paragraph 3 below if you used special service.)*
- ☐ mail. *(Go to paragraph 4 if you used mailed service.)*
- ☐ courier. *(Go to paragraph 5 if you used courier.)*
- ☐ deposit at a document exchange. *(Go to paragraph 6 if you used a document exchange.)*
- ☐ fax. *(Go to paragraph 7 if you used fax.)*
- ☐ substituted service or advertisement. *(Go to paragraph 8 if you used substituted service or advertisement.)*

3. I carried out special service of the document(s) on the person named in paragraph 1 at *(place or address)*

by: **X** leaving a copy with the person.

Check one box only. Strike out paragraphs 4 to 8 and go to paragraph 9.

- ☐ leaving a copy with *(name)*
    - ☐ who is the person's lawyer and who accepted service on the person's behalf.
    - ☐ who is the *(office or position)*
    of the corporation named in paragraph 1.
- ☐ mailing a copy to the person together with a prepaid return postcard in Form 6 in an envelope bearing the sender's return address. This postcard, in which receipt of the document(s) is acknowledged, was

Continued on other side. ➡

SELF-COUNSEL PRESS-DIVONT-FAM(204-1)00

138

Form 6B: Affidavit of
     Service dated .... (page 2)   Court file number ....

returned and is attached to this affidavit.

☐ leaving a copy in a sealed envelope addressed to the person at the person's place of residence with *(name)* who provided me with identification to show that he/she was an adult person residing at the same address and by mailing another copy of the same document(s) on the same or following day to the person named in paragraph 1 at that place of residence.

☐ *(Other; specify. See rule 6 for details.)*

4. I mailed the document(s) to be served by addressing the covering envelope to the person named in paragraph 1 at: *(Set out address.)*

which is the address   ☐ of the person's place of business.
Check appropriate   ☐ of the person's lawyer.
paragraph and strike   ☐ of the person's home.
out paragraphs 3, 5,   ☐ on the document most recently filed in court by the person.
6, 7, 8 and 9.   ☐ *(Other; specify.)*

5. The document(s) to be served was/were placed in an envelope that was picked up at .... a.m./p.m. on *(date)* .... by *(name of courier service)*

a private courier service, a copy of whose receipt is attached to this affidavit. The envelope was addressed to the person named in paragraph 1 at: *(Set out address.)*

which is the address   ☐ of the person's place of business.
Check appropriate   ☐ of the person's lawyer.
paragraph and strike   ☐ of the person's home.
out paragraphs 3, 4,   ☐ on the document most recently filed in court by the person.
6, 7, 8 and 9.   ☐ *(Other; specify.)*

6. The document(s) was/were deposited at a document exchange. The exchange's date stamp on the attached copy shows the date of deposit. *(Strike out paragraphs 3, 4, 5, 7, 8 and 9.)*

7. The document(s) to be served was/were faxed. The fax confirmation is attached to this affidavit. *(Strike out paragraphs 3, 4, 5, 6, 8 and 9.)*

8. An order of this court made on *(date)* .... allowed
    ☐ substituted service.
    ☐ service by advertisement. *(Attach advertisement.)*
The order was carried out as follows: *(Give details. Then go to paragraph 9 if you had to travel to serve substitutionally or by advertisement.)*

9. To serve the document(s), I had to travel .... kilometres. My fee for service of the document(s) is $ .... , including travel.

Sworn/Affirmed before me at ....
                                  municipality

in ....
        province, state or country

on ....
     date   *Commissioner for taking affidavits*
                       (Type or print name below if signature is illegible.)

Signature
(This form is to be signed in front of a lawyer, justice of the peace, notary public or commissioner for taking affidavits.)

SELF-COUNSEL PRESS-DIVONT-FAM(204-2)00

139

SAMPLE #34
FORM 36 — AFFIDAVIT FOR DIVORCE

SUPERIOR COURT OF JUSTICE FAMILY COURT	Court File Number
(Name of court)	
	Form 36: Affidavit for Divorce

at _____
Court office address

Applicant

Full legal name & address for service — street & number, municipality, postal code, telephone & fax and e-mail address (if any). Joan Public 322 Lakeshore Road London, Ontario L5N 3N2 (519) 123-4567	Lawyer's name & address — street & number, municipality, postal code, telephone & fax numbers and e-mail address (if any).

Respondent(s)

Full legal name & address for service — street & number, municipality, postal code, telephone & fax numbers and e-mail address (if any). John Que Public 1000 Yonge Street London, Ontario L5N 3N1 (519) 765-4321	Lawyer's name & address — street & number, municipality, postal code, telephone & fax numbers and e-mail address (if any).

My name is *(full legal name)* Joan Public

I live in *(municipality & province)* County of Middlesex, Ontario

and I swear/affirm that the following is true:

1. I am the applicant in this divorce case.

2. There is no chance of a reconciliation between the respondent and me.

3. All the information in the application in this case is correct, except: *(State any corrections or changes to the information in the application. Write "NONE" if there are no corrections or changes.)*

4. ☐ The certificate or registration of my marriage to the respondent has been signed and sealed by the Registrar General of Ontario and
    X has been filed with the application.
    ☐ is attached to this affidavit.
☐ The certificate of my marriage to the respondent was issued outside Ontario. It is called *(title of certificate)* .... It was issued
at *(place of issue)* ....
on *(date)* .... by
(name and title of person who issued certificate) ....
and the information in it about my marriage is correct.
☐ I have not been able to get a certificate or registration of my marriage. I was married to the respondent on
(date) .... at
(place of marriage) .... The marriage was
performed by *(name and title)* ....
who had the authority to perform marriages in that place.

5. The legal basis for the divorce is:
X that the respondent and I have been separated for at least one year. We separated on June 1, 1995.
☐ *(Other. Specify.)*

Continued on other side. ➡

SELF-COUNSEL PRESS-DIVONT-FAM(205-1)00

140

Form 36: **Affidavit for Divorce** (page 2)　　　　　　　　Court file number . . . .

6. I do not know about and I am not involved in any arrangement to make up or to hide evidence or to deceive the court in this divorce case.

Strike out the following paragraphs if they do not apply.

7. I do not want to make a claim for a division of property in this divorce case, even though I know that it may be legally impossible to make such a claim after the divorce.

8. I want the divorce order to include the following paragraph numbers of the attached consent, settlement, separation agreement or previous court order: *(List the numbers of the paragraphs that you want included in the divorce order.)*

9. There are (number) . . . . children of the marriage. They are:

Full legal name of child	Birthdate (d,m,y)

10. The custody and access arrangements for the child(ren) are as follows: *(Give summary.)*

. . . .
. . . .
. . . .
. . . .
. . . .
. . . .
. . . .
. . . .

11. These are the arrangements that have been made for the support of the child(ren) of the marriage:

　　(a) The income of the party paying child support is $ . . . . per year.

　　(b) The number of children for whom support is supposed to be paid is *(number)* . . . .

　　(c) The amount of support that should be paid according to the applicable table in the child support guidelines is $ . . . . per month.

　　(d) The amount of child support actually being paid is $ . . . . per month.
　　　　(**NOTE:—** *Where the dollar amounts in clauses (c) and (d) are different, you must fill out the frame on the next page. If the amounts in clauses (c) and (d) are the same, skip the frame and go directly to paragraph 12.)*

Continued on next sheet. ➡

SELF-COUNSEL PRESS-DIVONT-FAM(205-2)00

141

Form 36: Affidavit for Divorce (page 3)   Court file number . . . .

(Paragraph 11 continued.)
Fill out the information in this frame only if the amounts in paragraphs 11(c) and 11(d) are different. If they are the same, go to paragraph 12.

(a) Child support is already covered by:

    (i) ☐ a court order dated *(date)* . . . . that was made before the child support guidelines came into effect (before 1 May 1997). I attach a copy of the order

    (ii) ☐ a domestic contract order dated *(date)* . . . . that was made before the child support guidelines came into effect (before 1 May 1997). I attach a copy of the contract

    (iii) ☐ a court order or written agreement dated *(date)* . . . . made after the guidelines came into effect that has some direct or indirect benefits for the child(ren). I attach a copy.

    (iv) ☐ a written consent between the parties dated *(date)* . . . . agreeing to the payment of an amount different from that set out in the guidelines.

(b) The child support clauses of this order or agreement require payment of $ . . . . per . . . . in child support.

(c) These child support clauses   ☐ are not indexed for any automatic cost-of-living increases.
                                                   ☐ are indexed according to *(Give indexing formula)*

(d) These child support clauses   ☐ have not been changed since the day the order or agreement was made.
                                                   ☐ have been changed on *(Give dates and details of changes)*

(e) *(If you ticked off box (i) above, you can go to paragraph 12. If you ticked off boxes (ii), (iii) or (iv) above, then fill out the information after box of the corresponding number below. For example, if you ticked off box (iii) above, you would fill out the information alongside box (iii) below.)*

    (ii) ☐ The amount being paid under this agreement is a fair and reasonable arrangement for the support of the child(ren) because: *(Give reasons.)*

    (iii) ☐ The order or agreement directly or indirectly benefits the child(ren) because: *(Give details of benefits.)*

    (iv) ☐ The amount to which the parties have consented is reasonable for the support of the child(ren) because: *(Give reasons.)*

Continued on other side. ➡

SELF-COUNSEL PRESS-DIVONT-FAM(205-3)00

Form 36: Affidavit for Divorce (page 4)   Court file number . . . .

12.   I am claiming costs in this case. The details of this claim are as follows: *(Give details.)*

13.   The respondent's address last known to me is: *(Give address.)*

1000 Yonge Street

London, Ontario

L5N 3N1

(519) 765-4321

Put a line through any blank space left on this page.

Sworn/Affirmed before me at . . . .
    municipality

in . . . .
    province, state or country

on . . . .
    date

Commissioner for taking affidavits
(Type or print name below if signature is illegible.)

Signature
(This form is to be signed in front of a lawyer, justice of the peace, notary public or commissioner for taking affidavits.)

SELF-COUNSEL PRESS-DIVONT-FAM(205-4)00

Court File Number

....

Continuing Record

Ontario **Superior Court of Justice, Family Court**

(Name of court)

at_____

Court office address

Volume_____

Applicant(s)

Full legal name & address for service - street & number, municipality, postal code, telephone & fax numbers & e-mail address (if any).	*Lawyer's name & address – street & number, municipality, postal code, telephone & fax numbers & e-mail address (if any).*
Joan Public 322 Lakeshore Road London, Ontario L5N 3N2 (519) 123-4567	

Respondent(s)

Full legal name & address for service - street & number, municipality, postal code, telephone & fax numbers & e-mail address (if any).	*Lawyer's name & address – street & number, municipality, postal code, telephone & fax numbers & e-mail address (if any).*
John Que Public 1000 Yonge Street London, Ontario L5N 3N1 (519) 765-4321	

Note: No document shall be removed from the continuing record, except by court order.

SELF-COUNSEL PRESS-DIVONT-FAM(206-1)00

Court File Number

....

Ontario Superior Court of Justice, Family Court

(Name of court)

**Cumulative Table of Contents
(continuing record)**

at_____

Court office address

Applicant(s)

Full legal name & address for service - street & number, municipality, postal code, telephone & fax numbers & e-mail address (if any).	Lawyer's name & address – street & number, municipality, postal code, telephone & fax numbers & e-mail address (if any).
Joan Public 322 Lakeshore Road London, Ontario L5N 3N2 (519) 123-4567	

Respondent(s)

Full legal name & address for service - street & number, municipality, postal code, telephone & fax numbers & e-mail address (if any).	Lawyer's name & address – street & number, municipality, postal code, telephone & fax numbers & e-mail address (if any).
John Que Public 1000 Yonge Street London, Ontario L5N 3N1 (519) 765-4321	

Document *(For an affidavit or transcript of evidence, include the name of the person who gave the affidavit or the evidence.)*	Filed by *(A=applicant or R=respondent or O=other)*	Date of Document	Date of Filling	Tab/Page (...../ ..... to .....)

(When this volume has 100 sheets of documents filed in it, start a new volume.)

SELF-COUNSEL PRESS-DIVONT-FAM(206-2)00

145

SUPERIOR COURT OF JUSTICE FAMILY COURT

Court File Number

....

(Name of court)

**Form 36A: Certificate
of Clerk (Divorce)**

at _____
Court office address

**Applicant's
last name: Public** . . . .

**Respondent's
last name: Public** . . . .

If the appropriate box on the left cannot be checked, check the box on the right margin and describe the deficiency by that box
The clerk of the court certifies as follows:

Check if applicable and complete the
rest of the certificate as if the divorce
had been claimed by the applicant.   ☐ Divorce claimed only by the respondent.

Deficiency

1. PRELIMINARY
- (a) ☐ No answer filed
  - ☐ Answer was withdrawn — Continuing record tab/page number . . . . . .
  - ☐ Order dated . . . . , under subrule 12(6), splitting divorce from rest of the case — Continuing record tab/page number . . . . . .
  - ☐ Answer struck out by order dated . . . . — Continuing record tab/page number . . . . . .
  - ☐ Joint application — no respondent
- (b) ☐ Clearance certificate from Central Divorce Registry

1(a) ☐

1(b) ☐

2. PROOF OF SERVICE
- ☐ Affidavit of service
- ☐ Person's lawyer accepted service
- ☐ Joint application — no service necessary

2 ☐

3. METHOD OF SERVICE
- ☐ Left copy with person to be served
- ☐ Left copy with person's lawyer
- ☐ Mailed copy to person and received acknowledgement signed by person
- ☐ Left copy at person's residence with adult resident and mailed another copy
- ☐ Signed acknowledgement of service filed
- ☐ *(Other. Specify.)*

Service took place in *(province or country)* . . . .
Service was carried out on *(date)* . . . .

3 ☐

4. GROUNDS FOR DIVORCE
- ☐ Separation since *(date)* . . . . , affidavit sworn more that one year after separation.
- ☐ Adultery
- ☐ Cruelty

4 ☐

5. ONTARIO RESIDENCE
Application should indicate that at least one spouse must have been Ontario resident for at least a year.
- ☐ Wife resident in Ontario since *(date)* . . . .
- ☐ Husband resident in Ontario since *(date)* . . . .

5 ☐

6. CLAIMS
- ☐ Only claim for divorce
- ☐ Claim for child support *[details in part 8 above]*
- ☐ Claim for custody/access — details in application
- ☐ Claim for spousal support — details in application
- ☐ Claim for property — details in application
- ☐ Claim to include provisions of consent, agreement or previous court order — details in application
- ☐ costs

6 ☐

7. PROOF OF MARRIAGE

7 ☐

Continued on other side. ➡

SELF-COUNSEL PRESS-DIVONT-FAM(207-1)00

Form 36A: Certificate of Clerk (Divorce) (page 2) Court file number . . . .

Deficiency

Marriage took place ☐ in Canada ☐ outside Canada
☐ Marriage certificate or registration of marriage filed — details agree with those in application — Continuing record tab/page number . . . . . .
☐ No certificate — details of marriage set out in affidavit — Continuing record tab/page number . . . . . .
☐ Previous divorce or death certificate filed — Continuing record tab/page number . . . . . .

8. **AFFIDAVITS**   8 ☐
☐ Applicant's affidavit — Continuing record tab/page number . . . . . .
☐ Respondent's affidavit — Continuing record tab/page number . . . . . .
☐ Affidavit of *(name)* . . . .
— Continuing record tab/page number . . . . . .
☐ Affidavit complies with Form 35 and is properly completed — Continuing record tab/page number . . . . . .

9. **CHILDREN**   9 ☐
☐ No children of the marriage
☐ There are children of the marriage
☐ Child support guidelines information supplied — Continuing record tab/page number
. . . . . .
☐ payor's income
☐ table amount
☐ recipient's income *[REQUIRED for special expenses (add-ons), split custody, shared custody, payor is stepparent, child over 18, payor's income more than $150,000, claim of undue hardship]*
☐ details of special expenses (add-ons)
☐ agreement/consent with explanation for claim less than table amount

10. **DRAFT ORDER**   10 ☐
The following material has been filed:
☐ 3 copies of draft order — no support claimed
☐ 4 copies of draft order + 2 drafts of support deduction order — support claimed
☐ Stamped envelope for each party
☐ Address for service of order on respondent is same as
☐ on application
☐ on documents filed by respondent
☐ in applicant's affidavit
☐ Draft order in same terms as application
☐ Draft order in same terms as consent, minutes of settlement, or agreement filed — Continuing record tab/page number . . . . . .
☐ Request for early effective date for divorce; agreements and undertakings filed not to appeal — Continuing record tab/page number . . . . . .

11. **NOTICE TO APPLICANT**   11 ☐
☐ Applicant notified of deficiencies but requests to submit papers to judge despite them.

_____   _____
Signature of clerk of the court   *Date of signature*

SELF-COUNSEL PRESS-DIVONT-FAM(207-2)00

147

SUPERIOR COURT OF JUSTICE FAMILY COURT
(Name of court)

Court File Number
....

at _____
Court office address

Form 25A: Divorce Order

Applicant(s)

Full legal name & address for service — street & number, municipality, postal code, telephone & fax numbers and e-mail address (if any).	Lawyer's name & address — street & number, municipality, postal code, telephone & fax numbers and e-mail address (if any).
Joan Public 322 Lakeshore Road London, Ontario L5N 3N2 (519) 123-4567	

Judge (print or type name)

_____

Date of order

Respondent(s)

Full legal name & address for service — street & number, municipality, postal code, telephone & fax numbers and e-mail address (if any).	Lawyer's name & address — street & number, municipality, postal code, telephone & fax numbers and e-mail address (if any).
John Que Public 1000 Yonge Street London, Ontario L5N 3N1 (519) 765-4321	

The court considered an application of *(name)* Joan Public

on *(date)*

The following persons were in court *(Give names of parties and lawyers in court. This paragraph may be struck out if the divorce is uncontested.)*

The court received evidence and considered submissions on behalf of *(name or names)* Joan Public, no one appearing on behalf of the respondent.

THIS COURT ORDERS THAT:

1. *(full legal names of spouses)* Joan Public and John Que Public

    who were married at *(place)* London, Ontario

    on *(date)* December 27, 1984

    be divorced and that the divorce take effect . .31 . . . . days after the date of this order.

    (Add further paragraphs where the court orders other relief.)

Continued on other side. ➡

SELF-COUNSEL PRESS-DIVONT-FAM(208-1)00

148

Form 25A: Divorce Order (page 2)　　　　　　　　Court file number . . . .

Put a line through any blank space left on this page. If additional space is needed, extra pages may be attached.

_____　　　　_____
　　　　　　Date of signature　　　　　　　　　　　*Signature of judge or clerk of the court*

NOTE: *Neither spouse is free to remarry until this order takes effect, at which time you can get a **Certificate of Divorce** from the court office.*

SELF-COUNSEL PRESS-DIVONT-FAM(208-2)00

SAMPLE #38
FORM 36B — CERTIFICATE OF DIVORCE

SUPERIOR COURT OF JUSTICE FAMILY COURT _____

(Name of court)

Court File Number

....

Form 36B: Certificate of Divorce

SEAL

at _____

Court office address

Applicant

Full legal name & address for service — street and number, municipality, postal code, telephone & fax numbers and e-mail address (if any).	Lawyer's name & address — street and number, municipality, postal code, telephone & fax numbers and e-mail address (if any).
Joan Public 322 Lakeshore Road London, Ontario L5N 3N2 (519) 123-4567	

Respondent(s)

Full legal name & address for service — street and number, municipality, postal code, telephone & fax numbers and e-mail address (if any).	Lawyer's name & address — street and number, municipality, postal code, telephone & fax numbers and e-mail address (if any).
John Que Public 1000 Yonge Street London, Ontario L5N 3N1 (519) 765-4321	

I CERTIFY THAT the marriage of *(full legal names of the spouses)* Joan Public and John Que Public

that was solemnized at *(place of marriage)* London, Ontario

on *(date of marriage)* December 27, 1984

was dissolved by an order of this court made on *(date of divorce order)*

The divorce took effect on *(date when order took effect)*

_____   _____

Signature of clerk of the court   *Date of signature*

NOTE: *This certificate can only be issued on or after the date on which the divorce takes effect.*

SELF-COUNSEL PRESS-DIVONT-FAM(209-1)00

APPENDIX 1
STEP-BY-STEP CHECKLIST
FOR A TYPICAL DIVORCE

❑ Read the *Divorce Guide* carefully to determine whether or not your case is suitable for you to represent yourself.

❑ Purchase a package of forms at your book or department store or from the publisher (see order form at the front of the book). **Note:** There are two different packages available: one for sole petitioners, and one for joint petitioners. Both packages also contain sets of the forms needed if you and/or your spouse live in one of the jurisdictions now covered by the Family Law Rules (see Chapter 6 for the list of jurisdictions).

❑ Read through this book to determine which procedure you are going to follow and be sure to purchase the correct kit.

❑ Write for a copy of your Certificate of Marriage. If you live in the Toronto region, Algoma District, or Essex County, prepare the Case Information Statement.

❑ If the marriage for which you are seeking a divorce was outside Ontario, obtain a copy of a previous Certificate of Divorce for either party previously married.

IF YOU ARE PROCEEDING AS JOINT PETITIONERS IN ONTARIO SUPERIOR COURT OF JUSTICE

❑ Complete and check rough draft of Petition using information from Certificate of Marriage. Make a good copy and photocopy two copies.

❑ Prepare Record. Prepare Support Deduction Order and the Support Deduction Order Information Form. If you live in the Toronto region, Algoma District, or Essex County, prepare the Case Information Statement.

❑ File Petition, Record, and all other documents, pay fees, and set action down. Be sure to send along with your documents stamped, addressed envelopes for each of the parties (including yourself).

❑ Upon receipt of Divorce Judgment, wait 31 days and file Certificate of Divorce.

IF YOU ARE PROCEEDING AS SOLE PETITIONER IN ONTARIO SUPERIOR COURT OF JUSTICE

❏ Confirm your spouse's address and all the information needed for your Petition. Find address of other person if needed.

❏ Obtain a picture of your spouse if service may prove to be difficult.

❏ Complete and check rough draft of Petition using information from Certificate of Marriage.

❏ Make a good copy and one photocopy, then sign both the original and the copy.

❏ Take Certificate of Marriage and Petition to registrar's office and pay fees.

❏ Make necessary number of photocopies of original signed and sealed Petition.

❏ Take necessary number of copies of Petition and photograph to sheriff's office for service on spouse (and other person if necessary) or send to sheriff's office near spouse with covering letter and cheque or money order for $20 to $25.

    or

Have Petition served by other means, e.g., process server.

❏ Receive Affidavit of Service with Petition attached from whomever served Petition. Make copy of Affidavit of Service for your records.

❏ Attend Family Information Session if required to do so (Toronto only).

❏ Prepare Record. Prepare Support Deduction Order and the Support Deduction Order Information Form.

❏ Wait the length of time required for service, e.g., 20 days or 40 days, and then go to courthouse.

IF YOU ARE PROCEEDING IN ONTARIO SUPERIOR COURT OF JUSTICE FAMILY COURT

❏ Confirm your spouse's address and all the information needed for your application. Find address of other person if needed.

❏ Obtain a picture of your spouse if service may prove to be difficult.

❏ Complete and check rough draft of application using information from Certificate of Marriage. Make a good copy and one photocopy, then sign both the original and the copy.

- [ ] Complete a Financial Statement if you are claiming child or spousal support, or have any other monetary claims.

- [ ] Take the Application and Financial Statement (if applicable) to court. Get a date of hearing from the court registrar. Pay fees and file Marriage Certificate with the court.

- [ ] Serve the Application and Financial Statement (if applicable) on the respondent.

- [ ] Take necessary number of copies of Application and photograph to sheriff's office for service on spouse (and other person if necessary) or send to sheriff's office near spouse with covering letter and cheque or money order for $20 to $25.

  or

  Have Application served by other means, e.g., process server.

- [ ] Receive Affidavit of Service with Application attached from whomever served Application. Make copy of Affidavit of Service for your records.

- [ ] Prepare Continuing Record. Prepare Support Deduction Order and the Support Deduction Order Information Form if applicable. File, along with four copies of Divorce Order. Include stamped, self-addressed envelopes.

- [ ] Wait the length of time required for service, e.g., 30 days or 60 days, and then go to courthouse.

DO YOU NEED TO APPEAR IN COURT?

Read the two sections below to see if a court appearance is needed.

Where a court appearance is unnecessary

- [ ] File Record, Affidavit of Service, and all other documents, pay fee, and set action down. Be sure to send along with your documents stamped, addressed envelopes for each of the parties (including yourself).

- [ ] Upon receipt of Divorce Judgment or Order, wait 31 days from the date of the Judgment or Order, and file Certificate of Divorce.

Where a court appearance is necessary

- [ ] File Record, Affidavit of Service, and all other necessary documents, pay fee, and set action down.

- [ ] Call court office to find out when you are scheduled for hearing.

- [ ] Attend uncontested divorce hearings.

- ❑ One week before your hearing be certain that you have the following:

    (a) Certificate of Marriage

    (b) Original of any separation agreement or court order referred to in the Petition or Application

    (c) A witness

    or the agreement of your spouse to appear in court, if you are alleging adultery. (It is a good idea to have a witness for your one-year separation, too.)

- ❑ If any of the above are missing, call the court office and ask for an adjournment.

- ❑ Three days before your hearing, file a confirmation form with the court (a copy of the confirmation form can be obtained from the court office).

- ❑ The day before your hearing review the sample hearing and your documents. Be sure any needed witnesses will appear.

- ❑ Go early to court (i.e., no later than 9:30 a.m.) and to the proper courtroom. Note spelling of the presiding judge's name. When your name is called, go up and present your case. Be calm. If all of the other steps are properly done, you should have no problem.

- ❑ Be sure to note the terms of the Divorce Judgment or Order carefully. See the clerk if necessary.

- ❑ Type up your Divorce Judgment or Order in accordance with the terms and take it, along with stamped, addressed envelopes for all parties (including yourself and the Children's Lawyer, if one is involved).

- ❑ Thirty-one days from the date of your Divorce Judgment or Order, you may apply for a Divorce Certificate.

APPENDIX 2
ADDRESSES TO WRITE TO FOR
MARRIAGE CERTIFICATES

You will need a certificate as proof of a valid marriage in many of the proceedings described in this book. Here's where to get it.

PROVINCE/TERRITORY	ADDRESS
Alberta	Alberta Vital Statistics no longer provides certificates. Contact your local Alberta Registry private agent to order the certificate.
British Columbia	Vital Statistics Division Ministry of Health 818 Fort Street Victoria, BC V8W 1H8 (payable to Minister of Finance)
Manitoba	Division of Vital Statistics Consumer and Corporate Affairs 317 - 450 Broadway Winnipeg, MB R3C 0V8
New Brunswick	Registrar General Department of Health and Community Services P.O. Box 5100 Fredericton, NB E3B 5G8
Newfoundland	Vital Statistics Division Department of Health Confederation Building, East Block P.O. Box 8700 St. John's, NF A1B 4J6
Northwest Territories	Registrar General Vital Statistics Department of Safety and Public Services P.O. Box 1320 Yellowknife, NT X1A 2L9
Nova Scotia	Deputy Registrar General Department of Health 1723 Hollis Street P.O. Box 157 Halifax, NS B3J 2M9

Ontario	Registrar General
	Ministry of Consumer and Commercial Relations
	P.O. Box 4600
	Thunder Bay, ON P7B 6L8
	(payable to Minister of Finance)

Prince Edward Island	Vital Statistics
	Department of Health and Social Services
	P.O. Box 2000
	Charlottetown, PE C1A 7N8

Québec

Birth and marriage certificates are issued by the Civil Archives of the judicial district where the event was registered. Contact the address below for a list of the 32 offices in Québec.

Ministère de la Justice
Registre du reference
300 boul. Jean-Lesage, RC-20
Québec, QC   G1K 8K6

Saskatchewan	Division of Vital Statistics
	Saskatchewan Health
	1919 Rose Street
	Regina, SK S4P 3P1

Yukon	Deputy Registrar General of Vital Statistics
	Yukon Health and Social Services
	P.O. Box 2703
	Whitehorse, YT Y1A 2C6

APPENDIX 3
COURT ADDRESSES

TORONTO REGION

TORONTO
Court House
393 University Avenue
20th Floor
Toronto
M5G 1E6
(416) 327-5505 (general information)
(416) 327-5542 (divorce information)

CENTRAL EAST REGION

DURHAM
Court House
605 Rossland Road E.
Box 640
Whitby
L1N 9G7
(905) 430-5800

HALIBURTON
20 Newcastle Street
Box 270
Minden
K0M 2K0
(705) 286-6417

MUSKOKA
Court House
3 Dominion Street N.
P.O. Box 1080
Bracebridge
P1L 2E6
(705) 645-8793

NORTHUMBERLAND
Court House
860 William Street
P.O. Box 910
Cobourg
K9A 3A9
(905) 372-3751

PETERBOROUGH
County Court House
70 Simcoe Street
Peterborough
K9H 7G9
(705) 876-3816

SIMCOE
Court House
114 Worsley Street
P.O. Box 184
Barrie
L4M 1M1
(705) 739-6116

VICTORIA
Court House
440 Kent Street W.
Lindsay
K9V 5P2
(705) 324-1400

YORK
Court House
50 Eagle Street W.
Newmarket
L3Y 6B1
(905) 853-4809

CENTRAL SOUTH REGION

BRANT
Court House
70 Wellington Street
Brantford
N3T 2L0
(519) 752-7828

HALDIMAND
Court House
Munsee
P.O. Box 70
Cayuga
N0A 1E0
(905) 772-3335

HAMILTON-WENTWORTH
Court House
55 Main Street W.
Hamilton
L8P 1H4
(905) 525-1550

NIAGARA NORTH
Court House
59 Church Street, 1st Floor
St. Catharines
L2R 7N8
(905) 988-6200

NIAGARA SOUTH
Court House
102 E. Main Street
Welland
L3B 5R4
(905) 735-0010

NORFOLK
Court House
530 Queensway W.
Simcoe
N3Y 4S2
(519) 426-1408

WATERLOO
Court House
20 Weber Street E.
Kitchener
N2H 1C3
(519) 741-3203

CENTRAL WEST REGION

BRUCE
Court House
215 Cayley Street
P.O. Box 430
Walkerton
N0G 2V0
(519) 881-0211

DUFFERIN
Court House
10 Louisa Street, 1st Floor
Orangeville
L9W 3P9
(519) 941-4744

GREY
Court House
595-9th Avenue E.
Owen Sound
N4K 3E3
(519) 376-3812

HALTON
Court House
491 Steeles Avenue E.
Milton
L9T 1Y7
(905) 878-7281

PEEL
Court House
7755 Hurontario Street
Brampton
L6V 2M7
(905) 452-6617

WELLINGTON
Court House
74 Woolwich Street
Guelph
N1H 3T9
(519) 824-4100

EAST REGION

FRONTENAC
Court House
469 Montreal Street
Kingston
K7K 3H9
(613) 548-6789

HASTINGS
Court House
235 Pinnacle Street
Belleville
K8N 3A9
(613) 962-9106

LANARK
Court House
43 Drummond Street E.
Perth
K7H 1G1
(613) 267-2021

LEEDS AND GRENVILLE
Court House
P.O. Box 8
Brockville
K6V 7A8
(613) 342-2288

LENNOX AND ADDINGTON
Court House
41 Dundas Street W.
Napanee
K7R 1Z5
(613) 354-3845

OTTAWA-CARLETON
Court House
161 Elgin Street
Ottawa
K2P 2K1
(613) 239-1105

PRINCE EDWARD
Court House
44 Union Street
P.O. Drawer 680
Picton
K0K 2T0
(613) 476-2606

RENFREW
Court House
297 Pembroke Street E.
Pembroke
K8A 6Y6
(613) 732-8581

STORMONT, DUNDAS, AND
GLENGARRY
340 Pitt Street, 4th Floor
Cornwall
K6H 5R9
(613) 933-7500

NORTHEAST REGION

ALGOMA
Court House
426 Queen Street E.
Sault Ste. Marie
P6A 1Z7
(705) 759-9418

COCHRANE
149 Fourth Avenue
P.O. Box 2069
Cochrane
P0L 1C0
(705) 272-4256

MANITOULIN
Court House
27 Phipps Street
Gore Bay
P0P 1H0
(705) 282-2461

PARRY SOUND
Court House
89 James Street
Parry Sound
P2A 1T7
(705) 746-4251

SUDBURY
Court House
155 Elm Street W.
Sudbury
P3C 1T9
(705) 671-5958

TEMISKAMING
Court House
393 Main Street
Box 609
Haileybury
P0J 1K0
(705) 672-3321

NORTHWEST REGION

KENORA
Court House
216 Water Street, Room 211
Kenora
P9N 1S4
(807) 468-2842

RAINY RIVER
Court House
333 Church Street
Fort Frances
P9A 1C9
(807) 274-5961

THUNDER BAY
Court House
277 Camelot Street
Thunder Bay
P7A 4B3
(807) 343-2725

SOUTHWEST REGION

ELGIN
Justice Building
145 Curtis Street
St. Thomas
N5P 3Z7
(519) 633-1720

ESSEX
Court House
245 Windsor Avenue
Windsor
N9A 1J2
(519) 973-6620

HURON
Court House
1 Court House Square
Box 400
Goderich
N7A 1M2
(519) 524-2519

KENT
Court House
21-7th Street
Box 2021
Chatham
N7M 5L9
(519) 352-9070

LAMBTON
Court House
700 Christina Street N.
Sarnia
N7V 3C2
(519) 337-5314

MIDDLESEX
Court House
80 Dundas Street
Ground Floor, Unit A
London
N6A 6A3
(519) 660-3054

OXFORD
Court House
415 Hunter Street
Box 70
Woodstock
N4S 7W5
(519) 539-6187

PERTH
Court House
17 George Street W.
Stratford
N5A 1A6
(519) 271-1850

Divorce Act

R.S., 1985, c. 3 (2nd Supp.)

[D-3.4]

An Act respecting divorce and corollary relief

*[1986, c. 4, assented to
13th February, 1986]*

SHORT TITLE

Short title

1. This Act may be cited as the *Divorce Act*.

INTERPRETATION

Definitions

2. (1) In this Act,

"appellate court" *«cour d'appel»*

"appellate court", in respect of an appeal from a court, means the court exercising appellate jurisdiction with respect to that appeal;

"child of the marriage" *«enfant à charge»*

"child of the marriage" means a child of two spouses or former spouses who, at the material time,
     (*a*) is under the age of sixteen years, or
     (*b*) is sixteen years of age or over and under their charge but unable, by reason of illness, disability or other cause, to withdraw from their charge or to obtain the necessaries of life;

"corollary relief proceeding" *«action en mesures accessoires»*

"corollary relief proceeding" means a proceeding in a court in which either or both former spouses seek a support order or a custody order or both such orders;

"court" *«tribunal»*

"court", in respect of a province, means
     (*a*) for the Province of Ontario, the Ontario Court (General Division),

(*a*.1) for the Province of Prince Edward Island or Newfoundland, the trial division of the Supreme Court of the Province,

(*b*) for the Province of Quebec, the Superior Court,

(*c*) for the Provinces of Nova Scotia and British Columbia, the Supreme Court of the Province,

(*d*) for the Province of New Brunswick, Manitoba, Saskatchewan or Alberta, the Court of Queen's Bench for the Province, and

(*e*) for the Yukon Territory or the Northwest Territories, the Supreme Court thereof,

and includes such other court in the province the judges of which are appointed by the Governor General as is designated by the Lieutenant Governor in Council of the province as a court for the purposes of this Act;

"custody" «*garde*»

"custody" includes care, upbringing and any other incident of custody;

"custody order" «*ordonnance de garde*»

"custody order" means an order made under subsection 16(1);

"divorce proceeding" «*action en divorce*»

"divorce proceeding" means a proceeding in a court in which either or both spouses seek a divorce alone or together with a support order or a custody order or both such orders;

"spouse" «*époux*»

"spouse" means either of a man or woman who are married to each other;

"support order" «*ordonnance alimentaire*»

"support order" means an order made under subsection 15(2);

"variation order" «*ordonnance modificative*»

"variation order" means an order made under subsection 17(1);

"variation proceeding" «*action en modification*»

"variation proceeding" means a proceeding in a court in which either or both former spouses seek a variation order.

Child of the marriage

(2) For the purposes of the definition "child of the marriage" in subsection (1), a child of two spouses or former spouses includes

(*a*) any child for whom they both stand in the place of parents; and

(*b*) any child of whom one is the parent and for whom the other stands in the place of a parent.

Term not restrictive

(3) The use of the term "application" to describe a proceeding under this Act in a court shall not be construed as limiting the name under which and the form and manner in which that proceeding may be taken in that court, and the name, manner and form of the proceeding in that court shall be such as is provided for by the rules regulating the practice and procedure in that court.

(4) The use in section 21.1 of the terms "affidavit" and "pleadings" to describe documents shall not be construed as limiting the name that may be used to refer to those documents in a court and the form of those documents, and the name and form of the documents shall be such as is provided for by the rules regulating the practice and procedure in that court.

R.S., 1985, c. 3 (2nd Supp.), s. 2, c. 27 (2nd Supp.), s. 10; 1990, c. 18, s. 1; 1992, c. 51, s. 46.

JURISDICTION

Jurisdiction in divorce proceedings

3. (1) A court in a province has jurisdiction to hear and determine a divorce proceeding if either spouse has been ordinarily resident in the province for at least one year immediately preceding the commencement of the proceeding.

Jurisdiction where two proceedings commenced on different days

(2) Where divorce proceedings between the same spouses are pending in two courts that would otherwise have jurisdiction under subsection (1) and were commenced on different days and the proceeding that was commenced first is not discontinued within thirty days after it was commenced, the court in which a divorce proceeding was commenced first has exclusive jurisdiction to hear and determine any divorce proceeding then pending between the spouses and the second divorce proceeding shall be deemed to be discontinued.

Jurisdiction where two proceedings commenced on same day

(3) Where divorce proceedings between the same spouses are pending in two courts that would otherwise have jurisdiction under subsection (1) and were commenced on the same day and neither proceeding is discontinued within thirty days after it was commenced, the Federal Court—Trial Division has exclusive jurisdiction to hear and determine any divorce proceeding then pending between the spouses and the divorce proceedings in those courts shall be transferred to the Federal Court—Trial Division on the direction of that Court.

Jurisdiction in corollary relief proceedings

4. (1) A court in a province has jurisdiction to hear and determine a corollary relief proceeding if

(*a*) either former spouse is ordinarily resident in the province at the commencement of the proceeding; or

(*b*) both former spouses accept the jurisdiction of the court.

Jurisdiction where two proceedings commenced on different days

(2) Where corollary relief proceedings between the same former spouses and in respect of the same matter are pending in two courts that would otherwise have jurisdiction under subsection (1) and were commenced on different days and the proceeding that was commenced first is not discontinued within thirty days after it was commenced, the court in which a corollary relief proceeding was commenced first has exclusive jurisdiction to hear and determine any corollary relief proceeding then pending between the former spouses in respect of that matter and the second corollary relief proceeding shall be deemed to be discontinued.

(3) Where proceedings between the same former spouses and in respect of the same matter are pending in two courts that would otherwise have jurisdiction under subsection (1) and were commenced on the same day and neither proceeding is discontinued within thirty days after it was commenced, the Federal Court—Trial Division has exclusive jurisdiction to hear and determine any corollary relief proceeding then pending between the former spouses in respect of that matter and the corollary relief proceedings in those courts shall be transferred to the Federal Court—Trial Division on the direction of that Court.

R.S., 1985, c. 3 (2nd Supp.), s. 4; 1993, c. 8, s. 1.

Jurisdiction in variation proceedings

5. (1) A court in a province has jurisdiction to hear and determine a variation proceeding if

(*a*) either former spouse is ordinarily resident in the province at the commencement of the proceeding; or

(*b*) both former spouses accept the jurisdiction of the court.

Jurisdiction where two proceedings commenced on different days

(2) Where variation proceedings between the same former spouses and in respect of the same matter are pending in two courts that would otherwise have jurisdiction under subsection (1) and were commenced on different days and the proceeding that was commenced first is not discontinued within thirty days after it was commenced, the court in which a variation proceeding was commenced first has exclusive jurisdiction to hear and determine any variation proceeding then pending between the former spouses in respect of that matter and the second variation proceeding shall be deemed to be discontinued.

Jurisdiction where two proceedings commenced on same day

(3) Where variation proceedings between the same former spouses and in respect of the same matter are pending in two courts that would otherwise have jurisdiction under subsection (1) and were commenced on the same day and neither proceeding is discontinued within thirty days after it was commenced, the Federal Court—Trial Division has exclusive jurisdiction to hear and determine any variation proceeding then pending between the former spouses in respect of that matter and the variation proceedings in those courts shall be transferred to the Federal Court—Trial Division on the direction of that Court.

Transfer of divorce proceeding where custody application

6. (1) Where an application for an order under section 16 is made in a divorce proceeding to a court in a province and is opposed and the child of the marriage in respect of whom the order is sought is most substantially connected with another province, the court may, on application by a spouse or on its own motion, transfer the divorce proceeding to a court in that other province.

Transfer of corollary relief proceeding where custody application

(2) Where an application for an order under section 16 is made in a corollary relief proceeding to a court in a province and is opposed and the child of the marriage in respect of whom the order is sought is most substantially connected with another province, the court may, on application by a former spouse or on its own motion, transfer the corollary relief proceeding to a court in that other province.

(3) Where an application for a variation order in respect of a custody order is made in a variation proceeding to a court in a province and is opposed and the child of the marriage in respect of whom the variation order is sought is most substantially connected with another province, the court may, on application by a former spouse or on its own motion, transfer the variation proceeding to a court in that other province.

Exclusive jurisdiction

(4) Notwithstanding sections 3 to 5, a court in a province to which a proceeding is transferred under this section has exclusive jurisdiction to hear and determine the proceeding.

Exercise of jurisdiction by judge

7. The jurisdiction conferred on a court by this Act to grant a divorce shall be exercised only by a judge of the court without a jury.

DIVORCE

Divorce

8. (1) A court of competent jurisdiction may, on application by either or both spouses, grant a divorce to the spouse or spouses on the ground that there has been a breakdown of their marriage.

Breakdown of marriage

(2) Breakdown of a marriage is established only if

(*a*) the spouses have lived separate and apart for at least one year immediately preceding the determination of the divorce proceeding and were living separate and apart at the commencement of the proceeding; or

(*b*) the spouse against whom the divorce proceeding is brought has, since celebration of the marriage,

(i) committed adultery, or

(ii) treated the other spouse with physical or mental cruelty of such a kind as to render intolerable the continued cohabitation of the spouses.

Calculation of period of separation

(3) For the purposes of paragraph (2)(*a*),

(*a*) spouses shall be deemed to have lived separate and apart for any period during which they lived apart and either of them had the intention to live separate and apart from the other; and

(*b*) a period during which spouses have lived separate and apart shall not be considered to have been interrupted or terminated

(i) by reason only that either spouse has become incapable of forming or having an intention to continue to live separate and apart or of continuing to live separate and apart of the spouse's own volition, if it appears to the court that the separation would probably have continued if the spouse had not become so incapable, or

(ii) by reason only that the spouses have resumed cohabitation during a period of, or periods totalling, not more than ninety days with reconciliation as its primary purpose.

9. (1) It is the duty of every barrister, solicitor, lawyer or advocate who undertakes to act on behalf of a spouse in a divorce proceeding

(*a*) to draw to the attention of the spouse the provisions of this Act that have as their object the reconciliation of spouses, and

(*b*) to discuss with the spouse the possibility of the reconciliation of the spouses and to inform the spouse of the marriage counselling or guidance facilities known to him or her that might be able to assist the spouses to achieve a reconciliation,

unless the circumstances of the case are of such a nature that it would clearly not be appropriate to do so.

Idem

(2) It is the duty of every barrister, solicitor, lawyer or advocate who undertakes to act on behalf of a spouse in a divorce proceeding to discuss with the spouse the advisability of negotiating the matters that may be the subject of a support order or a custody order and to inform the spouse of the mediation facilities known to him or her that might be able to assist the spouses in negotiating those matters.

Certification

(3) Every document presented to a court by a barrister, solicitor, lawyer or advocate that formally commences a divorce proceeding shall contain a statement by him or her certifying that he or she has complied with this section.

Duty of court — reconciliation

10. (1) In a divorce proceeding, it is the duty of the court, before considering the evidence, to satisfy itself that there is no possibility of the reconciliation of the spouses, unless the circumstances of the case are of such a nature that it would clearly not be appropriate to do so.

Adjournment

(2) Where at any stage in a divorce proceeding it appears to the court from the nature of the case, the evidence or the attitude of either or both spouses that there is a possibility of the reconciliation of the spouses, the court shall

(*a*) adjourn the proceeding to afford the spouses an opportunity to achieve a reconciliation; and

(*b*) with the consent of the spouses or in the discretion of the court, nominate

(i) a person with experience or training in marriage counselling or guidance, or

(ii) in special circumstances, some other suitable person,

to assist the spouses to achieve a reconciliation.

Resumption

(3) Where fourteen days have elapsed from the date of any adjournment under subsection (2), the court shall resume the proceeding on the application of either or both spouses.

Nominee not competent or compellable

(4) No person nominated by a court under this section to assist spouses to achieve a

reconciliation is competent or compellable in any legal proceedings to disclose any admission or communication made to that person in his or her capacity as a nominee of the court for that purpose.

(5) Evidence of anything said or of any admission or communication made in the course of assisting spouses to achieve a reconciliation is not admissible in any legal proceedings.

Duty of court — bars

11. (1) In a divorce proceeding, it is the duty of the court

(*a*) to satisfy itself that there has been no collusion in relation to the application for a divorce and to dismiss the application if it finds that there was collusion in presenting it;

(*b*) to satisfy itself that reasonable arrangements have been made for the support of any children of the marriage and, if such arrangements have not been made, to stay the granting of the divorce until such arrangements are made; and

(*c*) where a divorce is sought in circumstances described in paragraph 8(2)(*b*), to satisfy itself that there has been no condonation or connivance on the part of the spouse bringing the proceeding, and to dismiss the application for a divorce if that spouse has condoned or connived at the act or conduct complained of unless, in the opinion of the court, the public interest would be better served by granting the divorce.

Revival

(2) Any act or conduct that has been condoned is not capable of being revived so as to constitute a circumstance described in paragraph 8(2)(*b*).

Condonation

(3) For the purposes of this section, a continuation or resumption of cohabitation during a period of, or periods totalling, not more than ninety days with reconciliation as its primary purpose shall not be considered to constitute condonation.

Definition of "collusion"

(4) In this section, "collusion" means an agreement or conspiracy to which an applicant for a divorce is either directly or indirectly a party for the purpose of subverting the administration of justice, and includes any agreement, understanding or arrangement to fabricate or suppress evidence or to deceive the court, but does not include an agreement to the extent that it provides for separation between the parties, financial support, division of property or the custody of any child of the marriage.

Effective date generally

12. (1) Subject to this section, a divorce takes effect on the thirty-first day after the day on which the judgment granting the divorce is rendered.

Special circumstances

(2) Where, on or after rendering a judgment granting a divorce,

(*a*) the court is of the opinion that by reason of special circumstances the divorce should take effect earlier than the thirty-first day after the day on which the judgment is rendered, and (*b*) the spouses agree and undertake that no appeal from the judgment will be taken, or any appeal from the judgment that was taken has been abandoned,

the court may order that the divorce takes effect at such earlier time as it considers appropriate.

Effective date where appeal

(3) A divorce in respect of which an appeal is pending at the end of the period referred to in subsection (1), unless voided on appeal, takes effect on the expiration of the time fixed by law for instituting an appeal from the decision on that appeal or any subsequent appeal, if no appeal has been instituted within that time.

Certain extensions to be counted

(4) For the purposes of subsection (3), the time fixed by law for instituting an appeal from a decision on an appeal includes any extension thereof fixed pursuant to law before the expiration of that time or fixed thereafter on an application instituted before the expiration of that time.

No late extensions of time for appeal

(5) Notwithstanding any other law, the time fixed by law for instituting an appeal from a decision referred to in subsection (3) may not be extended after the expiration of that time, except on an application instituted before the expiration of that time.

Effective date where decision of Supreme Court of Canada

(6) A divorce in respect of which an appeal has been taken to the Supreme Court of Canada, unless voided on the appeal, takes effect on the day on which the judgment on the appeal is rendered.

Certificate of divorce

(7) Where a divorce takes effect in accordance with this section, a judge or officer of the court that rendered the judgment granting the divorce or, where that judgment has been appealed, of the appellate court that rendered the judgment on the final appeal, shall, on request, issue to any person a certificate that a divorce granted under this Act dissolved the marriage of the specified persons effective as of a specified date.

Conclusive proof

(8) A certificate referred to in subsection (7), or a certified copy thereof, is conclusive proof of the facts so certified without proof of the signature or authority of the person appearing to have signed the certificate.

Legal effect throughout Canada

13. On taking effect, a divorce granted under this Act has legal effect throughout Canada.

Marriage dissolved

14. On taking effect, a divorce granted under this Act dissolves the marriage of the spouses.

COROLLARY RELIEF

Definition of "spouse"

15. (1) In this section and section 16, "spouse" has the meaning assigned by subsection 2(1) and includes a former spouse.

(2) A court of competent jurisdiction may, on application by either or both spouses, make an order requiring one spouse to secure or pay, or to secure and pay, such lump sum or periodic sums, or such lump sum and periodic sums, as the court thinks reasonable for the support of

(*a*) the other spouse;

(*b*) any or all children of the marriage; or

(*c*) the other spouse and any or all children of the marriage.

(3) Where an application is made under subsection (2), the court may, on application by either or both spouses, make an interim order requiring one spouse to secure or pay, or to secure and pay, such lump sum or periodic sums, or such lump sum and periodic sums, as the court thinks reasonable for the support of

(*a*) the other spouse,

(*b*) any or all children of the marriage, or

(*c*) the other spouse and any or all children of the marriage,

pending determination of the application under subsection (2).

(4) The court may make an order under this section for a definite or indefinite period or until the happening of a specified event and may impose such other terms, conditions or restrictions in connection therewith as it thinks fit and just.

(5) In making an order under this section, the court shall take into consideration the condition, means, needs and other circumstances of each spouse and of any child of the marriage for whom support is sought, including

(*a*) the length of time the spouses cohabited;

(*b*) the functions performed by the spouse during cohabitation; and

(*c*) any order, agreement or arrangement relating to support of the spouse or child.

(6) In making an order under this section, the court shall not take into consideration any misconduct of a spouse in relation to the marriage.

(7) An order made under this section that provides for the support of a spouse should

(*a*) recognize any economic advantages or disadvantages to the spouses arising from the marriage or its breakdown;

(*b*) apportion between the spouses any financial consequences arising from the care of any child of the marriage over and above the obligation apportioned between the spouses pursuant to subsection (8);

(*c*) relieve any economic hardship of the spouses arising from the breakdown of the marriage; and

(*d*) in so far as practicable, promote the economic self-sufficiency of each spouse within a reasonable period of time.

Objectives of order for support of child

(8) An order made under this section that provides for the support of a child of the marriage should

(*a*) recognize that the spouses have a joint financial obligation to maintain the child; and

(*b*) apportion that obligation between the spouses according to their relative abilities to contribute to the performance of the obligation.

Assignment of order

(9) An order made under this section may be assigned to

(*a*) any minister of the Crown for Canada designated by the Governor in Council;

(*b*) any minister of the Crown for a province designated by the Lieutenant Governor in Council of the province;

(*c*) any member of the Council of the Yukon Territory designated by the Commissioner of the Yukon Territory; or

(*d*) any member of the Council of the Northwest Territories designated by the Commissioner of the Northwest Territories.

Order for custody

16. (1) A court of competent jurisdiction may, on application by either or both spouses or by any other person, make an order respecting the custody of or the access to, or the custody of and access to, any or all children of the marriage.

Interim order for custody

(2) Where an application is made under subsection (1), the court may, on application by either or both spouses or by any other person, make an interim order respecting the custody of or the access to, or the custody of and access to, any or all children of the marriage pending determination of the application under subsection (1).

Application by other person

(3) A person, other than a spouse, may not make an application under subsection (1) or (2) without leave of the court.

Joint custody or access

(4) The court may make an order under this section granting custody of, or access to, any or all children of the marriage to any one or more persons.

Access

(5) Unless the court orders otherwise, a spouse who is granted access to a child of the marriage has the right to make inquiries, and to be given information, as to the health, education and welfare of the child.

Terms and conditions

(6) The court may make an order under this section for a definite or indefinite period or until the happening of a specified event and may impose such other terms, conditions or restrictions in connection therewith as it thinks fit and just.

Order respecting change of residence

(7) Without limiting the generality of subsection (6), the court may include in an order under this section a term requiring any person who has custody of a child of the marriage and who intends to change the place of residence of that child to notify, at least thirty days before the change or within such other period before the change as the court may specify, any person who is granted access to that child of the change, the time at which the change will be made and the new place of residence of the child.

Factors

(8) In making an order under this section, the court shall take into consideration only the best interests of the child of the marriage as determined by reference to the condition, means, needs and other circumstances of the child.

Past conduct

(9) In making an order under this section, the court shall not take into consideration the past conduct of any person unless the conduct is relevant to the ability of that person to act as a parent of a child.

Maximum contact

(10) In making an order under this section, the court shall give effect to the principle that a child of the marriage should have as much contact with each spouse as is consistent with the best interests of the child and, for that purpose, shall take into consideration the willingness of the person for whom custody is sought to facilitate such contact.

Order for variation, rescission or suspension

17. (1) A court of competent jurisdiction may make an order varying, rescinding or suspending, prospectively or retroactively,

(*a*) a support order or any provision thereof on application by either or both former spouses; or

(*b*) a custody order or any provision thereof on application by either or both former spouses or by any other person.

Application by other person

(2) A person, other than a former spouse, may not make an application under paragraph (1)(*b*) without leave of the court.

Terms and conditions

(3) The court may include in a variation order any provision that under this Act could have been included in the order in respect of which the variation order is sought.

Factors for support order

(4) Before the court makes a variation order in respect of a support order, the court shall

satisfy itself that there has been a change in the condition, means, needs or other circumstances of either former spouse or of any child of the marriage for whom support is or was sought occurring since the making of the support order or the last variation order made in respect of that order, as the case may be, and, in making the variation order, the court shall take into consideration that change.

Factors for custody order

(5) Before the court makes a variation order in respect of a custody order, the court shall satisfy itself that there has been a change in the condition, means, needs or other circumstances of the child of the marriage occurring since the making of the custody order or the last variation order made in respect of that order, as the case may be, and, in making the variation order, the court shall take into consideration only the best interests of the child as determined by reference to that change.

Conduct

(6) In making a variation order, the court shall not take into consideration any conduct that under this Act could not have been considered in making the order in respect of which the variation order is sought.

Objectives of variation order varying order for support of former spouse

(7) A variation order varying a support order that provides for the support of a former spouse should

(*a*) recognize any economic advantages or disadvantages to the former spouses arising from the marriage or its breakdown;

(*b*) apportion between the former spouses any financial consequences arising from the care of any child of the marriage over and above the obligation apportioned between the former spouses pursuant to subsection (8);

(*c*) relieve any economic hardship of the former spouses arising from the breakdown of the marriage; and

(*d*) in so far as practicable, promote the economic self-sufficiency of each former spouse within a reasonable period of time.

Objectives of variation order varying order for support of child

(8) A variation order varying a support order that provides for the support of a child of the marriage should

(*a*) recognize that the former spouses have a joint financial obligation to maintain the child; and

(*b*) apportion that obligation between the former spouses according to their relative abilities to contribute to the performance of the obligation.

Maximum contact

(9) In making a variation order varying a custody order, the court shall give effect to the principle that a child of the marriage should have as much contact with each former spouse as is consistent with the best interests of the child and, for that purpose, where the variation order would grant custody of the child to a person who does not currently have custody, the court shall take into consideration the willingness of that person to facilitate such contact.

Limitation

(10) Notwithstanding subsection (1), where a support order provides for support for a definite period or until the happening of a specified event, a court may not, on an application instituted after the expiration of that period or the happening of that event, make a variation order for the purpose of resuming that support unless the court is satisfied that

(*a*) a variation order is necessary to relieve economic hardship arising from a change described in subsection (4) that is related to the marriage; and

(*b*) the changed circumstances, had they existed at the time of the making of the support order or the last variation order made in respect of that order, as the case may be, would likely have resulted in a different order.

Copy of order

(11) Where a court makes a variation order in respect of a support order or a custody order made by another court, it shall send a copy of the variation order, certified by a judge or officer of the court, to that other court.

Variation order by affidavit, etc.

17.1 Where both former spouses are ordinarily resident in different provinces, a court of competent jurisdiction may, in accordance with any applicable rules of the court, make a variation order pursuant to subsection 17(1) on the basis of the submissions of the former spouses, whether presented orally before the court or by means of affidavits or any means of telecommunication, if both former spouses consent thereto.

1993, c. 8, s. 2.

Definitions

18. (1) In this section and section 19,

"Attorney General" *«procureur général»*

"Attorney General", in respect of a province, means

(*a*) for the Yukon Territory, the member of the Council of the Yukon Territory designated by the Commissioner of the Yukon Territory,

(*b*) for the Northwest Territories, the member of the Council of the Northwest Territories designated by the Commissioner of the Northwest Territories, and

(*c*) for the other provinces, the Attorney General of the province,

and includes any person authorized in writing by the member or Attorney General to act for the member or Attorney General in the performance of a function under this section or section 19;

"provisional order" *«ordonnance conditionnelle»*

"provisional order" means an order made pursuant to subsection (2).

Provisional order

(2) Notwithstanding paragraph 5(1)(*a*) and subsection 17(1), where an application is made to a court in a province for a variation order in respect of a support order and

(*a*) the respondent in the application is ordinarily resident in another province and has not accepted the jurisdiction of the court, or both former spouses have not consented to the application of section 17.1 in respect of the matter, and

173

(*b*) in the circumstances of the case, the court is satisfied that the issues can be adequately determined by proceeding under this section and section 19,

the court shall make a variation order with or without notice to and in the absence of the respondent, but such order is provisional only and has no legal effect until it is confirmed in a proceeding under section 19 and, where so confirmed, it has legal effect in accordance with the terms of the order confirming it.

Transmission

(3) Where a court in a province makes a provisional order, it shall send to the Attorney General for the province

(*a*) three copies of the provisional order certified by a judge or officer of the court;

(*b*) a certified or sworn document setting out or summarizing the evidence given to the court; and

(*c*) a statement giving any available information respecting the identification, location, income and assets of the respondent.

Idem

(4) On receipt of the documents referred to in subsection (3), the Attorney General shall send the documents to the Attorney General for the province in which the respondent is ordinarily resident.

Further evidence

(5) Where, during a proceeding under section 19, a court in a province remits the matter back for further evidence to the court that made the provisional order, the court that made the order shall, after giving notice to the applicant, receive further evidence.

Transmission

(6) Where evidence is received under subsection (5), the court that received the evidence shall forward to the court that remitted the matter back a certified or sworn document setting out or summarizing the evidence, together with such recommendations as the court that received the evidence considers appropriate.

R.S., 1985, c. 3 (2nd Supp.), s. 18; 1993, c. 8, s. 3.

Transmission

19. (1) On receipt of any documents sent pursuant to subsection 18(4), the Attorney General for the province in which the respondent is ordinarily resident shall send the documents to a court in the province.

Procedure

(2) Subject to subsection (3), where documents have been sent to a court pursuant to subsection (1), the court shall serve on the respondent a copy of the documents and a notice of a hearing respecting confirmation of the provisional order and shall proceed with the hearing, in the absence of the applicant, taking into consideration the certified or sworn document setting out or summarizing the evidence given to the court that made the provisional order.

Return to Attorney General

(3) Where documents have been sent to a court pursuant to subsection (1) and the respondent apparently is outside the province and is not likely to return, the court shall send the documents to the Attorney General for that province, together with any available information respecting the location and circumstances of the respondent.

Idem

(4) On receipt of any documents and information sent pursuant to subsection (3), the Attorney General shall send the documents and information to the Attorney General for the province of the court that made the provisional order.

Right of respondent

(5) In a proceeding under this section, the respondent may raise any matter that might have been raised before the court that made the provisional order.

Further evidence

(6) Where, in a proceeding under this section, the respondent satisfies the court that for the purpose of taking further evidence or for any other purpose it is necessary to remit the matter back to the court that made the provisional order, the court may so remit the matter and adjourn the proceeding for that purpose.

Order of confirmation or refusal

(7) At the conclusion of a proceeding under this section, the court shall make an order

(*a*) confirming the provisional order without variation;

(*b*) confirming the provisional order with variation; or

(*c*) refusing confirmation of the provisional order.

Further evidence

(8) The court, before making an order confirming the provisional order with variation or an order refusing confirmation of the provisional order, shall decide whether to remit the matter back for further evidence to the court that made the provisional order.

Interim order for support

(9) Where a court remits a matter pursuant to this section, the court may make an interim order requiring the respondent to secure or pay, or to secure and pay, such lump sum or periodic sums, or such lump sum and periodic sums, as the court thinks reasonable for the support of

(*a*) the applicant,

(*b*) any or all children of the marriage, or

(*c*) the applicant and any or all children of the marriage,

pending the making of an order under subsection (7).

Terms and conditions

(10) The court may make an order under subsection (9) for a definite or indefinite period or until the happening of a specified event and may impose such other terms, conditions or restrictions in connection therewith as it thinks fit and just.

Provisions applicable

(11) Subsections 17(4) and (6) to (8) apply, with such modifications as the circumstances require, in respect of an order made under subsection (9) as if it were a variation order referred to in those subsections.

Report and filing

(12) On making an order under subsection (7), the court in a province shall

(*a*) send a copy of the order, certified by a judge or officer of the court, to the Attorney General for that province, to the court that made the provisional order and, where that court is not the court that made the support order in respect of which the provisional order was made, to the court that made the support order;

(*b*) where an order is made confirming the provisional order with or without variation, file the order in the court; and

(*c*) where an order is made confirming the provisional order with variation or refusing confirmation of the provisional order, give written reasons to the Attorney General for that province and to the court that made the provisional order.

R.S., 1985, c. 3 (2nd Supp.), s. 19; 1993, c. 8, s. 4.

Definition of "court"

20. (1) In this section, "court", in respect of a province, has the meaning assigned by subsection 2(1) and includes such other court having jurisdiction in the province as is designated by the Lieutenant Governor in Council of the province as a court for the purposes of this section.

Legal effect throughout Canada

(2) Subject to subsection 18(2), an order made under section 15, 16 or 17 or subsection 19(9) has legal effect throughout Canada.

Enforcement

(3) An order that has legal effect throughout Canada pursuant to subsection (2) may be

(*a*) registered in any court in a province and enforced in like manner as an order of that court; or

(*b*) enforced in a province in any other manner provided for by the laws of that province.

APPEALS

Appeal to appellate court

21. (1) Subject to subsections (2) and (3), an appeal lies to the appellate court from any judgment or order, whether final or interim, rendered or made by a court under this Act.

Restriction on divorce appeals

(2) No appeal lies from a judgment granting a divorce on or after the day on which the divorce takes effect.

Restriction on order appeals

(3) No appeal lies from an order made under this Act more than thirty days after the day on which the order was made.

(4) An appellate court or a judge thereof may, on special grounds, either before or after the expiration of the time fixed by subsection (3) for instituting an appeal, by order extend that time.

(5) The appellate court may

(*a*) dismiss the appeal; or

(*b*) allow the appeal and

(i) render the judgment or make the order that ought to have been rendered or made, including such order or such further or other order as it deems just, or

(ii) order a new hearing where it deems it necessary to do so to correct a substantial wrong or miscarriage of justice.

(6) Except as otherwise provided by this Act or the rules or regulations, an appeal under this section shall be asserted, heard and decided according to the ordinary procedure governing appeals to the appellate court from the court rendering the judgment or making the order being appealed.

GENERAL

21.1 (1) In this section, "spouse" has the meaning assigned by subsection 2(1) and includes a former spouse.

(2) In any proceedings under this Act, a spouse (in this section referred to as the "deponent") may serve on the other spouse and file with the court an affidavit indicating

(*a*) that the other spouse is the spouse of the deponent;

(*b*) the date and place of the marriage, and the official character of the person who solemnized the marriage;

(*c*) the nature of any barriers to the remarriage of the deponent within the deponent's religion the removal of which is within the other spouse's control;

(*d*) where there are any barriers to the remarriage of the other spouse within the other spouse's religion the removal of which is within the deponent's control, that the deponent

(i) has removed those barriers, and the date and circumstances of that removal, or

(ii) has signified a willingness to remove those barriers, and the date and circumstances of that signification;

(*e*) that the deponent has, in writing, requested the other spouse to remove all of the barriers to the remarriage of the deponent within the deponent's religion the removal of which is within the other spouse's control;

(*f*) the date of the request described in paragraph (*e*); and

(*g*) that the other spouse, despite the request described in paragraph (*e*), has failed to remove all of the barriers referred to in that paragraph.

(3) Where a spouse who has been served with an affidavit under subsection (2) does not

(*a*) within fifteen days after that affidavit is filed with the court or within such longer period as the court allows, serve on the deponent and file with the court an affidavit indicating that all of the barriers referred to in paragraph (2)(*e*) have been removed, and

(*b*) satisfy the court, in any additional manner that the court may require, that all of the barriers referred to in paragraph (2)(*e*) have been removed,

the court may, subject to any terms that the court considers appropriate,

(*c*) dismiss any application filed by that spouse under this Act, and

(*d*) strike out any other pleadings and affidavits filed by that spouse under this Act.

Special case

(4) Without limiting the generality of the court's discretion under subsection (3), the court may refuse to exercise its powers under paragraphs (3)(*c*) and (*d*) where a spouse who has been served with an affidavit under subsection (2)

(*a*) within fifteen days after that affidavit is filed with the court or within such longer period as the court allows, serves on the deponent and files with the court an affidavit indicating genuine grounds of a religious or conscientious nature for refusing to remove the barriers referred to in paragraph (2)(*e*); and

(*b*) satisfies the court, in any additional manner that the court may require, that the spouse has genuine grounds of a religious or conscientious nature for refusing to remove the barriers referred to in paragraph (2)(*e*).

Affidavits

(5) For the purposes of this section, an affidavit filed with the court by a spouse must, in order to be valid, indicate the date on which it was served on the other spouse.

Where section does not apply

(6) This section does not apply where the power to remove the barrier to religious remarriage lies with a religious body or official.

1990, c. 18, s. 2.

Recognition of foreign divorce

22. (1) A divorce granted, on or after the coming into force of this Act, pursuant to a law of a country or subdivision of a country other than Canada by a tribunal or other authority having jurisdiction to do so shall be recognized for all purposes of determining the marital status in Canada of any person, if either former spouse was ordinarily resident in that country or subdivision for at least one year immediately preceding the commencement of proceedings for the divorce.

Idem

(2) A divorce granted, after July 1, 1968, pursuant to a law of a country or subdivision of a country other than Canada by a tribunal or other authority having jurisdiction to do so, on the

basis of the domicile of the wife in that country or subdivision determined as if she were unmarried and, if she was a minor, as if she had attained the age of majority, shall be recognized for all purposes of determining the marital status in Canada of any person.

Other recognition rules preserved

(3) Nothing in this section abrogates or derogates from any other rule of law respecting the recognition of divorces granted otherwise than under this Act.

Provincial laws of evidence

23. (1) Subject to this or any other Act of Parliament, the laws of evidence of the province in which any proceedings under this Act are taken, including the laws of proof of service of any document, apply to such proceedings.

Presumption

(2) For the purposes of this section, where any proceedings are transferred to the Federal Court—Trial Division under subsection 3(3) or 5(3), the proceedings shall be deemed to have been taken in the province specified in the direction of the Court to be the province with which both spouses or former spouses, as the case may be, are or have been most substantially connected.

Proof of signature or office

24. A document offered in a proceeding under this Act that purports to be certified or sworn by a judge or an officer of a court shall, unless the contrary is proved, be proof of the appointment, signature or authority of the judge or officer and, in the case of a document purporting to be sworn, of the appointment, signature or authority of the person before whom the document purports to be sworn.

Definition of "competent authority"

25. (1) In this section, "competent authority", in respect of a court, or appellate court, in a province means the body, person or group of persons ordinarily competent under the laws of that province to make rules regulating the practice and procedure in that court.

Rules

(2) Subject to subsection (3), the competent authority may make rules applicable to any proceedings under this Act in a court, or appellate court, in a province, including, without limiting the generality of the foregoing, rules

(*a*) regulating the practice and procedure in the court, including the addition of persons as parties to the proceedings;

(*b*) respecting the conduct and disposition of any proceedings under this Act without an oral hearing;

(*b*.1) respecting the application of section 17.1 in respect of proceedings for a variation order;

(*c*) regulating the sittings of the court;

(*d*) respecting the fixing and awarding of costs;

(*e*) prescribing and regulating the duties of officers of the court;

(*f*) respecting the transfer of proceedings under this Act to or from the court; and (*g*) prescribing and regulating any other matter considered expedient to attain the ends of justice and carry into effect the purposes and provisions of this Act.

Exercise of power

(3) The power to make rules for a court or appellate court conferred by subsection (2) on a competent authority shall be exercised in the like manner and subject to the like terms and conditions, if any, as the power to make rules for that court conferred on that authority by the laws of the province.

Not statutory instruments

(4) Rules made pursuant to this section by a competent authority that is not a judicial or quasi-judicial body shall be deemed not to be statutory instruments within the meaning and for the purposes of the *Statutory Instruments Act.*

R.S., 1985, c. 3 (2nd Supp.), s. 25; 1993, c. 8, s. 5.

Regulations

26. (1) The Governor in Council may make regulations for carrying the purposes and provisions of this Act into effect and, without limiting the generality of the foregoing, may make regulations

(*a*) respecting the establishment and operation of a central registry of divorce proceedings in Canada; and

(*b*) providing for uniformity in the rules made pursuant to section 25.

Regulations prevail

(2) Any regulations made pursuant to subsection (1) to provide for uniformity in the rules prevail over those rules.

Fees

27. (1) The Governor in Council may, by order, authorize the Minister of Justice to prescribe a fee to be paid by any person to whom a service is provided under this Act or the regulations.

Agreements

(2) The Minister of Justice may, with the approval of the Governor in Council, enter into an agreement with the government of any province respecting the collection and remittance of any fees prescribed pursuant to subsection (1).

CONSEQUENTIAL AMENDMENTS

28. to **31.** [Amendments]

TRANSITIONAL PROVISIONS

Proceedings based on facts arising before commencement of Act

32. Proceedings may be commenced under this Act notwithstanding that the material facts or circumstances giving rise to the proceedings or to jurisdiction over the proceedings occurred wholly or partly before the day on which this Act comes into force.

33. Proceedings commenced under the *Divorce Act*, chapter D-8 of the Revised Statutes of Canada, 1970, before the day on which this Act comes into force and not finally disposed of before that day shall be dealt with and disposed of in accordance with that Act as it read immediately before that day, as though it had not been repealed.

Variation and enforcement of orders previously made

34. (1) Any order made under subsection 11(1) of the *Divorce Act*, chapter D-8 of the Revised Statutes of Canada, 1970, including any such order made pursuant to section 33 of this Act, and any order to the like effect made corollary to a decree of divorce granted in Canada before July 2, 1968 or granted on or after that day pursuant to subsection 22(2) of that Act may be varied, rescinded, suspended or enforced in accordance with sections 17 to 20, other than subsection 17(10), of this Act as if

(*a*) the order were a support order or custody order, as the case may require; and

(*b*) in subsections 17(4) and (5), the words "or the last order made under subsection 11(2) of the *Divorce Act*, chapter D-8 of the Revised Statutes of Canada, 1970, varying that order" were added immediately before the words "or the last variation order made in respect of that order".

Enforcement of orders previously made

(2) Any order made under section 10 of the *Divorce Act*, chapter D-8 of the Revised Statutes of Canada, 1970, including any such order made pursuant to section 33 of this Act, may be enforced in accordance with section 20 of this Act as if it were an order made under section 15 or 16 of this Act, as the case may require.

Assignment of orders previously made

(3) Any order for the maintenance of a spouse or child of the marriage made under section 10 or 11 of the *Divorce Act*, chapter D-8 of the Revised Statutes of Canada, 1970, including any such order made pursuant to section 33 of this Act, and any order to the like effect made corollary to a decree of divorce granted in Canada before July 2, 1968 or granted on or after that day pursuant to subsection 22(2) of that Act may be assigned to any person designated pursuant to subsection 15(9).

Procedural laws continued

35. The rules and regulations made under the *Divorce Act*, chapter D-8 of the Revised Statutes of Canada, 1970, and the provisions of any other law or of any rule, regulation or other instrument made thereunder respecting any matter in relation to which rules may be made under subsection 25(2) that were in force in Canada or any province immediately before the day on which this Act comes into force and that are not inconsistent with this Act continue in force as though made or enacted by or under this Act until they are repealed or altered by rules or regulations made under this Act or are, by virtue of the making of rules or regulations under this Act, rendered inconsistent with those rules or regulations.

COMMENCEMENT

Commencement

*36. This Act shall come into force on a day to be fixed by proclamation.

*[Note: Act in force June 1, 1986, *see* SI/86-70.]

RELATED PROVISIONS

—　　　　　**R.S., 1985, c. 27 (2nd Supp.), s. 11:**

Transitional: proceedings

"**11.** Proceedings to which any of the provisions amended by the schedule apply that were commenced before the coming into force of section 10 shall be continued in accordance with those amended provisions without any further formality."

—　　　　　**1990, c. 18, s. 3:**

Application of amendments

"**3.** Subsection 2(4) and section 21.1 of the *Divorce Act*, as enacted by this Act, apply in respect of proceedings commenced under the *Divorce Act* either before or after the coming into force of this Act."

—　　　　　**1992, c. 51, s. 67(1):**

Transitional: proceedings

67. (1) Every proceeding commenced before the coming into force of this subsection and in respect of which any provision amended by this Act applies shall be taken up and continued under and in conformity with that amended provision without any further formality.

—　　　　　**1992, c. 51, s. 68:**

Transitional: salary

68. (1) Notwithstanding the *Judges Act*, a person who holds the office of Chief Judge of the County Court of Nova Scotia immediately before the coming into force of section 6 shall continue to be paid the salary then annexed to that office until the salary annexed to the office of judge of the Supreme Court of Nova Scotia exceeds that salary, at which time that person shall be paid the salary annexed to the last-mentioned office.

Transitional: annuity

(2) Notwithstanding the *Judges Act*, the Chief Judge of the County Court of Nova Scotia shall, on the coming into force of this subsection, be deemed to have made an election in accordance with section 32 of that Act for the purposes of subsection 43(2) of that Act, and if, at the time of resignation, removal or attaining the age of retirement, is holding office as a puisne judge of the Supreme Court of Nova Scotia or the Nova Scotia Court of Appeal, the annuity payable under section 42 of that Act shall be an annuity equal to two thirds of the result obtained by subtracting five thousand dollars from the salary annexed at that time to the office of Chief Justice of the Supreme Court of Nova Scotia.

Idem

(3) Where, before the coming into force of this subsection, an annuity has been granted to or in respect of a judge of a county or district court of any province pursuant to sections 42, 43, 44 and 47 of the *Judges Act*, payment of that annuity shall continue in accordance with those sections, as they read immediately before the coming into force of this subsection.

— 1993, c. 8, ss. 19(1), (2):

Transitional

19. (1) Sections 4 and 17.1 and subsection 18(2) of the *Divorce Act*, as enacted by sections 1, 2 and 3, respectively, of this Act, apply only to corollary relief proceedings commenced under the *Divorce Act* after the coming into force of those sections.

Idem

(2) Subsections 19(2) and (7) of the *Divorce Act*, as enacted by section 4 of this Act, apply to corollary relief proceedings commenced under the *Divorce Act* before or after the coming into force of that section.

AMENDMENTS NOT IN FORCE

— 1993, c. 28, s. 78 (Sch. III, ss. 41 to 43):

41. Paragraph (*e*) of the definition "court" in subsection 2(1) is repealed and the following substituted therefor:

(*e*) for the Yukon Territory, the Northwest Territories or Nunavut, the Supreme Court thereof,

42. Subsection 15(9) is amended by striking out the word "or" at the end of paragraph (*c*) thereof, by adding the word "or" at the end of paragraph (*d*) thereof and by adding thereto the following paragraph:

(*e*) any member of the Executive Council of Nunavut designated by the Commissioner of Nunavut.

43. The definition "Attorney General" in subsection 18(1) is amended by striking out the word "and" at the end of paragraph (*b*) thereof and by adding thereto, immediately after paragraph (*b*) thereof, the following paragraph:

(*b*.1) for Nunavut, the member of the Executive Council of Nunavut designated by the Commissioner of Nunavut, and

45-46 ELIZABETH II

CHAPTER 1

An Act to amend the Divorce Act, the Family Orders and Agreements Enforcement Assistance Act, the Garnishment, Attachment and Pension Diversion Act and the Canada Shipping Act

[Assented to 19th February, 1997]

Her Majesty, by and with the advice and consent of the Senate and House of Commons of Canada, enacts as follows:

Divorce Act

R.S., c. 3 (2nd Supp.); R.S., c. 27 (2nd Supp.); 1990, c. 18; 1992. c. 51; 1993. cc. 8, 28

1. (1) The definitions "corollary relief proceeding", "divorce proceeding" and "support order" in subsection 2(1) of the *Divorce Act* are replaced by the following:

"corollary relief proceeding"

"corollary relief proceeding" means a proceeding in a court in which either or both former spouses seek a child support order, a spousal support order or a custody order;

"divorce proceeding" means a proceeding in a court in which either or both spouses seek a divorce alone or together with a child support order, a spousal support order or a custody order;

"support order"

"support order" means a child support order or a spousal support order;

(2) Paragraphs (*a*) and (*b*) of the definition "child of the marriage" in subsection 2(1) of the Act are replaced by the following:

(*a*) is under the age of majority and who has not withdrawn from their charge, or

(*b*) is the age of majority or over and under their charge but unable, by reason of illness, disability or other cause, to withdraw from their charge or to obtain the necessaries of life;

(3) Subsection 2(1) of the Act is amended by adding the following in alphabetical order:

"age of majority"

"age of majority", in respect of a child, means the age of majority as determined by the laws of the province where the child ordinarily resides, or, if the child ordinarily resides outside of Canada, eighteen years of age;

"applicable guidelines"

"applicable guidelines" means

(*a*) where both spouses or former spouses are ordinarily resident in the same province at the time an application for a child support order or a variation order in respect of a child support order is made, or the amount of a child support order is to be recalculated pursuant to section 25.1, and that province has been designated by an order made under subsection (5), the laws of the province specified in the order, and

(*b*) in any other case, the Federal Child Support Guidelines;

"child support order"

"child support order" means an order made under subsection 15.1(1);

"Federal Child Support Guidelines"

"Federal Child Support Guidelines" means the guidelines made under section 26.1;

"provincial child support service" means any service, agency or body designated in an agreement with a province under subsection 25.1(1);

"spousal support order" means an order made under subsection 15.2(1);

(4) Section 2 of the Act is amended by adding the following after subsection (4):

Provincial child support guidelines

(5) The Governor in Council may, by order, designate a province for the purposes of the definition "applicable guidelines" in subsection (1) if the laws of the province establish comprehensive guidelines for the determination of child support that deal with the matters referred to in section 26.1. The order shall specify the laws of the province that constitute the guidelines of the province.

Amendments included

(6) The guidelines of a province referred to in subsection (5) include any amendments made to them from time to time.

1.1 Paragraph 11(1)(*b*) of the Act is replaced by the following:

(*b*) to satisfy itself that reasonable arrangements have been made for the support of any children of the marriage, having regard to the applicable guidelines, and, if such arrangements have not been made, to stay the granting of the divorce until such arrangements are made; and

2. Section 15 of the Act is replaced by the following:

Interpretation

Definition of "spouse"

15. In sections 15.1 to 16, "spouse" has the meaning assigned by subsection 2(1), and includes a former spouse.

Child Support Orders

Child support order

15.1 (1) A court of competent jurisdiction may, on application by either or both spouses, make an order requiring a spouse to pay for the support of any or all children of the marriage.

Interim order

(2) Where an application is made under subsection (1), the court may, on application by either or both spouses, make an interim order requiring a spouse to pay for the support of any or all children of the marriage, pending the determination of the application under subsection (1).

Guidelines apply

(3) A court making an order under subsection (1) or an interim order under subsection (2) shall do so in accordance with the applicable guidelines.

Terms and conditions

(4) The court may make an order under subsection (1) or an interim order under subsection (2) for a definite or indefinite period or until a specified event occurs, and may impose terms, conditions or restrictions in connection with the order or interim order as it thinks fit and just.

Court may take agreement, etc., into account

(5) Notwithstanding subsection (3), a court may award an amount that is different from the amount that would be determined in accordance with the applicable guidelines if the court is satisfied

(*a*) that special provisions in an order, a judgment or a written agreement respecting the financial obligations of the spouses, or the division or transfer of their property, directly or indirectly benefit a child, or that special provisions have otherwise been made for the benefit of a child; and

(*b*) that the application of the applicable guidelines would result in an amount of child support that is inequitable given those special provisions.

185

(6) Where the court awards, pursuant to subsection (5), an amount that is different from the amount that would be determined in accordance with the applicable guidelines, the court shall record its reasons for having done so.

(7) Notwithstanding subsection (3), a court may award an amount that is different from the amount that would be determined in accordance with the applicable guidelines on the consent of both spouses if it is satisfied that reasonable arrangements have been made for the support of the child to whom the order relates.

(8) For the purposes of subsection (7), in determining whether reasonable arrangements have been made for the support of a child, the court shall have regard to the applicable guidelines. However, the court shall not consider the arrangements to be unreasonable solely because the amount of support agreed to is not the same as the amount that would otherwise have been determined in accordance with the applicable guidelines.

Spousal Support Orders

15.2 (1) A court of competent jurisdiction may, on application by either or both spouses, make an order requiring a spouse to secure or pay, or to secure and pay, such lump sum or periodic sums, or such lump sum and periodic sums, as the court thinks reasonable for the support of the other spouse.

(2) Where an application is made under subsection (1), the court may, on application by either or both spouses, make an interim order requiring a spouse to secure or pay, or to secure and pay, such lump sum or periodic sums, or such lump sum and periodic sums, as the court thinks reasonable for the support of the other spouse, pending the determination of the application under subsection (1).

(3) The court may make an order under subsection (1) or an interim order under subsection (2) for a definite or indefinite period or until a specified event occurs, and may impose terms, conditions or restrictions in connection with the order as it thinks fit and just.

(4) In making an order under subsection (1) or an interim order under subsection (2), the court shall take into consideration the condition, means, needs and other circumstances of each spouse, including

(a) the length of time the spouses cohabited;

(b) the functions performed by each spouse during cohabitation; and

(c) any order, agreement or arrangement relating to support of either spouse.

(5) In making an order under subsection (1) or an interim order under subsection (2), the court shall not take into consideration any misconduct of a spouse in relation to the marriage.

(6) An order made under subsection (1) or an interim order under subsection (2) that provides for the support of a spouse should

(a) recognize any economic advantages or disadvantages to the spouses arising from the marriage or its breakdown;

(b) apportion between the spouses any financial consequences arising from the care of any child of the marriage over and above any obligation for the support of any child of the marriage;

(c) relieve any economic hardship of the spouses arising from the breakdown of the marriage; and

(d) in so far as practicable, promote the economic self-sufficiency of each spouse within a reasonable period of time.

Priority

15.3 (1) Where a court is considering an application for a child support order and an application for a spousal support order, the court shall give priority to child support in determining the applications.

(2) Where, as a result of giving priority to child support, the court is unable to make a spousal support order or the court makes a spousal support order in an amount that is less than it otherwise would have been, the court shall record its reasons for having done so.

(3) Where, as a result of giving priority to child support, a spousal support order was not made, or the amount of a spousal support order is less than it otherwise would have been, any subsequent reduction or termination of that child support constitutes a change of circumstances for the purposes of applying for a spousal support order, or a variation order in respect of the spousal support order, as the case may be.

3. The Act is amended by adding the following before section 16:

Custody Orders

4. The Act is amended by adding the following before section 17:

Variation, Rescission or Suspension of Orders

5. (1) Subsection 17(4) of the Act is replaced by the following:

(4) Before the court makes a variation order in respect of a child support order, the court shall satisfy itself that a change of circumstances as provided for in the applicable guidelines has occurred since the making of the child support order or the last variation order made in respect of that order.

(4.1) Before the court makes a variation order in respect of a spousal support order, the court shall satisfy itself that a change in the condition, means, needs or other circumstances of either former spouse has occurred since the making of the spousal support order or the last variation order made in respect of that order, and, in making the variation order, the court shall take that change into consideration.

(2) Section 17 of the Act is amended by adding the following after subsection (6):

(6.1) A court making a variation order in respect of a child support order shall do so in accordance with the applicable guidelines.

(6.2) Notwithstanding subsection (6.1), in making a variation order in respect of a child support order, a court may award an amount that is different from the amount that would be determined in accordance with the applicable guidelines if the court is satisfied

(*a*) that special provisions in an order, a judgment or a written agreement respecting the financial obligations of the spouses, or the division or transfer of their property, directly or indirectly benefit a child, or that special provisions have otherwise been made for the benefit of a child; and

(*b*) that the application of the applicable guidelines would result in an amount of child support that is inequitable given those special provisions.

(6.3) Where the court awards, pursuant to subsection (6.2), an amount that is different from the amount that would be determined in accordance with the applicable guidelines, the court shall record its reasons for having done so.

(6.4) Notwithstanding subsection (6.1), a court may award an amount that is different from the amount that would be determined in accordance with the applicable guidelines on the consent of both spouses if it is satisfied that reasonable arrangements have been made for the support of the child to whom the order relates.

(6.5) For the purposes of subsection (6.4), in determining whether reasonable arrangements have been made for the support of a child, the court shall have regard to the applicable guidelines. However, the court shall not consider the arrangements to be unreasonable solely because the amount of support agreed to is not the same as the amount that would otherwise have been determined in accordance with the applicable guidelines.

(3) The portion of subsection 17(7) of the Act before paragraph (*a*) is replaced by the following:

(7) A variation order varying a spousal support order should

187

(4) Paragraph 17(7)(*b*) of the Act is replaced by the following:

(*b*) apportion between the former spouses any financial consequences arising from the care of any child of the marriage over and above any obligation for the support of any child of the marriage;

(5) Subsection 17(8) of the Act is repealed.

(6) Subsection 17(10) of the Act is replaced by the following:

Limitation

(10) Notwithstanding subsection (1), where a spousal support order provides for support for a definite period or until a specified event occurs, a court may not, on an application instituted after the expiration of that period or the occurrence of the event, make a variation order for the purpose of resuming that support unless the court is satisfied that

(*a*) a variation order is necessary to relieve economic hardship arising from a change described in subsection (4.1) that is related to the marriage; and

(*b*) the changed circumstances, had they existed at the time of the making of the spousal support order or the last variation order made in respect of that order, as the case may be, would likely have resulted in a different order.

6. The Act is amended by adding the following before section 18:

Provisional Orders

1993, c. 8,
s. 4(2)

7. (1) The portion of subsection 19(7) of the Act before paragraph (*a*) is replaced by the following:

Order of
confirmation
or refusal

(7) Subject to subsection (7.1), at the conclusion of a proceeding under this section, the court shall make an order

(2) Section 19 of the Act is amended by adding the following after subsection (7):

Guidelines
apply

(7.1) A court making an order under subsection (7) in respect of a child support order shall do so in accordance with the applicable guidelines.

(3) Subsections 19(9) to (11) of the Act are replaced by the following:

Interim order
for support of
children

(9) Where a court remits a matter pursuant to this section in relation to a child support order, the court may, pending the making of an order under subsection (7), make an interim order in accordance with the applicable guidelines requiring a spouse to pay for the support of any or all children of the marriage.

Interim order
for support of
spouse

(9.1) Where a court remits a matter pursuant to this section in relation to a spousal support order, the court may make an interim order requiring a spouse to secure or pay, or to secure and pay, such lump sum or periodic sums, or such lump sum and periodic sums, as the court thinks reasonable for the support of the other spouse, pending the making of an order under subsection (7).

Terms and
conditions

(10) The court may make an order under subsection (9) or (9.1) for a definite or indefinite period or until a specified event occurs, and may impose terms, conditions or restrictions in connection with the order as it thinks fit and just.

Provisions
applicable

(11) Subsections 17(4), (4.1) and (6) to (7) apply, with such modifications as the circumstances require, in respect of an order made under subsection (9) or (9.1) as if it were a variation order referred to in those subsections.

8. (1) Subsection 20(2) of the Act is replaced by the following:

Legal effect
throughout
Canada

(2) Subject to subsection 18(2), an order made under any of sections 15.1 to 17 or subsection 19(7), (9) or (9.1) has legal effect throughout Canada.

(2) Paragraph 20(3)(b) of the Act is replaced by the following:

(b) enforced in a province in any other manner provided for by the laws of that province, including its laws respecting reciprocal enforcement between the province and a jurisdiction outside Canada.

(3) Section 20 of the Act is amended by adding the following after subsection (3):

(4) Notwithstanding subsection (3), a court may only vary an order that has legal effect throughout Canada pursuant to subsection (2) in accordance with this Act.

9. The Act is amended by adding the following after section 20:

20.1 (1) A support order may be assigned to

(a) any minister of the Crown for Canada designated by the Governor in Council;

(b) any minister of the Crown for a province, or any agency in a province, designated by the Lieutenant Governor in Council of the province;

(c) any member of the Council of the Yukon Territory, or any agency in the Yukon Territory, designated by the Commissioner of the Yukon Territory; or

(d) any member of the Council of the Northwest Territories, or any agency in the Northwest Territories, designated by the Commissioner of the Northwest Territories.

(2) A minister, member or agency referred to in subsection (1) to whom an order is assigned is entitled to the payments due under the order, and has the same right to be notified of, and to participate in, proceedings under this Act to vary, rescind, suspend or enforce the order as the person who would otherwise be entitled to the payments.

10. The Act is amended by adding the following after section 25:

25.1 (1) With the approval of the Governor in Council, the Minister of Justice may, on behalf of the Government of Canada, enter into an agreement with a province authorizing a provincial child support service designated in the agreement to

(a) assist courts in the province in the determination of the amount of child support; and

(b) recalculate, at regular intervals, in accordance with the applicable guidelines, the amount of child support orders on the basis of updated income information.

(2) Subject to subsection (5), the amount of a child support order as recalculated pursuant to this section shall for all purposes be deemed to be the amount payable under the child support order.

(3) The former spouse against whom a child support order was made becomes liable to pay the amount as recalculated pursuant to this section thirty-one days after both former spouses to whom the order relates are notified of the recalculation in the manner provided for in the agreement authorizing the recalculation.

(4) Where either or both former spouses to whom a child support order relates do not agree with the amount of the order as recalculated pursuant to this section, either former spouse may, within thirty days after both former spouses are notified of the recalculation in the manner provided for in the agreement authorizing the recalculation, apply to a court of competent jurisdiction for an order under subsection 17(1).

(5) Where an application is made under subsection (4), the operation of subsection (3) is suspended pending the determination of the application, and the child support order continues in effect.

(6) Where an application made under subsection (4) is withdrawn before the determination of the application, the former spouse against whom the order was made becomes

liable to pay the amount as recalculated pursuant to this section on the day on which the former spouse would have become liable had the application not been made.

11. The Act is amended by adding the following after section 26:

26.1 (1) The Governor in Council may establish guidelines respecting the making of orders for child support, including, but without limiting the generality of the foregoing, guidelines

(*a*) respecting the way in which the amount of an order for child support is to be determined;

(*b*) respecting the circumstances in which discretion may be exercised in the making of an order for child support;

(*c*) authorizing a court to require that the amount payable under an order for child support be paid in periodic payments, in a lump sum or in a lump sum and periodic payments;

(*d*) authorizing a court to require that the amount payable under an order for child support be paid or secured, or paid and secured, in the manner specified in the order;

(*e*) respecting the circumstances that give rise to the making of a variation order in respect of a child support order;

(*f*) respecting the determination of income for the purposes of the application of the guidelines;

(*g*) authorizing a court to impute income for the purposes of the application of the guidelines; and

(*h*) respecting the production of income information and providing for sanctions when that information is not provided.

(2) The guidelines shall be based on the principle that spouses have a joint financial obligation to maintain the children of the marriage in accordance with their relative abilities to contribute to the performance of that obligation.

(3) In subsection (1), "order for child support" means

(*a*) an order or interim order made under section 15.1;

(*b*) a variation order in respect of a child support order; or

(*c*) an order or an interim order made under section 19.

12. The headings before section 28 and sections 28 to 31 of the Act are replaced by the following:

28. The Minister of Justice shall undertake a comprehensive review of the provisions and operation of the Federal Child Support Guidelines and the determination of child support under this Act and shall cause a report on the review to be laid before each House of Parliament within five years after the coming into force of this section.

13. The Act is amended by adding the following before section 33:

Divorce Act, R.S. 1970, c. D-8

14. Section 34 of the Act is replaced by the following:

34. (1) Subject to subsection (1.1), any order made under subsection 11(1) of the *Divorce Act*, chapter D-8 of the Revised Statutes of Canada, 1970, including any order made pursuant to section 33 of this Act, and any order to the like effect made corollary to a decree of divorce granted in Canada before July 2, 1968 or granted on or after that day pursuant to subsection 22(2) of that Act may be varied, rescinded, suspended or enforced in accordance with sections 17 to 20, other than subsection 17(10), of this Act as if

(*a*) the order were a support order or custody order, as the case may be; and

(*b*) in subsections 17(4), (4.1) and (5), the words "or the last order made under subsection 11(2) of the *Divorce Act*, chapter D-8 of the Revised Statutes of Canada,

1970, varying that order" were added immediately before the words "or the last variation order made in respect of that order".

Combined orders

(1.1) Where an application is made, under subsection 17(1) to vary an order referred to in subsection (1) that provides a single amount of money for the combined support of one or more children and a former spouse, the court shall rescind the order and treat the application as an application for a child support order and an application for a spousal support order.

Enforcement of interim orders

(2) Any order made under section 10 of the *Divorce Act*, chapter D-8 of the Revised Statutes of Canada, 1970, including any order made pursuant to section 33 of this Act, may be enforced in accordance with section 20 of this Act as if it were an order made under subsection 15.1(1) or 15.2(1) or section 16 of this Act, as the case may be.

Assignment of orders previously made

(3) Any order for the maintenance of a spouse or child of the marriage made under section 10 or 11 of the *Divorce Act*, chapter D-8 of the Revised Statutes of Canada, 1970, including any order made pursuant to section 33 of this Act, and any order to the like effect made corollary to a decree of divorce granted in Canada before July 2, 1968 or granted on or after that day pursuant to subsection 22(2) of that Act may be assigned to any minister, member or agency designated pursuant to section 20.1.

15. The Act is amended by adding the following after section 35:

Divorce Act, R.S. 1985, c. 3 (2nd Supp.)

Variation and enforcement of support orders previously made

35.1 (1) Subject to subsection (2), any support order made under this Act before the coming into force of this section may be varied, rescinded, suspended or enforced in accordance with sections 17 to 20 as if the support order were a child support order or a spousal support order, as the case may be.

Combined orders

(2) Where an application is made under subsection 17(1) to vary a support order made under this Act before the coming into force of this section that provides for the combined support of one or more children and a former spouse, the court shall rescind the order and treat the application as an application for a child support order and an application for a spousal support order.

Assignment of orders previously made

(3) Any support order made under this Act before the coming into force of this section may be assigned to any minister, member or agency designated pursuant to section 20.1.

APPENDIX 5
RULE 36: DIVORCE

APPLICATION FOR DIVORCE

36. (1) Either spouse may start a divorce case by,

   (a) filing an application naming the other spouse as a respondent; or

   (b) filing a joint application with no respondent

JOINT APPLICATION

(2) In a joint application the divorce and any other order sought shall be made only with the consent of both spouses

ALLEGATION OF ADULTERY

(3) In an application for divorce claiming that the other spouse committed adultery with another person, that person does not need to be named, but if named, shall be served with the application and has all the rights of a respondent in the case.

MARRIAGE CERTIFICATE AND CENTRAL DIVORCE REGISTRY CERTIFICATE

(4) The court shall not grant a divorce until the following have been filed:

   1. A marriage certificate or marriage registration certificate, unless the application states that it is impractical to obtain a certificate and explains why.

   2. A report on earlier divorce cases started by either spouse, issued under the *Central Registry of Divorce Proceedings Regulations* (Canada).

DIVORCE BASED ON AFFIDAVIT EVIDENCE

(5) If the respondent files no answer, or files one and later withdraws it, the applicant shall file an affidavit (Form 36) that,

   (a) confirms that all the information in the application is correct except as stated in the affidavit;

   (b) if no marriage certificate or marriage registration certificate has been filed, provides sufficient information to prove the marriage;

   (c) contains proof of any previous divorce or the death of a party's previous spouse, unless the marriage took place in Canada;

   (d) contains the information about arrangements for support for any children of the marriage by paragraph 11 (1) (b) of the *Divorce Act* (Canada), and attaches as exhibits the income and financial information required by section 21 of the child support guidelines and

   (e) contains any other information necessary for the court to grant the divorce.

DRAFT DIVORCE ORDER

(6) The applicant shall file with the affidavit,

(a) three copies of a draft divorce order (Form 25A),

(b) a stamped envelope addressed to each party; and

(c) if the divorce order is to contain a support order,

(i) an extra copy of the draft divorce order for the clerk to file with The Director of the Family Responsibility Office and

(ii) two copies of a draft support deduction order.

CLERK TO PRESENT PAPERS TO JUDGE

(7) When the documents mentioned in subrules (4) to (6) have been filed, the clerk shall prepare a certificate (Form 36A) and present the documents to a judge, who may,

(a) grant the divorce as set out in the draft order;

(b) have the clerk return the document to the applicant to make any needed corrections; or

(c) grant the divorce but make changes to the draft order, or refuse to grant the divorce, after giving the applicant a chance to file an additional affidavit or come to court to explain why the order should be made without change.

DIVORCE CERTIFICATE

(8) When a divorce takes effect the clerk shall, on either party's request,

(a) check the continuing record to verify that,

(i) no appeal has been taken from the divorce order, or any appeal from it has been disposed of and

(ii) no order has been made extending the time for an appeal, or any extended time has expired without an appeal; and

(b) if satisfied of those matters, issue a divorce certificate (Form 36B) and mail it to the parties, unless the court orders otherwise.

REGISTRATION OF ORDERS MADE OUTSIDE ONTARIO

(9) If a court outside Ontario has made an order for support, custody or access under the *Divorce Act* (Canada), a person who wants it registered for enforcement in Ontario under paragraph 20 (3) (a) of that Act shall mail a certified copy of the order to the clerk at the office of the Superior Court of Justice in a municipality where the order may be enforced under subrule 5 (6).

APPENDIX 6
CHILD SUPPORT GUIDELINES FOR ONTARIO

PROVINCE: *ONTARIO*

NO. OF CHILDREN/N^{BRE} D'ENFANTS: *One/Un*

FEDERAL CHILD SUPPORT TABLES/
TABLES FÉDÉRALES DE PENSIONS ALIMENTAIRES POUR ENFANTS

Income/Revenu ($) From/De	To/À	Basic Amount/ Montant de base	Plus (%)	of Income over/ du revenu dépassant
0	6729	0	5.00	0
6730	6999	0	4.81	6730
7000	7999	14	0.86	7000
8000	8999	62	0.86	8000
9000	9999	70	0.86	9000
10000	10999	79	0.86	10000
11000	11999	87	0.86	11000
12000	12999	96	0.86	12000
13000	13999	105	0.86	13000
14000	14999	113	0.68	14000
15000	15999	120	0.68	15000
16000	16999	127	0.68	16000
17000	17999	134	0.68	17000
18000	18999	140	0.72	18000
19000	19999	148	1.50	19000
20000	20999	163	1.50	20000
21000	21999	178	1.50	21000
22000	22999	192	1.06	22000
23000	23999	203	0.95	23000
24000	24999	213	0.95	24000
25000	25999	222	0.95	25000
26000	26999	232	0.88	26000
27000	27999	240	0.88	27000
28000	28999	249	0.88	28000
29000	29999	258	0.80	29000
30000	30999	266	0.71	30000
31000	31999	273	0.76	31000
32000	32999	281	0.83	32000
33000	33999	289	0.83	33000
34000	34999	297	0.79	34000
35000	35999	305	0.78	35000
36000	36999	313	0.81	36000
37000	37999	321	0.81	37000
38000	38999	329	0.81	38000
39000	39999	337	0.81	39000
40000	40999	345	0.84	40000
41000	41999	354	0.84	41000
42000	42999	362	0.84	42000
43000	43999	371	0.84	43000
44000	44999	379	0.84	44000
45000	45999	387	0.84	45000
46000	46999	396	0.84	46000
47000	47999	404	0.84	47000
48000	48999	413	0.84	48000
49000	49999	421	0.84	49000
50000	50999	429	0.84	50000
51000	51999	438	0.84	51000
52000	52999	446	0.76	52000
53000	53999	454	0.72	53000

Income/Revenu ($) From/De	To/À	Basic Amount/ Montant de base	Plus (%)	of Income over/ du revenu dépassant
54000	54999	461	0.72	54000
55000	55999	468	0.73	55000
56000	56999	475	0.80	56000
57000	57999	483	0.80	57000
58000	58999	492	0.80	58000
59000	59999	500	0.75	59000
60000	60999	507	0.74	60000
61000	61999	514	0.74	61000
62000	62999	522	0.74	62000
63000	63999	529	0.70	63000
64000	64999	536	0.67	64000
65000	65999	543	0.51	65000
66000	66999	548	0.52	66000
67000	67999	553	0.55	67000
68000	68999	559	0.64	68000
69000	69999	565	0.67	69000
70000	70999	572	0.67	70000
71000	71999	578	0.67	71000
72000	72999	585	0.67	72000
73000	73999	592	0.67	73000
74000	74999	599	0.67	74000
75000	75999	605	0.67	75000
76000	76999	612	0.67	76000
77000	77999	619	0.67	77000
78000	78999	625	0.67	78000
79000	79999	632	0.67	79000
80000	80999	639	0.67	80000
81000	81999	645	0.67	81000
82000	82999	652	0.67	82000
83000	83999	659	0.67	83000
84000	84999	666	0.67	84000
85000	85999	672	0.67	85000
86000	86999	679	0.67	86000
87000	87999	686	0.67	87000
88000	88999	692	0.67	88000
89000	89999	699	0.67	89000
90000	90999	706	0.67	90000
91000	91999	712	0.67	91000
92000	92999	719	0.67	92000
93000	93999	726	0.67	93000
94000	94999	733	0.67	94000
95000	95999	739	0.67	95000
96000	96999	746	0.67	96000
97000	97999	753	0.67	97000
98000	98999	759	0.67	98000
99000	99999	766	0.67	99000
100000	100999	773	0.67	100000
101000	101999	779	0.67	101000
102000	102999	786	0.67	102000

Income/Revenu ($) From/De	To/À	Basic Amount/ Montant de base	Plus (%)	of Income over/ du revenu dépassant
103000	103999	793	0.67	103000
104000	104999	799	0.67	104000
105000	105999	806	0.67	105000
106000	106999	813	0.67	106000
107000	107999	820	0.67	107000
108000	108999	826	0.67	108000
109000	109999	833	0.67	109000
110000	110999	840	0.67	110000
111000	111999	846	0.67	111000
112000	112999	853	0.67	112000
113000	113999	860	0.67	113000
114000	114999	866	0.67	114000
115000	115999	873	0.67	115000
116000	116999	880	0.67	116000
117000	117999	887	0.67	117000
118000	118999	893	0.67	118000
119000	119999	900	0.67	119000
120000	120999	907	0.67	120000
121000	121999	913	0.67	121000
122000	122999	920	0.67	122000
123000	123999	927	0.67	123000
124000	124999	933	0.67	124000
125000	125999	940	0.67	125000
126000	126999	947	0.67	126000
127000	127999	954	0.67	127000
128000	128999	960	0.67	128000
129000	129999	967	0.67	129000
130000	130999	974	0.67	130000
131000	131999	980	0.67	131000
132000	132999	987	0.67	132000
133000	133999	994	0.67	133000
134000	134999	1000	0.67	134000
135000	135999	1007	0.67	135000
136000	136999	1014	0.67	136000
137000	137999	1020	0.67	137000
138000	138999	1027	0.67	138000
139000	139999	1034	0.67	139000
140000	140999	1041	0.67	140000
141000	141999	1047	0.67	141000
142000	142999	1054	0.67	142000
143000	143999	1061	0.67	143000
144000	144999	1067	0.67	144000
145000	145999	1074	0.67	145000
146000	146999	1081	0.67	146000
147000	147999	1087	0.67	147000
148000	148999	1094	0.67	148000
149000	149999	1101	0.67	149000
150000 or greater/ou plus		1108	0.67	150000

FEDERAL CHILD SUPPORT TABLES/
TABLES FÉDÉRALES DE PENSIONS ALIMENTAIRES POUR ENFANTS

Income/Revenu ($) From/De	To/À	Basic Amount/ Montant de base	Plus (%)	of income over/ du revenu dépassant
0	6729	0		
6730	6999	0	5.42	6730
7000	7999	15	5.23	7000
8000	8999	67	3.54	8000
9000	9999	102	1.65	9000
10000	10999	119	2.86	10000
11000	11999	147	2.90	11000
12000	12999	176	2.21	12000
13000	13999	198	1.24	13000
14000	14999	211	1.24	14000
15000	15999	223	1.24	15000
16000	16999	236	1.24	16000
17000	17999	248	1.24	17000
18000	18999	260	1.24	18000
19000	19999	273	1.24	19000
20000	20999	285	1.24	20000
21000	21999	297	1.24	21000
22000	22999	310	1.24	22000
23000	23999	322	1.80	23000
24000	24999	340	1.96	24000
25000	25999	360	1.95	25000
26000	26999	379	1.85	26000
27000	27999	398	1.85	27000
28000	28999	416	1.66	28000
29000	29999	433	1.25	29000
30000	30999	446	1.10	30000
31000	31999	456	1.15	31000
32000	32999	468	1.26	32000
33000	33999	481	1.26	33000
34000	34999	493	1.26	34000
35000	35999	506	1.26	35000
36000	36999	518	1.30	36000
37000	37999	531	1.30	37000
38000	38999	544	1.26	38000
39000	39999	557	1.26	39000
40000	40999	570	1.31	40000
41000	41999	583	1.31	41000
42000	42999	596	1.31	42000
43000	43999	609	1.31	43000
44000	44999	622	1.31	44000
45000	45999	635	1.31	45000
46000	46999	648	1.31	46000
47000	47999	661	1.31	47000
48000	48999	674	1.31	48000
49000	49999	687	1.31	49000
50000	50999	700	1.31	50000
51000	51999	713	1.31	51000
52000	52999	726	1.22	52000
53000	53999	739	1.17	53000

Income/Revenu ($) From/De	To/À	Basic Amount/ Montant de base	Plus (%)	of income over/ du revenu dépassant
54000	54999	750	1.17	54000
55000	55999	762	1.18	55000
56000	56999	774	1.25	56000
57000	57999	786	1.25	57000
58000	58999	799	1.25	58000
59000	59999	811	1.16	59000
60000	60999	823	1.15	60000
61000	61999	834	1.15	61000
62000	62999	846	1.15	62000
63000	63999	857	1.10	63000
64000	64999	868	1.07	64000
65000	65999	879	0.91	65000
66000	66999	888	0.91	66000
67000	67999	897	0.94	67000
68000	68999	907	1.02	68000
69000	69999	917	1.04	69000
70000	70999	927	1.04	70000
71000	71999	938	1.04	71000
72000	72999	948	1.04	72000
73000	73999	959	1.04	73000
74000	74999	969	1.04	74000
75000	75999	979	1.04	75000
76000	76999	990	1.04	76000
77000	77999	1000	1.04	77000
78000	78999	1011	1.04	78000
79000	79999	1021	1.04	79000
80000	80999	1031	1.04	80000
81000	81999	1042	1.04	81000
82000	82999	1052	1.04	82000
83000	83999	1063	1.04	83000
84000	84999	1073	1.04	84000
85000	85999	1084	1.04	85000
86000	86999	1094	1.04	86000
87000	87999	1104	1.04	87000
88000	88999	1115	1.04	88000
89000	89999	1125	1.04	89000
90000	90999	1136	1.04	90000
91000	91999	1146	1.04	91000
92000	92999	1156	1.04	92000
93000	93999	1167	1.04	93000
94000	94999	1177	1.04	94000
95000	95999	1188	1.04	95000
96000	96999	1198	1.04	96000
97000	97999	1209	1.04	97000
98000	98999	1219	1.04	98000
99000	99999	1229	1.04	99000
100000	100999	1240	1.04	100000
101000	101999	1250	1.04	101000
102000	102999	1261	1.04	102000

Income/Revenu ($) From/De	To/À	Basic Amount/ Montant de base	Plus (%)	of income over/ du revenu dépassant
103000	103999	1271	1.04	103000
104000	104999	1281	1.04	104000
105000	105999	1292	1.04	105000
106000	106999	1302	1.04	106000
107000	107999	1313	1.04	107000
108000	108999	1323	1.04	108000
109000	109999	1334	1.04	109000
110000	110999	1344	1.04	110000
111000	111999	1354	1.04	111000
112000	112999	1365	1.04	112000
113000	113999	1375	1.04	113000
114000	114999	1386	1.04	114000
115000	115999	1396	1.04	115000
116000	116999	1406	1.04	116000
117000	117999	1417	1.04	117000
118000	118999	1427	1.04	118000
119000	119999	1438	1.04	119000
120000	120999	1448	1.04	120000
121000	121999	1459	1.04	121000
122000	122999	1469	1.04	122000
123000	123999	1479	1.04	123000
124000	124999	1490	1.04	124000
125000	125999	1500	1.04	125000
126000	126999	1511	1.04	126000
127000	127999	1521	1.04	127000
128000	128999	1531	1.04	128000
129000	129999	1542	1.04	129000
130000	130999	1552	1.04	130000
131000	131999	1563	1.04	131000
132000	132999	1573	1.04	132000
133000	133999	1584	1.04	133000
134000	134999	1594	1.04	134000
135000	135999	1604	1.04	135000
136000	136999	1615	1.04	136000
137000	137999	1625	1.04	137000
138000	138999	1636	1.04	138000
139000	139999	1646	1.04	139000
140000	140999	1656	1.04	140000
141000	141999	1667	1.04	141000
142000	142999	1677	1.04	142000
143000	143999	1688	1.04	143000
144000	144999	1698	1.04	144000
145000	145999	1709	1.04	145000
146000	146999	1719	1.04	146000
147000	147999	1729	1.04	147000
148000	148999	1740	1.04	148000
149000	149999	1750	1.04	149000
150000 or greater/ou plus		1761	1.04	150000

FEDERAL CHILD SUPPORT TABLES/
TABLES FÉDÉRALES DE PENSIONS ALIMENTAIRES POUR ENFANTS

PROVINCE: *ONTARIO*

NO. OF CHILDREN/N^{bre} D'ENFANTS: *Three/Trois*

Income/Revenu ($) From/De	To/À	Basic Amount/ Montant de base	Plus (%)	of income over/ du revenu dépassant	Income/Revenu ($) From/De	To/À	Basic Amount/ Montant de base	Plus (%)	of income over/ du revenu dépassant	Income/Revenu ($) From/De	To/À	Basic Amount/ Montant de base	Plus (%)	of income over/ du revenu dépassant
0	6729	0			54000	54999	982	1.54	54000	103000	103999	1654	1.34	103000
6730	6999	0	5.83	6730	55000	55999	997	1.55	55000	104000	104999	1667	1.34	104000
7000	7999	16	5.65	7000	56000	56999	1013	1.61	56000	105000	105999	1680	1.34	105000
8000	8999	72	3.95	8000	57000	57999	1029	1.61	57000	106000	106999	1694	1.34	106000
9000	9999	112	2.06	9000	58000	58999	1045	1.61	58000	107000	107999	1707	1.34	107000
10000	10999	132	3.27	10000	59000	59999	1061	1.50	59000	108000	108999	1721	1.34	108000
11000	11999	165	3.32	11000	60000	60999	1076	1.47	60000	109000	109999	1734	1.34	109000
12000	12999	198	3.20	12000	61000	61999	1091	1.47	61000	110000	110999	1747	1.34	110000
13000	13999	230	3.20	13000	62000	62999	1105	1.47	62000	111000	111999	1761	1.34	111000
14000	14999	262	3.20	14000	63000	63999	1120	1.43	63000	112000	112999	1774	1.34	112000
15000	15999	294	2.81	15000	64000	64999	1134	1.39	64000	113000	113999	1788	1.34	113000
16000	16999	323	1.68	16000	65000	65999	1148	1.22	65000	114000	114999	1801	1.34	114000
17000	17999	339	1.68	17000	66000	66999	1160	1.22	66000	115000	115999	1814	1.34	115000
18000	18999	356	1.68	18000	67000	67999	1173	1.24	67000	116000	116999	1828	1.34	116000
19000	19999	373	1.68	19000	68000	68999	1185	1.32	68000	117000	117999	1841	1.34	117000
20000	20999	390	1.68	20000	69000	69999	1198	1.34	69000	118000	118999	1855	1.34	118000
21000	21999	407	1.68	21000	70000	70999	1212	1.34	70000	119000	119999	1868	1.34	119000
22000	22999	424	1.68	22000	71000	71999	1225	1.34	71000	120000	120999	1881	1.34	120000
23000	23999	440	1.68	23000	72000	72999	1238	1.34	72000	121000	121999	1895	1.34	121000
24000	24999	457	1.68	24000	73000	73999	1252	1.34	73000	122000	122999	1908	1.34	122000
25000	25999	474	1.67	25000	74000	74999	1265	1.34	74000	123000	123999	1922	1.34	123000
26000	26999	491	1.54	26000	75000	75999	1279	1.34	75000	124000	124999	1935	1.34	124000
27000	27999	506	1.88	27000	76000	76999	1292	1.34	76000	125000	125999	1948	1.34	125000
28000	28999	525	2.20	28000	77000	77999	1305	1.34	77000	126000	126999	1962	1.34	126000
29000	29999	547	2.14	29000	78000	78999	1319	1.34	78000	127000	127999	1975	1.34	127000
30000	30999	568	2.09	30000	79000	79999	1332	1.34	79000	128000	128999	1988	1.34	128000
31000	31999	589	2.14	31000	80000	80999	1346	1.34	80000	129000	129999	2002	1.34	129000
32000	32999	611	2.28	32000	81000	81999	1359	1.34	81000	130000	130999	2015	1.34	130000
33000	33999	633	1.64	33000	82000	82999	1372	1.34	82000	131000	131999	2029	1.34	131000
34000	34999	650	1.60	34000	83000	83999	1386	1.34	83000	132000	132999	2042	1.34	132000
35000	35999	666	1.60	35000	84000	84999	1399	1.34	84000	133000	133999	2055	1.34	133000
36000	36999	682	1.66	36000	85000	85999	1413	1.34	85000	134000	134999	2069	1.34	134000
37000	37999	698	1.66	37000	86000	86999	1426	1.34	86000	135000	135999	2082	1.34	135000
38000	38999	715	1.66	38000	87000	87999	1439	1.34	87000	136000	136999	2096	1.34	136000
39000	39999	732	1.67	39000	88000	88999	1453	1.34	88000	137000	137999	2109	1.34	137000
40000	40999	748	1.72	40000	89000	89999	1466	1.34	89000	138000	138999	2122	1.34	138000
41000	41999	765	1.70	41000	90000	90999	1480	1.34	90000	139000	139999	2136	1.34	139000
42000	42999	782	1.68	42000	91000	91999	1493	1.34	91000	140000	140999	2149	1.34	140000
43000	43999	799	1.68	43000	92000	92999	1506	1.34	92000	141000	141999	2163	1.34	141000
44000	44999	816	1.68	44000	93000	93999	1520	1.34	93000	142000	142999	2176	1.34	142000
45000	45999	833	1.68	45000	94000	94999	1533	1.34	94000	143000	143999	2189	1.34	143000
46000	46999	850	1.68	46000	95000	95999	1546	1.34	95000	144000	144999	2203	1.34	144000
47000	47999	866	1.68	47000	96000	96999	1560	1.34	96000	145000	145999	2216	1.34	145000
48000	48999	883	1.68	48000	97000	97999	1573	1.34	97000	146000	146999	2230	1.34	146000
49000	49999	900	1.68	49000	98000	98999	1587	1.34	98000	147000	147999	2243	1.34	147000
50000	50999	917	1.68	50000	99000	99999	1600	1.34	99000	148000	148999	2256	1.34	148000
51000	51999	934	1.68	51000	100000	100999	1613	1.34	100000	149000	149999	2270	1.34	149000
52000	52999	950	1.59	52000	101000	101999	1627	1.34	101000	150000 or greater/ ou plus		2283	1.34	150000
53000	53999	966	1.54	53000	102000	102999	1640	1.34	102000					

FEDERAL CHILD SUPPORT TABLES/
TABLES FÉDÉRALES DE PENSIONS ALIMENTAIRES POUR ENFANTS

PROVINCE: *ONTARIO*

NO. OF CHILDREN/N^BRE D'ENFANTS: *Four/Quatre*

Income/Revenu ($) From/De	To/À	Basic Amount/Montant de base	Plus (%)	of Income over/du revenu dépassant
0	6729	0		
6730	6999	0	6.25	6730
7000	7999	17	6.06	7000
8000	8999	78	4.37	8000
9000	9999	121	2.48	9000
10000	10999	146	3.69	10000
11000	11999	183	3.74	11000
12000	12999	220	3.62	12000
13000	13999	256	3.62	13000
14000	14999	293	3.62	14000
15000	15999	329	3.62	15000
16000	16999	365	3.62	16000
17000	17999	401	3.34	17000
18000	18999	435	2.05	18000
19000	19999	455	2.05	19000
20000	20999	476	2.05	20000
21000	21999	496	2.05	21000
22000	22999	517	2.05	22000
23000	23999	537	2.05	23000
24000	24999	558	2.05	24000
25000	25999	578	2.04	25000
26000	26999	598	1.88	26000
27000	27999	617	1.88	27000
28000	28999	636	1.88	28000
29000	29999	655	1.66	29000
30000	30999	672	1.37	30000
31000	31999	685	2.33	31000
32000	32999	709	2.50	32000
33000	33999	733	2.50	33000
34000	34999	758	2.50	34000
35000	35999	783	2.51	35000
36000	36999	809	2.58	36000
37000	37999	834	2.03	37000
38000	38999	855	1.95	38000
39000	39999	874	1.96	39000
40000	40999	894	2.02	40000
41000	41999	914	2.02	41000
42000	42999	934	2.02	42000
43000	43999	954	2.02	43000
44000	44999	975	2.02	44000
45000	45999	995	1.99	45000
46000	46999	1015	1.99	46000
47000	47999	1034	1.99	47000
48000	48999	1054	1.99	48000
49000	49999	1074	1.99	49000
50000	50999	1094	1.99	50000
51000	51999	1114	1.99	51000
52000	52999	1134	1.89	52000
53000	53999	1153	1.84	53000

Income/Revenu ($) From/De	To/À	Basic Amount/Montant de base	Plus (%)	of Income over/du revenu dépassant
54000	54999	1171	1.84	54000
55000	55999	1189	1.85	55000
56000	56999	1208	1.90	56000
57000	57999	1227	1.90	57000
58000	58999	1246	1.90	58000
59000	59999	1265	1.77	59000
60000	60999	1283	1.74	60000
61000	61999	1300	1.74	61000
62000	62999	1317	1.74	62000
63000	63999	1335	1.69	63000
64000	64999	1352	1.66	64000
65000	65999	1368	1.48	65000
66000	66999	1383	1.48	66000
67000	67999	1398	1.50	67000
68000	68999	1413	1.56	68000
69000	69999	1428	1.58	69000
70000	70999	1444	1.58	70000
71000	71999	1460	1.58	71000
72000	72999	1476	1.58	72000
73000	73999	1492	1.58	73000
74000	74999	1508	1.58	74000
75000	75999	1523	1.58	75000
76000	76999	1539	1.58	76000
77000	77999	1555	1.58	77000
78000	78999	1571	1.58	78000
79000	79999	1587	1.58	79000
80000	80999	1603	1.58	80000
81000	81999	1618	1.58	81000
82000	82999	1634	1.58	82000
83000	83999	1650	1.58	83000
84000	84999	1666	1.58	84000
85000	85999	1682	1.58	85000
86000	86999	1698	1.58	86000
87000	87999	1713	1.58	87000
88000	88999	1729	1.58	88000
89000	89999	1745	1.58	89000
90000	90999	1761	1.58	90000
91000	91999	1777	1.58	91000
92000	92999	1793	1.58	92000
93000	93999	1808	1.58	93000
94000	94999	1824	1.58	94000
95000	95999	1840	1.58	95000
96000	96999	1856	1.58	96000
97000	97999	1872	1.58	97000
98000	98999	1888	1.58	98000
99000	99999	1903	1.58	99000
100000	100999	1919	1.58	100000
101000	101999	1935	1.58	101000
102000	102999	1951	1.58	102000

Income/Revenu ($) From/De	To/À	Basic Amount/Montant de base	Plus (%)	of Income over/du revenu dépassant
103000	103999	1967	1.58	103000
104000	104999	1983	1.58	104000
105000	105999	1998	1.58	105000
106000	106999	2014	1.58	106000
107000	107999	2030	1.58	107000
108000	108999	2046	1.58	108000
109000	109999	2062	1.58	109000
110000	110999	2077	1.58	110000
111000	111999	2093	1.58	111000
112000	112999	2109	1.58	112000
113000	113999	2125	1.58	113000
114000	114999	2141	1.58	114000
115000	115999	2157	1.58	115000
116000	116999	2172	1.58	116000
117000	117999	2188	1.58	117000
118000	118999	2204	1.58	118000
119000	119999	2220	1.58	119000
120000	120999	2236	1.58	120000
121000	121999	2252	1.58	121000
122000	122999	2267	1.58	122000
123000	123999	2283	1.58	123000
124000	124999	2299	1.58	124000
125000	125999	2315	1.58	125000
126000	126999	2331	1.58	126000
127000	127999	2347	1.58	127000
128000	128999	2362	1.58	128000
129000	129999	2378	1.58	129000
130000	130999	2394	1.58	130000
131000	131999	2410	1.58	131000
132000	132999	2426	1.58	132000
133000	133999	2442	1.58	133000
134000	134999	2457	1.58	134000
135000	135999	2473	1.58	135000
136000	136999	2489	1.58	136000
137000	137999	2505	1.58	137000
138000	138999	2521	1.58	138000
139000	139999	2537	1.58	139000
140000	140999	2552	1.58	140000
141000	141999	2568	1.58	141000
142000	142999	2584	1.58	142000
143000	143999	2600	1.58	143000
144000	144999	2616	1.58	144000
145000	145999	2631	1.58	145000
146000	146999	2647	1.58	146000
147000	147999	2663	1.58	147000
148000	148999	2679	1.58	148000
149000	149999	2695	1.58	149000
150000	or greater/ou plus	2711	1.53	150000

Income/Revenu ($)		Monthly Award/Paiement mensuel ($)		
From/De	To/À	Basic Amount/Montant de base	Plus (%)	of income over/du revenu dépassant
0	6729	0		
6730	6999	0	6.25	6730
7000	7999	17	6.06	7000
8000	8999	78	4.37	8000
9000	9999	121	2.48	9000
10000	10999	146	3.69	10000
11000	11999	183	3.74	11000
12000	12999	220	3.62	12000
13000	13999	256	3.62	13000
14000	14999	293	3.62	14000
15000	15999	329	3.62	15000
16000	16999	365	3.62	16000
17000	17999	401	3.62	17000
18000	18999	437	3.62	18000
19000	19999	474	3.62	19000
20000	20999	510	3.62	20000
21000	21999	546	3.62	21000
22000	22999	582	3.54	22000
23000	23999	618	2.35	23000
24000	24999	641	2.34	24000
25000	25999	665	2.17	25000
26000	26999	688	2.17	26000
27000	27999	710	2.17	27000
28000	28999	731	2.17	28000
29000	29999	753	1.92	29000
30000	30999	772	1.58	30000
31000	31999	788	1.64	31000
32000	32999	805	1.83	32000
33000	33999	823	2.07	33000
34000	34999	844	2.68	34000
35000	35999	870	2.69	35000
36000	36999	897	2.77	36000
37000	37999	925	2.77	37000
38000	38999	953	2.77	38000
39000	39999	980	2.78	39000
40000	40999	1008	2.86	40000
41000	41999	1037	2.35	41000
42000	42999	1060	2.27	42000
43000	43999	1083	2.27	43000
44000	44999	1106	2.27	44000
45000	45999	1129	2.27	45000
46000	46999	1151	2.27	46000
47000	47999	1174	2.27	47000
48000	48999	1197	2.26	48000
49000	49999	1219	2.24	49000
50000	50999	1242	2.24	50000
51000	51999	1264	2.24	51000
52000	52999	1287	2.14	52000
53000	53999	1308	2.09	53000
54000	54999	1329	2.09	54000
55000	55999	1350	2.10	55000
56000	56999	1371	2.15	56000
57000	57999	1392	2.15	57000
58000	58999	1414	2.15	58000
59000	59999	1435	1.99	59000
60000	60999	1455	1.97	60000
61000	61999	1475	1.97	61000
62000	62999	1494	1.97	62000
63000	63999	1514	1.92	63000
64000	64999	1533	1.88	64000
65000	65999	1552	1.69	65000
66000	66999	1569	1.69	66000
67000	67999	1586	1.71	67000
68000	68999	1603	1.77	68000
69000	69999	1620	1.79	69000
70000	70999	1638	1.79	70000
71000	71999	1656	1.79	71000
72000	72999	1674	1.79	72000
73000	73999	1692	1.79	73000
74000	74999	1710	1.79	74000
75000	75999	1728	1.79	75000
76000	76999	1745	1.79	76000
77000	77999	1763	1.79	77000
78000	78999	1781	1.79	78000
79000	79999	1799	1.79	79000
80000	80999	1817	1.79	80000
81000	81999	1835	1.79	81000
82000	82999	1853	1.79	82000
83000	83999	1870	1.79	83000
84000	84999	1888	1.79	84000
85000	85999	1906	1.79	85000
86000	86999	1924	1.79	86000
87000	87999	1942	1.79	87000
88000	88999	1960	1.79	88000
89000	89999	1978	1.79	89000
90000	90999	1995	1.79	90000
91000	91999	2013	1.79	91000
92000	92999	2031	1.79	92000
93000	93999	2049	1.79	93000
94000	94999	2067	1.79	94000
95000	95999	2085	1.79	95000
96000	96999	2103	1.79	96000
97000	97999	2120	1.79	97000
98000	98999	2138	1.79	98000
99000	99999	2156	1.79	99000
100000	100999	2174	1.79	100000
101000	101999	2192	1.79	101000
102000	102999	2210	1.79	102000
103000	103999	2228	1.79	103000
104000	104999	2245	1.79	104000
105000	105999	2263	1.79	105000
106000	106999	2281	1.79	106000
107000	107999	2299	1.79	107000
108000	108999	2317	1.79	108000
109000	109999	2335	1.79	109000
110000	110999	2353	1.79	110000
111000	111999	2370	1.79	111000
112000	112999	2388	1.79	112000
113000	113999	2406	1.79	113000
114000	114999	2424	1.79	114000
115000	115999	2442	1.79	115000
116000	116999	2460	1.79	116000
117000	117999	2478	1.79	117000
118000	118999	2495	1.79	118000
119000	119999	2513	1.79	119000
120000	120999	2531	1.79	120000
121000	121999	2549	1.79	121000
122000	122999	2567	1.79	122000
123000	123999	2585	1.79	123000
124000	124999	2603	1.79	124000
125000	125999	2620	1.79	125000
126000	126999	2638	1.79	126000
127000	127999	2656	1.79	127000
128000	128999	2674	1.79	128000
129000	129999	2692	1.79	129000
130000	130999	2710	1.79	130000
131000	131999	2728	1.79	131000
132000	132999	2745	1.79	132000
133000	133999	2763	1.79	133000
134000	134999	2781	1.79	134000
135000	135999	2799	1.79	135000
136000	136999	2817	1.79	136000
137000	137999	2835	1.79	137000
138000	138999	2853	1.79	138000
139000	139999	2870	1.79	139000
140000	140999	2888	1.79	140000
141000	141999	2906	1.79	141000
142000	142999	2924	1.79	142000
143000	143999	2942	1.79	143000
144000	144999	2960	1.79	144000
145000	145999	2978	1.79	145000
146000	146999	2995	1.79	146000
147000	147999	3013	1.79	147000
148000	148999	3031	1.79	148000
149000	149999	3049	1.79	149000
150000 or greater/ou plus		3067	1.79	150000

Income/Revenu ($) From/De	To/À	Basic Amount/Montant de base	Monthly Award/Paiement mensuel ($) Plus (%)	of income over/du revenu dépassant
0	6729	0		
6730	6999	0	6.25	6730
7000	7999	17	6.06	7000
8000	8999	78	4.37	8000
9000	9999	121	2.48	9000
10000	10999	146	3.69	10000
11000	11999	183	3.74	11000
12000	12999	220	3.62	12000
13000	13999	256	3.62	13000
14000	14999	293	3.62	14000
15000	15999	329	3.62	15000
16000	16999	365	3.62	16000
17000	17999	401	3.62	17000
18000	18999	437	3.62	18000
19000	19999	474	3.62	19000
20000	20999	510	3.62	20000
21000	21999	546	3.62	21000
22000	22999	582	3.62	22000
23000	23999	618	3.62	23000
24000	24999	655	3.62	24000
25000	25999	691	3.59	25000
26000	26999	727	3.20	26000
27000	27999	759	3.20	27000
28000	28999	791	3.20	28000
29000	29999	823	2.74	29000
30000	30999	850	2.10	30000
31000	31999	871	2.18	31000
32000	32999	893	2.15	32000
33000	33999	914	2.05	33000
34000	34999	935	2.06	34000
35000	35999	955	2.58	35000
36000	36999	976	2.93	36000
37000	37999	1002	2.93	37000
38000	38999	1031	2.94	38000
39000	39999	1060	3.03	39000
40000	40999	1090	3.03	40000
41000	41999	1120	3.03	41000
42000	42999	1151	3.03	42000
43000	43999	1181	3.03	43000
44000	44999	1211	3.03	44000
45000	45999	1241	2.53	45000
46000	46999	1267	2.49	46000
47000	47999	1292	2.49	47000
48000	48999	1316	2.49	48000
49000	49999	1341	2.49	49000
50000	50999	1366	2.49	50000
51000	51999	1391	2.49	51000
52000	52999	1416	2.36	52000
53000	53999	1439	2.30	53000

Income/Revenu ($) From/De	To/À	Basic Amount/Montant de base	Monthly Award/Paiement mensuel ($) Plus (%)	of income over/du revenu dépassant
54000	54999	1462	2.30	54000
55000	55999	1485	2.31	55000
56000	56999	1508	2.35	56000
57000	57999	1532	2.35	57000
58000	58999	1555	2.35	58000
59000	59999	1579	2.19	59000
60000	60999	1601	2.15	60000
61000	61999	1622	2.15	61000
62000	62999	1644	2.15	62000
63000	63999	1665	2.10	63000
64000	64999	1686	2.07	64000
65000	65999	1707	1.87	65000
66000	66999	1726	1.87	66000
67000	67999	1744	1.88	67000
68000	68999	1763	1.94	68000
69000	69999	1783	1.96	69000
70000	70999	1802	1.96	70000
71000	71999	1822	1.96	71000
72000	72999	1841	1.96	72000
73000	73999	1861	1.96	73000
74000	74999	1881	1.96	74000
75000	75999	1900	1.96	75000
76000	76999	1920	1.96	76000
77000	77999	1939	1.96	77000
78000	78999	1959	1.96	78000
79000	79999	1978	1.96	79000
80000	80999	1998	1.96	80000
81000	81999	2018	1.96	81000
82000	82999	2037	1.96	82000
83000	83999	2057	1.96	83000
84000	84999	2076	1.96	84000
85000	85999	2096	1.96	85000
86000	86999	2115	1.96	86000
87000	87999	2135	1.96	87000
88000	88999	2155	1.96	88000
89000	89999	2174	1.96	89000
90000	90999	2194	1.96	90000
91000	91999	2213	1.96	91000
92000	92999	2233	1.96	92000
93000	93999	2253	1.96	93000
94000	94999	2272	1.96	94000
95000	95999	2292	1.96	95000
96000	96999	2311	1.96	96000
97000	97999	2331	1.96	97000
98000	98999	2350	1.96	98000
99000	99999	2370	1.96	99000
100000	100999	2390	1.96	100000
101000	101999	2409	1.96	101000
102000	102999	2429	1.96	102000

Income/Revenu ($) From/De	To/À	Basic Amount/Montant de base	Monthly Award/Paiement mensuel ($) Plus (%)	of income over/du revenu dépassant
103000	103999	2448	1.96	103000
104000	104999	2468	1.96	104000
105000	105999	2487	1.96	105000
106000	106999	2507	1.96	106000
107000	107999	2527	1.96	107000
108000	108999	2546	1.96	108000
109000	109999	2566	1.96	109000
110000	110999	2585	1.96	110000
111000	111999	2605	1.96	111000
112000	112999	2624	1.96	112000
113000	113999	2644	1.96	113000
114000	114999	2664	1.96	114000
115000	115999	2683	1.96	115000
116000	116999	2703	1.96	116000
117000	117999	2722	1.96	117000
118000	118999	2742	1.96	118000
119000	119999	2761	1.96	119000
120000	120999	2781	1.96	120000
121000	121999	2801	1.96	121000
122000	122999	2820	1.96	122000
123000	123999	2840	1.96	123000
124000	124999	2859	1.96	124000
125000	125999	2879	1.96	125000
126000	126999	2899	1.96	126000
127000	127999	2918	1.96	127000
128000	128999	2938	1.96	128000
129000	129999	2957	1.96	129000
130000	130999	2977	1.96	130000
131000	131999	2996	1.96	131000
132000	132999	3016	1.96	132000
133000	133999	3036	1.96	133000
134000	134999	3055	1.96	134000
135000	135999	3075	1.96	135000
136000	136999	3094	1.96	136000
137000	137999	3114	1.96	137000
138000	138999	3133	1.96	138000
139000	139999	3153	1.96	139000
140000	140999	3173	1.96	140000
141000	141999	3192	1.96	141000
142000	142999	3212	1.96	142000
143000	143999	3231	1.96	143000
144000	144999	3251	1.96	144000
145000	145999	3270	1.96	145000
146000	146999	3290	1.96	146000
147000	147999	3310	1.96	147000
148000	148999	3329	1.96	148000
149000	149999	3349	1.96	149000
150000 or greater/ou plus		3368	1.96	150000

199

GLOSSARY

ADULTERY

Sexual intercourse with a person other than your spouse. For purposes of evidence, it is not necessary to have someone actually see the act.

AFFIDAVIT

A form of declaration made voluntarily, sworn before a lawyer or notary public and thus admissible in court as a statement of fact.

CERTIFICATE OF DIVORCE

Order that terminates the marriage and is irrevocable. It is granted after a waiting period of 31 days from the date of the Divorce Judgment.

CHAMBERS

It is best described as the private office of a judge where the only evidence allowed is affidavit evidence. There are no witnesses or juries, simply a judge who listens to applications, peruses the affidavit evidence, and grants (or refuses) orders based on this evidence. It is less formal than open court and because of this can be used only to obtain certain orders.

CHILD

Defined in section 2 of the Divorce Act and refers to any child under the age of 16 or over 16 but dependent on a parent because of illness, disability, or other cause.

CHILD OF THE MARRIAGE

A child of two spouses or former spouses who is under the age of 16 or 16 or over and under their charge but unable to withdraw from his or her dependency because of illness, disability, or other cause.

COLLUSION

An agreement between husband and wife that one of them shall commit, or appear to have committed, acts constituting a cause for divorce for the purpose of enabling the other to obtain a divorce.

COMMISSIONER

Person to whom is charged the administration of the legal process. All lawyers in Ontario are commissioners, but not all commissioners are lawyers. Commissioners must witness your signature to any and all affidavits.

CONDONATION

Forgiveness of any act or acts which are now being used as grounds for divorce. It means, in practical terms, that you continued to live with your spouse, or returned to live with your spouse, after learning of the act(s) in question.

CONNIVANCE

Active encouragement of your spouse's conduct by standing idly by and doing nothing about it could also be construed as a form of condonation.

COURT REGISTRY (Registrar's Office)

Place where all legal actions are processed. It is part of the machinery of the legal process. The employees are civil servants and not lawyers, but they are very knowledgeable in all phases of court proceedings and will help anyone who politely requests such help.

CRUELTY

Can be either mental or physical but must be of such a kind as to render intolerable the continued cohabitation of the parties. The test of cruelty is a personal one and can vary in the circumstances, i.e., what is cruel for one spouse may not be for another.

DIVORCE JUDGMENT

An order that you receive when you appear in court or once your documents have been processed. It is not the final order dissolving the marriage. A 31-day waiting period is required following the granting of the Divorce Judgment before you can obtain a Certificate of Divorce.

MOTION FOR JUDGMENT

This is a procedure by which you apply to a judge of the Ontario Court (General Division) for a Divorce Judgment. The Motion is made where the respondent is in default and has not filed an Answer within the prescribed time and requires a Requisition to the registrar and a Notice of Motion for Judgment. The Notice of Motion should set out the documentary evidence to be relied upon and should also set out whether you intend to present oral evidence at the hearing; otherwise the matter will proceed by way of Affidavit evidence.

NOTARY PUBLIC

Public officer whose function is to attest and certify certain documents and to perform other official acts. (**Note:** All lawyers are notaries public; not all notaries public are lawyers.)

NOTICE OF MOTION

Notice in writing to the other side stating that on a certain designated day at a specific place a motion will be made to the court for the purpose or relief stated in the Notice. A motion is different from a trial in that the procedure is more summary.

PERSON NAMED IN THE PETITION

Person named in the petition (usually the co-adulterer) where no claim is made against that person for damages or costs.

PETITION

Written document containing an application by a person or persons and addressed to another person requesting the court to exercise its authority to redress some wrong or grant some privilege (e.g., divorce).

PETITIONER

Person who presents the petition to the court.

PLEADINGS

Formal allegations by the parties of their respective claims and defences submitted to the court for arbitration.

REQUISITION

Instructions to the registrar to take a certain step. In the usual case, to note the respondent in default. Such a step can be taken only when the Petition for Divorce has been filed with proof of service.

RESPONDENT AND CO-RESPONDENT

Person to whom the petition is addressed and usually defined as the opposing party. The co-respondent usually means the person charged with adultery with the respondent in a suit for divorce for that cause and joined as a defendant with such party if and only if some form of relief is claimed against the person. If no form of relief is claimed, the person may be named in the petition but is not a party to the action.

SUBSTITUTED SERVICE

Service upon a person in a manner other than by personal service. The method of serving substitutionally is authorized by statute, the most common being the publishing of notices in local newspapers in areas where they are most likely to be seen by the parties to whom the notices are addressed.

TITLE OF PROCEEDINGS

Title of the action including (in the case of divorce petitions) the court and registry numbers and the full names of the petitioner and the respondent.

TRIAL COHABITATION

An attempt by a couple that has separated to live together again. This does not affect the one-year separation period unless the period or periods of cohabitation total more than 90 days.